Abraham Lincoln And Mexico

A History of Courage, Intrigue And Unlikely Friendships

MICHAEL HOGAN

EGRETBOOKS.COM,
SAN DIEGO, CALIFORNIA

FONDO EDITORIAL UNIVERSITARIO,
GUADALAJARA, JALISCO

USA Publisher's Cataloging-In-Publication Data
(Prepared by The Donohue Group, Inc.)

Names: Hogan, Michael, 1943-
Title: Abraham Lincoln and Mexico : a history of courage, intrigue and unlikely friendships / Michael Hogan.
Description: San Diego, California : EgretBooks.com, 2016. | Interest age level: 13 and up. | Includes bibliographical references and index.
Identifiers: LCCN 2016934399 | ISBN 978-0-9857744-9-3 (USA paperback) | ISBN 978-0-692-69454-1 (eBook)
Subjects: LCSH: Mexican War, 1846-1848–Diplomatic history. | Lincoln, Abraham, 1809-1865. | Juárez, Benito, 1806-1872. | United States–History–Civil War, 1861-1865. | United States–Foreign relations–Mexico. | Mexico–Foreign relations–United States. | United States–History–19th century. | Mexico–History–19th century.
Classification: LCC E407 .H64 2016 | DDC 973.621–dc23

Editing by Mikel Miller, **Interior Design** by Ediciones de la Noche, **Front Cover design concept** by Tania Romero Topete, **Full Cover final design** by Ediciones de la Noche, **Indexing** by Emmanuel Carballo
Cover photograph: Abraham Lincoln, 1863. Alexander Gardner, photographer. Prints and Photographs Division, Library of Congress, Washington, DC

USA paperback edition 978-0-9857744-9-3
EgretBooks.com, San Diego, California

TABLE OF CONTENTS

A large part of the value of this book comes from the author's extensive research based on primary source documents from museums, libraries, and archives in both the United States and Mexico. Where possible, the author has included the complete text of archival documents in the Appendix. The author has chosen to present the original material without modification even though some quoted material and archival documents contain spellings, sentence construction, capitalization, and punctuation that might appear to be errors.

ACCLAIM FOR
ABRAHAM LINCOLN AND MEXICO

Michael Hogan's important new study of US expansionist policy in the mid-nineteenth century provides an illuminating and un-varnished account of United States imperialist ambitions vis-à-vis Mexico. His book is a powerful indictment of and a necessary cor-rective to the frequently heard simplistic and self-serving national-ist claims of American exceptionalism. It is also a spirited defense against and rebuttal of simplistic thinking about Abraham Lincoln's ideas about slavery, Mexico, and American hegemony. Hogan sets the record straight on these and other controversial historical mat-ters, and in his generous and open-minded approach to historiog-raphy, offers a positive way forward in considering Mexican-Amer-ican relations. – *Robert DiYanni, Professor, Center for the Advancement of Teaching, New York University.*

In this shining contribution to the literature on Abraham Lincoln and that of the US-Mexican War, Michael Hogan illuminates the stance of a young politician against that terrible war, telling a story that is both urgently necessary and well more than a century over-due. – *C.M. Mayo, author of The Last Prince of the Mexican Empire*

Michael Hogan, in *Abraham Lincoln and Mexico*, brings together a passion for Mexico and an understanding of the United States during the nineteenth century so that he narrates their history with a sense of the intertwining of international relevance with an engrossing story. Here Abraham Lincoln becomes a human being of keen ideas and political know-how rather than the marble statue of his monument; here Benito Juarez also becomes an individual beyond the dour lawyer portrayed in textbooks, movies, and television. There is a scope about this book that finds a kind of grandeur in the events as they are eloquently described. – *William H. Beezley, Professor of History, University of Arizona. Author of The Essential Mexico (Oxford University Press).*

The story of Lincoln's evolving defense of Mexico's autonomy and rights as a sovereign nation is an excellent forum for understanding related topics including the limitations of presidential power, the interpretation of the power to wage war, and the limits of the use of a pre-emptive attack on another country. This thoughtful, well-balanced presentation of primary document resources illuminates Lincoln's rising stature as a voice of protest against the crimes of war and the unjustifiable invasion of another republic. Like his earlier work, *The Irish Soldiers of Mexico*, Michael Hogan's Lincoln narrative will soon become a primary resource for scholars and teachers interested in the politics of civil war, territorial expansion, and human slavery. – *Victoria M. Breting-Garcia, Independent scholar/ historian.*

While *Abraham Lincoln and Mexico* undoubtedly privileges the U.S. context, it nevertheless adds to the vital pedagogical mission of challenging triumphalist narratives of U.S. identity with more critical renderings of the past. Building on one of his previous books, *The Irish Soldiers of Mexico* (1997), and based on decades of experience teaching U.S. history in Guadalajara, Hogan reiterates what Mexicans have been voicing since 1848: the war with the United States was clearly a war of northern aggression. – *Carlos R. Hernández, Department of History, Yale University.*

These neglected connections between Lincoln and Mexico provide valuable insights into U.S.-Mexico relations and international history. This is an important book which is far-reaching in its contemporary implications. It should be a resource in every high school and college classroom. – *Victor Gonzalez Pérez, Facultad de Estudios Sociales, Colegio Americano, Guadalajara.*

Abraham Lincoln and Mexico is a great read. As an AP teacher, I believe that books like these are worth their weight in gold. Michael Hogan has not only broken ground on undiscovered sources covering Lincoln's relationship with Mexico, but has also generously annexed the sources in their entirety. It is a godsend for history teachers who are constantly looking for new material and ways to challenge their students' analytical skills. – *Liam O'Hara, Chair, Department of History and Social Studies, American School Foundation of Guadalajara, A.C.*

Dr. Hogan has done it again, finding a grand tale lost in the shadows of history. His meticulous research brings to light a period of Lincoln's life often ignored by other biographers. Although Lincoln's opposition to the Mexican War is well-documented, some have dismissed it as political posturing or partisan bluster. The historical record, however, shows us that Lincoln's opposition came from his personal belief that the war represented a terrible injustice unworthy of his beloved United States of America. – *Christopher Minster, Ph.D., Founder and Editor of About.com's Latin American History site.*

The research that went into *Abraham Lincoln and Mexico* is excellent. Dr. Hogan has backed up his thesis with solid facts. I also like the way in which he dealt with so many "minor" characters and factors in describing the complex relations between the US, Mexico, and foreign powers, instead of concentrating only on the principal actors and events. It gives a more complete and realistic picture of the whole era, although the wealth of detail might prove a little overwhelming for some general readers. I think this is a very important book which deserves a wide circulation. I am in complete agreement with Michael Hogan's research methods to back up everything as far as possible with the earliest most authentic source materials and, if possible, "set the record straight." Michael Hogan has done this to perfection. – *Ronald Barnett, Ph.D., former Professor of Classics, Universidad Autonoma de Guadalajara.*

Abraham Lincoln and Mexico brings to light that which for too long has hidden in the shadows: the interest, integrity, and involvement of our sixteenth President in the struggles and victories of our southern neighbor, be they internal or external with the United States and France. Through the extensive use of primary documents, Hogan reveals the insight and intelligence with which Lincoln and his closest associates approached Mexico. He brings to light little known roles played by actors such as Matías Romero, Charge d'Affaires of Juárez to Washington DC; Philip Sheridan, Lew Wallace, and Ulysses Grant of Civil War fame; or the unknown Buffalo Soldier who fought with and for the Republican Army of Mexico against the Imperial Armies of France, Austria and Belgium as they sought to impose their emperor on Mexico. It is a story full of complicated motivations and characters. It is a tale well told. – *Philip Stover, former Deputy Superintendent, San Diego Unified School District, and author of Religion and Revolution in Mexico's North.*

PREFACE

American students might be forgiven if they know little about the Mexican-American War of 1846-48. It was a conflict not covered in high school history texts until recently. When it did finally appear in such texts as a subset of Westward Expansion, the result was to make it look like a fight for freedom on the part of patriotic Texans, migration to the territories, and the subsequent acquisition via the Treaty of Guadalupe Hidalgo. To most students it appeared to be a simple real estate deal much like the Louisiana Purchase.

In fact, the Mexican War was a preemptive invasion by US forces with the primary purpose of acquiring California, and a land route across the southwest to connect the Atlantic with the Pacific. It was unjustified and unconstitutional. It resulted in the largest land acquisition in modern history. More than half of Mexico was taken by the stroke of a pen and that country was relegated to Third World status; whereas the United States with its acquisition of 1,972,550 km² (761,606 sq. mi.) of new territory, "from sea to shining sea," rose to be a world power with deep ports on both the Atlantic and Pacific coasts. From the seized territories, the US carved out the present-day states of California, Utah, Arizona, and Nevada, along with parts of Kansas, New Mexico, Colorado, and Wyoming. In addition, the lower part of Texas from the Nueces River to the Rio Grande became officially part of the US.

Despite the continuing impact on the people of Mexico and the problems created by the artificially-imposed borders as a result of that treaty, the acquisition still does not merit much space in the US history books, nor in the Advanced Placement curriculum. Few know that the Mexican people living in the territory seized by the Americans were promised citizenship by the Treaty of Guadalupe Hidalgo. Few know that these same people were assured that their property rights would be respected. Neither one of these "legally binding" promises was fully kept.

As a history teacher working at an American School in Mexico, I have tried to at least bring my class into a fuller awareness of the importance of this war, its impact both nationally and internationally, its troubling legacy, and the result of the silences that have been pervasive over the years regarding this conflict and the resulting territorial seizures by the United States. It has been an uphill battle.

In 1997, I wrote a book entitled *The Irish Soldiers of Mexico* that explored the history of a group of Irish immigrants who fought on the side of Mexico during the conflict and their reasons for doing so. I also noted how this war was quite unpopular for a good many conscientious Americans at the time. Henry David Thoreau went to jail rather than pay taxes to support the war. He later wrote a fine essay "On Civil Disobedience" reflecting how it was the duty of every citizen to resist this kind of warmongering and preemptive strike. John Quincy Adams, who lost a son in the conflict, held that the war was started unconstitutionally. Ulysses S. Grant, an army captain in the invasion and subsequent occupation of Mexico, called it "the most unjust war ever waged against a weaker nation by a stronger." Nevertheless, despite a long history of US military interventions in foreign countries, twelve years after my book on the Mexican War was written, President Obama addressed the cadets of West Point and told them:

> And finally, we must draw on the strength of our values – for the challenges that we face may have changed, but the things that we believe in must not. That's why we must promote our values by living them at home.... And we must make it clear to every man, woman and child around the world who lives under the dark cloud of tyranny that America will speak out on be-

half of their human rights, and tend to the light of freedom and justice and opportunity and respect for the dignity of all peoples. That is who we are. That is the source, the moral source, of America's authority. For unlike the great powers of old, we have not sought world domination. Our union was founded in resistance to oppression. We do not seek to occupy other nations. We will not claim another nation's resources or target other peoples because their faith or ethnicity is different from ours.[1]

What a narrow view of world history these future military leaders were being given. What an un-nuanced view of America's actions abroad. The President went on to say that he is a believer in "American exceptionalism." From the text of the speech one is inclined to believe that this might be defined as always putting a positive spin on US relationships with other countries, including one of the two republics which share the continent of North America with us, despite our seizure of their territory, our confiscation of private property in violation of treaties, and our subsequent denial of citizenship.

I also observed in my book how a Whig congressman, Abraham Lincoln, risked his political career by making several forceful speeches in Congress denouncing President Polk for his unilateral decision to declare war against a neighboring and peaceful republic, and how Lincoln showed that the president purposely distorted the facts in efforts to get the Congress to ratify his decision.

In the ensuing years since the publication of that book, very little has been done to examine the war through a lens other than American exceptionalism. When the new Lincoln movie was released in 2012 to critical acclaim and the announcement that there would be "new historical information" and "insights into Lincoln's political courage," all of my students felt certain that the story of Lincoln and the Mexican War would finally be told. However, they were disappointed. The movie was mostly about slavery and the Emancipation Proclamation, subjects about which most students

---

1.   Barack Obama, Address to the Nation. Office of the Press Secretary. The White House. December 01, 2009. https://www.whitehouse.gov/the-press-office/remarks-president-address-nation-way-forward-afghanistan-and-pakistan

both in the United States and Mexico had been amply informed through dozens of readings, lectures, and films.

So, when my students suggested that I write a book about Lincoln and the Mexican-American War, I decided to check and see what had been written. I was delighted to find and read two monographs that appeared since the publication of my book, and which were especially helpful for an extended discussion. The first was a compilation on Lincoln's "spot resolutions" that he introduced in Congress, compiled by Louis Fisher of the Law Library of Congress and published by Penny Hill Press in 2009. It is a very short monograph, only twelve pages, but a valuable source for any serious student of the War since he lists and references the original documents. The second helpful essay on the same subject was a chapter from *A Wicked War: Polk, Clay, Lincoln and the 1846 US Invasion of Mexico* by Amy S. Greenberg. The chapter was entitled "Lincoln and the War," and it is also highly recommended because Greenberg sets out how Lincoln was later vilified in the press for his stand against Polk's declaration of war, which he considered unconstitutional and unprovoked by Mexico. I will be referring to both of these in this text and am grateful to both authors for their contribution to this study.

I thought this book might end at this point in Lincoln's career until, in the course of my perusal through Lincoln's papers, I discovered a note he had written for the Mexican president, Benito Juárez, in support of his efforts to form a republican government. It would be a valuable asset during the French Occupation of 1861-1867, a time that coincided with our own Civil War. It would help the Mexican president raise money, arms and men to overthrow Maximilian. In the process of following up on this item, I found out how much Lincoln actually did to support the liberal cause in Mexico and help rid the country of the French imperialists. I also uncovered the little-known role that his generals, Grant and Sheridan, played in that liberation.

Einstein famously wrote that: "If we knew what we were doing, we wouldn't call it research." So it might come as no surprise to the reader that another of the research pathways led to the black troops in the Civil War after the Emancipation Proclamation (another group not represented in the Lincoln movie), and how these brave men fought for their own freedom. And, what is even more remarkable, how at the end of the Civil War, many went south to fight for Mexico. This last episode is unknown to most Americans and Mexicans alike. I am grateful to William A. Dobak, author of *Freedom by the Sword, The US Colored Troops, 1863-1867*, and John David Smith, author of *Lincoln and the US Colored Troops*, for providing insights into the formation and accomplishments of this group of courageous soldiers.

My thanks to the Presidency Project begun in 1999 to organize all the papers, documents and speeches of the presidents from 1789 to the present. It is an on-line searchable site where one can find many primary resources. For the convenience of the reader, I have included an appendix to this work that provides the most relevant documents of Lincoln's concerns with Mexico, the consistency of his moral stance, and letters between him and his confidants who shared his views. I am also grateful to the John Hay Library at Brown University that provided me with additional letters and documents illustrating this historical period. On the Mexican side I am extremely grateful to the Banco de México, which has made the papers of Matías Romero (special envoy and later Mexican ambassador to the United States from 1861-67), available to scholars, and also to the Biblioteca Nacional de Antropología e Historia in Mexico City, which filled in some of the gaps in my research.

Finally, I wish to thank the American School Foundation of Guadalajara and the students of my Advanced Placement US History (APUSH) class of 2014. This was the largest group of Latin American students enrolled in an APUSH course in the history of the College Board's AP program.[2] They were a challenging cadre of students who researched many primary source documents independently and always had probing questions about the role of the United States, especially in Latin American affairs. We occasionally got away from the course description and syllabus, but it made for a dynamic interaction and a fascinating class. I hope I have answered

---

2. Luciana Mendez, "American School has largest U.S. History class in Latin America." *Guadalajara Reporter.* Dec. 27, 2014, p 6.

some of their questions here and have done them the honor of clarifying the role of the United States in Mexico during two of the most controversial and complex periods in American history, and how decisions made then continue to permeate the daily lives of citizens and residents of both countries.

Michael Hogan
Guadalajara, Jalisco, México

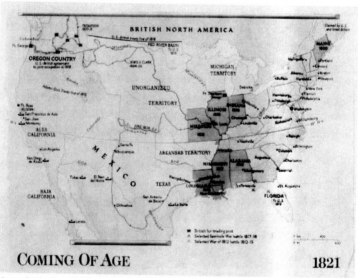

Map of Mexico, 1821. Its territory extended from Louisiana to the Pacific in the east and west, and from Guatemala to Oregon Territory in the south and north.

1

MEXICO BEFORE THE CONFLICT

In order to get a clear picture of Mexico prior to the US invasion, it is important to see the country as it was in the year following its independence from Spain in 1821. The northern Mexican state of Coahuila y Tejas (wherein is located today's state of Texas) was sparsely populated but still a viable national entity. While there was little in the way of municipal structures, there were several small settlements or *pueblos*, a dozen large ranchos, some missions founded by the Franciscans, and a scattering of military outposts. Wichita, Apache, Kiowa, and Comanche also roamed the area pretty much at will, attacking travelers and raiding the missions.

In 1822, Stephen F. Austin led several American families into the region to make their home. Two years before, his father had persuaded the Spanish government to grant him a huge tract of land for American settlers. After his father died, Austin went ahead with the plan. By that time, Mexico had gained its independence, so Austin had to make arrangements with the new government. Mexico agreed to honor the Spanish land grant under the conditions that the colonists would belong to the Catholic faith, that they would become Mexican citizens, and that they would obey Mexican laws.[3]

---

3.   Robert Ryal Miller, *Mexico: A History* (Norman: University of Oklahoma, 1985), 210.

At first, the government was pleased with the colonization of this area. There were several reasons for this. The original settlers, sometimes known as the Three Hundred, were grateful to Mexico for the opportunity to settle there and were willing to work hard to become good citizens. In addition, the local inhabitants saw that they were good neighbors and were integrating themselves into Mexican society, thus helping to secure a territory that was distant from and unprofitable to the capital. So the government opened up more of the region to settlement under the same conditions. As these new arrivals came, buying as much as 4,000 acres for $40, considerably less than the cost of land in the States, dissension began. Unlike Austin's original First Families, many of the new arrivals were malcontents, restless adventurers, and others uncomfortable with the restrictions of American society. Several brought their slaves with them.

Few of the new breed of settlers bothered to learn Spanish; most of those who made the formal declaration of Faith were not Catholics and moreover often had contempt for that religion, which they considered a superstitious cult. The social differences between these rough Anglo settlers and the local Mexicans were considerable. Most of the Anglos were single men, unattached to any community or tradition. The Mexicans had lived in the region for decades prior to independence from Spain in 1821. They had raised families, developed the land, built homes, and formed local governments. Dissension was beginning to grow.

Some of the settlers were small farmers who bought land in Texas because their own farms had become overworked and un-profitable. This was especially true of cotton plantation owners who moved into the region with their families and their slaves. They considered the local inhabitants to be racially inferior to the Anglo-Saxon. In addition, the majority of the new settlers were Protestants who held the Catholic religion to be a "misdirected and misbegotten religion,"[4] and "idolatrous Popery." The American Bible Society urged the unity of Protest-

---

4.   K. Jack Bauer, *The Mexican War. 1846-1848.* (New York: Macmillan Co., 1974), 14.

ant sects to combat Rome's influence in the Americas. The stage was set for both religious and racial conflict.

In 1827, there were 12,000 Anglos living in Texas. By 1835, there were 30,000 colonists, mostly impervious to the local traditions and unwilling to assimilate. Many of them were also contemptuous of the people whom they considered half-breeds, "more degraded even than our Blacks."[5] In addition, they grew increasingly unwilling to abide by many of the Mexican laws as well, including those concerned with ownership (slavery was outlawed in Mexico in 1829), possession of unregistered firearms, and payment of federal and state taxes. Because of this, the Mexican government sought to put a stop to further settlement of this area by foreigners.

Santa Anna and the Texas Rebellion

Mexico was a federalist government at this time, with state governments usually capable of settling differences between settlers and longtime inhabitants. However, President Antonio López de Santa Anna was elected in 1833 as a reaction of the military and the Church against the previous liberal government that had confiscated Church property, limited the power of the Mexican Army, and established local militias. Santa Anna established the Plan of Cuernavaca in 1834 that mandated a change in the Constitution to replace the federal form of government with one that was fully centralized in Mexico City with the states organized into military districts. He also restored confiscated properties to the Church, eliminated the local militias, and restored the army to its previous standing.

The centralist cast of the new Mexican administration was just the catalyst that the Anglo settlers had been waiting for. Knowing that the state governments were no longer effective and that the central government would take much longer to respond to any crisis, they saw an opportunity. Encouraged by expansionists in the

---

5.   George Frederick Ruxton, *Adventures in Mexico and the Rocky Mountains* (New York: Harper and Bros., 1846), 26.

US, and using the election of Santa Anna as the final straw, they made plans for a revolt.

Who was this Santa Anna and how did his rise to power bring the Texas pot to a boil? There is no question that, in the history of the Americas, Santa Anna is one of the most colorful characters. He was born in 1794 in Veracruz. He was a *criollo*, that is, a native of the Americas whose parents were pure or "white" Christian Spaniards, with no mixture of Moor or Indian blood. He joined the Spanish Army at age sixteen and saw combat a year later. For ten years, he was a cavalry officer who supported the cause of the King in New Spain, fought against insurgents and Indians, was injured by arrows in one major Indian uprising, and had been commended for valor in battle. He rose fairly quickly through the officer ranks from second lieutenant in 1812 to captain in 1816. Here he witnessed the Spanish Army's "no quarter" policy for rebels. All prisoners were summarily executed. Nonetheless, in 1821, Santa Anna left the Spanish Army and joined the Mexican rebels with the rank of general in their fight for independence. His personal risk was extreme and his courage was notable. When the Mexican Republic devolved to a repressive imperial phase, he turned against the forces of Emperor Iturbide and helped to restore a representative government. In 1829, when Spain attempted to re-conquer Mexico (similar to England's invasion of the US in 1812), Santa Anna again took to the field and crushed the Spanish forces at Tampico. He was named "Savior of His Country" and a medal was struck in his honor by the Mexican Congress.[6]

Wisely, Santa Anna did not run for office during this turbulent time. Four of the original leaders of the War of Independence died violently. When he did finally run for president in 1833, the charismatic general received an overwhelming majority. It was the first of many political victories. Day-to-day administration was not his strength, however. Moreover, since he was elected as a liberal, he would be expected to make reforms that would weaken his popularity with the Church and his friends in the military. He retreated

---

6.   Rafael F. Muñoz, Santa Anna, El dictador resplandesciente (México: Fondo de Cultura Económica, 1983), 107-122.

to his estate in Jalapa, Veracruz, and left the daily administration of the government to his vice-president, Gomez Farías. When Farías secularized the Church, confiscated its funds, and then reduced the power of the army, the conservatives rushed to Santa Anna's estate to persuade him to return to power. He did so with a vigor that troubled the Texans who had grown used to the benevolent disregard of the federal government and their untaxed, unfettered way of life.

It should be noted that among the laws they found most onerous was one stating that anyone living in Texas with an unregistered gun would be considered a pirate and subject to immediate execution. The unlimited right to bear arms was one Texans took seriously even in those days, and they vowed to shoot any Mexican trying to enforce the law. Led by Sam Houston, who left a career in politics in Tennessee to come to Texas in 1829, the settlers declared their independence on March 2, 1836. They chose David Burnett as the first president of their new nation.[7]

Several other states also openly rebelled against the new government. In addition to Texas (which would become the Republic of Texas), the Yucatán, Tamaulipas, and Zacatecas also revolted. Some of these states formed their own brief governments as well: the Republic of the Rio Grande and the Republic of Yucatán. The Zacatecan militia, the largest of the northern Mexican states, was well armed with .753 caliber British 'Brown Bess' muskets and Baker .61 rifles and posed the most immediate threat. But, after two hours of combat on May 12, 1835, Santa Anna defeated the Zacatecan militia and took almost 3,000 prisoners. After that signal victory, he planned to move on to Coahuila y Tejas to quell the revolt there, which was being supported by settlers from the United States (aka *Texians*). In his northern march, however, Santa Anna faced many obstacles including scarcity of supplies, inadequate manpower, and untrained Indian troops. In addition, the troops were not used to or dressed for the colder weather of the north, water sources were polluted, and Apache attacks cut down strag-

---

7.   Josefina Vásquez, *The Texas Question in Mexican Politics, 1836-1845*, in *Southwestern Historical Quarterly 89* (1986), 309-344.

glers. Santa Anna, however, was confident that a show of force would intimidate the Texas troops. Not only had he successfully defeated a larger, well-equipped Zacatecan force but now with his announcement that "all foreigners who might be caught under arms on Mexican soil would be treated as pirates and shot," he expected the rebels would surrender. He also reinforced his edict by having his buglers sound *el degüello* to signal that the Texas rebels would receive no quarter if they did not.

At the Battle of the Alamo on March 6, 1836, his troops handily defeated the defenders led by William Barrett Travis after they barricaded themselves in the Alamo, a Franciscan mission on the outskirts of San Antonio de Bexar. They held out for thirteen days but, at the end of the battle, the Texans were dead. However, the lengthy siege of the Alamo gave ships manned by Texas rebels time to plunder Mexican ports along the coast, and provided other Texas land forces time to gain both weapons and ammunition from the United States.

But one more defeat would follow before the Texan forces could rally. On March 26, 1836, the Mexicans surrounded a large force of Texas rebels at Goliad. Lt. Col. Nicolás de la Portilla accepted their surrender and intended to hold them as prisoners. However, Santa Anna ordered them all summarily executed, citing the national law of piracy and the illegal bearing of arms as a justification. These excesses of Santa Anna were to give the Texas rebels a new solidarity and a desperation of purpose.

Aroused by Santa Anna's brutality, and using "Remember the Alamo, remember Goliad" as a battle cry, on April 21, 1836, the Texas rebels, reinforced by supplies and men from all over the United States, retaliated at the Battle of San Jacinto. The Mexican Army, weakened by lack of supplies and wearied by forced marches, was overwhelmed and almost the entire force was killed or captured at the Battle of San Jacinto. Santa Anna himself was taken and held captive.

While a prisoner, Santa Anna was "persuaded" by the Texans to sign two "treaties." In the first, he stipulated that he would cease all hostilities and would take his remaining troops across the Rio Grande. In the second, he stipulated that in exchange for his release and transportation to Veracruz, he would endeavor to persuade the Mexican government to formally recognize Texas independence. The Mexican Congress responded by enacting a law stipulating that any agreement made by a Mexican president while being held prisoner was null and void. It also refused to recognize Texas as an independent nation. Santa Anna returned to Mexico in disgrace and retired to his hacienda in Jalapa, Veracruz.[8] Within two years, however, he would once again have an opportunity to seize the stage and become a military hero.

8.   Summary based on facts generally agreed on by both US and Mexican historians. See Cecil Robinson's *The View from Chapultepec: Mexican Writers on the U.S.-Mexican War* (Tucson: University of Arizona, 1979) and Josefina Vázquez and Lorenzo Meyer, *Mexicanos y Norteamericanos ante la Guerra de 47* (México: Ediciones Ateneo, 1977), Chap 2.

2

TEXAS STATEHOOD AND GENERAL TAYLOR'S ARMY

In September 1836, Texas voted overwhelmingly in favor of annexation and had support from the pro-slavery faction in Congress. Mexico did not recognize the new republic, however, and many inhabitants of Texas did not feel safe. They felt it was just a matter of time before efforts were made to recover the lost territory. But when the Texas minister in Washington, DC, proposed annexation to the Martin Van Buren administration in August 1837, he was told that the proposition could not be entertained. While the United States recognized Texas independence in 1837, many Americans objected to Texas statehood on the grounds that Texas would become a slave state with its entrance into the Union and the slave states would then outnumber the free states.

The debate raged on. Many southern politicians saw Texas statehood simply as a way to spread the institution of slavery, since the federal law provided no express restrictions on slavery in newly-acquired territories. In fact, some hoped that Texas, because of its size, might yield two or three slave states each with their own senators and representatives in Congress. Northerners, fearing that the admission of Texas would give the South control of Congress, opposed its annexation. Still others, who opposed slavery on principle, argued the moral issue of admitting to the Union a territory already populated by slaveholders. Others were opposed to annexation because they felt that the Texans had deliberately provoked the Mexicans by refusing to obey Mexican laws. This group, called the Anti-Texass Legion, persisted in purposely misspelling the name of the territory.[9]

The controversy over the issue of slavery, and the balance of power that would be subverted by admission of Texas as a slave state, grew so heated that John Quincy Adams, the former president, felt that the Union itself might not survive the controversy. In 1839, the outgoing president, Andrew Jackson, favored Texas statehood but thought it untimely coming right on the heels of the Texans' military victory. He felt that it would appear to the rest of the world as if the US had simply infiltrated Mexican territory with armed bands with the sole intent of seizing the territory for the US. This, indeed, was the opinion of the Mexican government.

William Henry Harrison was elected in 1840, and he was a moderate on the issue as well. His vice-president, however, a compromise candidate chosen to get the Southern vote, was committed to Texas annexation. The Whig party reasoned that vice-presidents have no power and so John Tyler's opinion on the question would have no effect. But as fate would have it, Harrison died after less than a month in office and Tyler acquired the presidency. He would try to push annexation through Congress with little success until just prior to the inauguration of his successor. So, for nearly ten years, Texas remained an independent nation, viz., "The Lone Star Republic."

Santa Anna Returns

Meanwhile, Mexico, torn with internal conflicts and power struggles, was unable to muster sufficient manpower or resources to retake its captured territory in the north. Santa Anna was driven into exile for making concessions to the Texans in 1837. However, in 1838, Mexico became involved in a war with France. During the chaos following the independence of Mexico, the property of for-

9.   Benjamin Lundy, "Anti-Texass Legion: Protest of some free men, states and presses against the Texass rebellion, against the laws of nature and of nations." (Albany: n/p, 1845.) http://texashistory.unt.edu/ark:/67531/metapth2356/

eign nationals was often damaged or confiscated. As a result, claims were filed by these nations. France's claim, based in part upon pastries consumed without compensation by hungry Mexican soldiers who had raided a French bakery in Mexico City, was one of these nations. Called the "Pastry War" by Mexico City journalists, it began when France had launched an invasion to secure reparations for her ten-year-old claim.

Santa Anna offered his services to defend Mexico and was invited to return home. He personally led an army that repulsed the French invasion and forced the French to settle their claims for a reduced sum and withdraw their troops. His horse was shot from under him while he was leading his men, and he was severely wounded in the knee. A few days later his leg was amputated. The victorious and wounded general was once again seen as a hero by the Mexican people.

Santa Anna, capitalizing on his popularity as a victorious general, had his leg buried with military honors and had a sumptuous new theater built in Mexico City, which he named after himself. Then followed a political vacuum, during which time Santa Anna had retreated to his villa to recover from his wounds. A revolt in 1841 brought him "reluctantly" back to power for three years, after which he was ousted in a military coup by a rival general. He then was exiled in 1845 to Cuba for ten years.[10]

Meanwhile, there were Indian uprisings in the Yucatán, and near bankruptcy in the capital. Mexico could still not afford to pay its foreign debts, including an embarrassing one to the United States for which the payments were overdue. Rival generals fought for control of the country, as taxes and domestic instability increased.

Polk Plans Aggressive Action

In 1844, while Mexico was busy dealing with its internal problems, James K. Polk was elected president of the United States on a platform that advocated Texas statehood. Shortly after the election,

---

10. Muñoz, *op. Cit.*, p. 196.

but prior to Polk's actual inauguration, Tyler, the lame duck president, had an annexation measure introduced to Congress. He had failed previously to get a two-thirds vote required for a treaty, but a joint resolution was finally approved in the closing hours of his administration. It was not ratified until July, however, and Texas did not formally become a state of the Union until December 1845.

Mexico had never recognized the independence of Texas. In addition, Mexico had previously warned the US that annexation would be an act of war. The US ignored these warnings. Additionally, the US claimed that the southern boundary of their new state was the Rio Grande del Norte (Rio Bravo) and not the southwest boundary marked on all existing maps at the Rio Nueces, considerably to the north.

The new administration was also responding to business interests who wanted the US to acquire Santa Fe, a valuable trading post, in the area now known as New Mexico. Additionally, California seemed attractive to expansionists in Congress. In late 1845, Polk sent his representative John Slidell to Mexico City to make an offer to buy both California and New Mexico. He was willing to forgive the Mexican debts, pay $5 million for New Mexico, and up to $25 million for California. The Mexican press got wind of it, and broadsides threatened revolution if the Mexican president even considered negotiation. The Mexican president, José Joaquín Herrera, although a moderate on the issue, felt that his hands were tied. Any attempt to negotiate might lead to his own fall from power. Accordingly, he refused to receive Slidell. Annoyed, Polk decided to become more aggressive. He wrote in his journal that he felt the status quo was impossible and he needed to take action.[11]

In mid-June 1845, a month before Texas had ratified annexation by the US and six months before Texas became a state, President Polk had the Secretary of War, William Marcy, order General Zachary Taylor to take a position south of the Nueces River with a force of approximately 4,000 men. By the end of July, there was a major US encampment in the Mexican village of Corpus Christi.

---

11.   Milo Milton Quife, *The Diary of James K. Polk* (Chicago: A.C. McClurg & Co., 1910). Facsimile Edition, University of Chicago. Entry of May 8, 1846, Vol 2. 81.

Polk's intention was clear. This was a show of force intended to give the Mexicans a sense of reality in the settlement of various matters he intended to take up, among them the purchase of California.[12]

In January 1846, Polk, in an effort to increase the pressure on the Mexicans to agree to a settlement, ordered Taylor to take a position on the Rio Grande, well beyond the official boundary of Mexico prior to the Santa Anna debacle. By March, Taylor had done so and constructed a fort on a bluff on the north bank of the river just opposite the Mexican town of Matamoros. Originally called Fort Texas, it was later to be re-named Fort Brown because of the death of its commander Major Jacob Brown in battle, and is the present site of Brownsville. Since the American Army had already crossed the Nueces River, Taylor's forces had actually been in Mexican (or at least disputed) territory, since June of the previous year. Now, building a fort on the banks of the Rio Grande and moving up artillery on the bluffs above a large Mexican settlement, the actions of the Americans seemed to the Mexicans to be calculated aggression.

---

12.   Bernard de Voto, *The Year of Decision: 1846* (Boston: Little, Brown & Co, 1943), 14.

Fig. 1. General Zachary Taylor, circa 1845. Daguerrotype, cropped. Library of Congress.

Fig. 2. General Antonio López de Santa Anna. Official portrait. ca. 1830.

3

THE THORNTON AFFAIR
AND MR. POLK'S WAR

Zachary Taylor was an unlikely general. Small in stature, overweight, with a grandfatherly face, he rarely wore the standard military uniform. He preferred an old straw hat, backwoods clothes, and a dirty bandanna around his neck. He often sat in front of his quarters to take the air. In spite of his unsoldierly appearance, however, Taylor was highly respected by his men and had combat experience in the War of 1812 and the Seminole War. After the latter conflict, he retired with the rank of colonel.

Called affectionately "Old Zack" and "Rough and Ready" by his soldiers, General Taylor was old for field command, almost sixty-one, and had been looking forward to settling down permanently to the life of a gentleman farmer. He had bought plantations in Louisiana and in Mississippi and had made plans for their increased production. He was a Whig and a slave owner; President Polk was a Democrat and an expansionist. Political differences were put aside, however, because of the high marks as a commander that Andrew Jackson gave Taylor in his conversations with Polk.

Taylor's official rank was that of Colonel of the 6th Infantry. His title of Brigadier General was a "brevet" title, that is, an honorary rank usually given for valor and not carrying with it the pay scale or emoluments for the higher grade. Notwithstanding the honorary nature of his rank, Taylor would become effectively the Commander-in-Chief of the US Army in Northern Mexico. Despite his casual style, reviewing his troops side-saddle on "Old Whitey," his leg casually cocked over the pommel, he would command the respect not only of his soldiers but of the entire United States.

On July 25, 1845, Taylor was ordered to leave New Orleans with eight companies of the Third Regiment and proceed to Corpus Christi at the mouth of the Nueces River. This was the border between Texas and Mexico on all the current maps. There they were joined by additional infantry as well as artillery troops and volunteers. It was thought by Polk that such a movement would convince the Mexicans of the seriousness of his negotiations for the purchase of California and the land route in the southwest. The Mexican government, however, remained adamant in its refusal to sell.

On January 13, 1846, Polk, in an effort to increase the pressure on the Mexicans to agree to a settlement, instructed Secretary of War William L. Marcy to give the critical order: "Advance and occupy, with the troops under your command, positions on or near the east bank of the Rio del Norte (Rio Grande) as soon as can be conveniently done."[13] When American troops crossed the Nueces, Mexico was certain to consider her territory invaded, and, in the language of Secretary Marcy, as "the commencement of hostilities." General Taylor privately agreed, and in his letters noted that this action was "unnecessary and provocative." Nevertheless, he followed his orders.

The construction of fortifications on the Rio Grande was further evidence of US aggression, not only to the Mexicans but also to several members of Congress in the United States. One US Whig senator observed that ordering Taylor to cross the River Nueces with his army and advancing to the banks of the Rio Grande was "as much an act of aggression on our part as is a man's pointing a pistol at another's breast."[14]

---

13.   William Holland Samson, ed., *Letters of Zachary Taylor from the Battlefields of the Mexican War.* (Rochester: Genesee Press, 1908, Amazon Kindle 2012). xix.

14.   William R. Everdell, *The End of Kings: A History of Republics and Republicans.* (Chicago: University of Chicago, 2000), 215.

On April 25, 1846, a scout suggested that a Mexican cavalry troop may have crossed the Rio Grande upstream of Taylor's army. Captain Seth Thornton was ordered by Taylor to take a patrol and see if his information was correct.

The Thornton Affair

According to the after-battle reports of Captain William J. Hardee, Captain Seth B. Thornton and 52 dragoons under his command were sent by Gen. Taylor to reconnoiter the Mexican positions to see if they had crossed the Rio Grande on April 26th. About 23 miles from camp, their guide refused to go farther and said that there were signs of Mexican cavalry. But Thornton persisted. They came to a large fenced property called Rancho Carricitos, which bordered the river. Once there, they opened the gate and entered the property in force through a narrow roadway. It was casually and contemptuously done without any guard or sentinel placed outside the gate in case they should be surprised. Captain Thornton was "convinced that the Mexicans would not fight" even if they later arrived at the ranch.[15]

An old man was found on the property, and while Thornton was talking with him the Mexican cavalry arrived. Thornton gave the signal to charge. However, his men who had been scattered about exploring the property were in "a perfect state of disorder" and were soon overwhelmed, with several killed or wounded. Capt. Hardee, the author of the report writes as follows:

> I rode up to Captain Thornton and told him that our only hope for safety was tearing down the fence: he gave the order, but could not stop his horse, nor would the men stop. Foreseeing that the direction Captain Thornton was pursuing would lead to the certain destruction of himself and men, without the possibility of resistance, I turned to the right and had the men follow me. I made for the river, intending to either swim it or place myself in a position

---

15. Steven R. Butler, ed. *A Documentary History of the Mexican War* (Richardson, Texas: Descendants of Mexican War Veterans, 1995), p. 53

of defense. I found the bank too bogging to accomplish the former...and almost everyone had lost a sabre, a pistol or carbine....[16]

Seeing that they were outnumbered, and believing that Capt. Thornton was among the fallen, Hardee surrendered his men with the understanding from the Mexican commander that they would be "treated with all the consideration to which such unfortunates are entitled by the rules of civilized warfare."

He was not mistaken in his expectation. As befitting the rules of war with a legitimate army, the Mexican general treated the American invaders honorably even though they were invaders. Unlike the Texans, they were a legitimate army—not a rebel horde— and the officers were given traditional Mexican hospitality and respect. In the words of Captain W. J. Hardee:

> I take pleasure in stating that since our surrender I and my brave companions in misfortune have been treated with uniform kindness and attention. It may soften the rigor of war for you to be informed of this fact. Lieutenant Kane and myself are living with General Ampudia, we lodge in his hotel, eat at his table, and his frank, agreeable manner and generous hospitality, almost make us forget our captivity. General Arista received us in the most gracious manner, said that his nation had been regarded as barbarous, and that he wished to prove to us the contrary. Told Lieutenant Kane and myself that we should receive half pay, and our men should receive ample rations, and in lieu of it for today 25 cents apiece. On declining the boon of the money, on the part of Lieutenant Kane and myself, I asked that we might be permitted to send to camp for money and he said that he could not permit it, that he intended to supply all our wants himself. These promises have already been fulfilled in part. [17]

In the battle, eleven Americans were killed and five wounded. The wounded were sent back to the American lines by Lieutenant Torrejon who stated he did not have "the medical facilities to care for them."[18] All the officers and men were later released as part of a prisoner exchange including Capt. Thornton who did not fall in

---

16. *Ibid.*
17. *Ibid.*
18. *Ibid.*

the battle, but went on to participate in the September 1847 takeover of Mexico City.

Mr. Polk's War

Meanwhile, although Polk had already decided to declare war and had drafted his declaration, he was not sure how Congress would respond. He called his cabinet together to consult with them on the afternoon of May 8th, and at the end of the meeting resolved to submit his war message on Tuesday, May 11th. However, that evening he received Taylor's dispatch of April 26th stating that hostilities had commenced. That gave Polk the opportunity for which he had been waiting. He revised his original draft to include news of the Thornton incident, which he interpreted as a *casus belli*. He sent his message to Congress on Monday, a day early, declaring that, since the Mexicans had "shed American blood on American soil," a state of war existed between the US and Mexico.

In the original draft, which he included in his address to Congress, he stated the real reason for calling up the troops. Mexico refused to sell California, refused even to negotiate with the American envoy despite his persistence. To Polk, this behavior of a weaker nation was intolerable, as can be seen, in the first paragraph of his war message to Congress.

The Government of Mexico, though solemnly pledged by official acts in October last to receive and accredit an American envoy, violated their plighted faith and refused the offer of a peaceful adjustment of our difficulties. Not only was the offer rejected, but the indignity of its rejection was enhanced by the manifest breach of faith in refusing to admit the envoy who came because they had bound themselves to receive him. Nor can it be said that the offer was fruitless from want of opportunity of discussing it; our envoy was present on their own soil. Nor can it be ascribed to a want of sufficient powers; our envoy had full powers to adjust every question of difference. Nor was there room for complaint that our propositions for settlement were unreasonable; permission was not even given our envoy to make any proposition whatever. Nor can it be objected that we, on our part, would not listen to any reasonable terms of their suggestion; the Mexican Government refused all negotiation, and have made no proposition of any kind.[19]

In the next paragraph, he justified sending General Taylor and his army to the Rio Nueces on the pretext that he wished to prevent an invasion by Mexico!

> In my message at the commencement of the present session I informed you that upon the earnest appeal both of the Congress and convention of Texas I had ordered an efficient military force to take a position "between the Nueces and Del Norte." This had become necessary to meet a threatened invasion of Texas by the Mexican forces, for which extensive military preparations had been made. The invasion was threatened solely because Texas had determined, in accordance with a solemn resolution of the Congress of the United States, to annex herself to our Union, and under these circumstances it was plainly our duty to extend our protection over her citizens and soil.[20]

In the third paragraph, he confirmed what the original motivation was: the failure to receive the envoy and conclude the sale of Mexican land to the United States. It was then and only then that he ordered Secretary Marcy to relay the order to Taylor to send the troops down to the Rio Grande.

> This force was concentrated at Corpus Christi, and remained there until after I had received such information from Mexico as rendered it probable, if not certain, that the Mexican Government would refuse to receive our envoy….[21]

Finally, he added the last argument, the disastrous American raid on the Mexican rancho. The Thornton Affair gave Polk what was in his opinion the most convincing reason for the declaration of war. Polk boldly contended that the Mexicans themselves caused the war by defending themselves against Thornton's dragoons who had not only crossed the border illegally and entered Mexican terri-

---

19.   James K. Polk, Address to Congress, May 11, 1846. http://www.dmwv.org/mexwar/
      documents/polk.htm
20.   *Ibid.*
21.   *Ibid.*

tory but had also trespassed on private property within Mexico and attacked Mexican cavalry who were there to protect that property.

> The cup of forbearance had been exhausted even before the recent information from the frontier of the Del Norte. But now, after reiterated menaces, *Mexico has passed the boundary of the United States, has invaded our territory and shed American blood upon the American soil.* [Emphasis supplied.] She has proclaimed that hostilities have commenced, and that the two nations are now at war.
>
> *As war exists,* [Emphasis supplied] and, notwithstanding all our efforts to avoid it, exists by the act of Mexico herself, we are called upon by every consideration of duty and patriotism to vindicate with decision the honor, the rights, and the interests of our country.[22]

There are two significant problems with the two paragraphs above where the emphasis is supplied. The first is that there was no existing map that showed the frontier to be the Rio del Norte (Rio Grande), nor was such a frontier recognized by any country, or established by a treaty ratified by any country. So, Polk's argument that Mexico passed the boundary of the United States was false, as was his assertion that American blood was shed on American soil.

The second problem is Polk's assertion that "war exists" and that it "exists by the act of Mexico herself." What existed at the time of this assertion were hostilities, certainly, but they could have been resolved by thoughtful negotiation. War was by no means inevitable and obviously did not "exist" at the time of the declaration. It was up to Congress to declare war after every reasonable attempt to resolve differences had been exhausted. Polk's assumption of the war powers from Congress, as well as his ordering the preemptive invasion of Mexican territory a month earlier and building fortifications, were both overreaching acts and abuses of the executive power.

But, of course, Polk was not naïve. He knew this all along. His intent, formed prior to even taking office, was to extend American territory across the southwest and, if he could not purchase the southwest land route and California, to wrest these territories from

22.   *Ibid.*

Mexico. In fact, soon after Texas statehood was accomplished, he ordered Taylor to begin recruiting troops. As Polk himself noted:

> Anticipating the possibility of a crisis like that which has arrived, instructions were given in August last, "as a precautionary measure" against invasion or threatened invasion, authorizing General Taylor, if the emergency required it, to accept volunteers, not from Texas only, but from the States of Louisiana, Alabama, Mississippi, Tennessee, and Kentucky, and corresponding letters were addressed to the respective governors of those States. These instructions were repeated, and in January last, soon after the incorporation of "Texas into our Union of States," General Taylor was further "authorized by the President to make a requisition upon the executive of that State for such of its militia force as may be needed to repel invasion or to secure the country against apprehended invasion." On the 2d day of March, he was again reminded, "in the event of the approach of any considerable Mexican force, promptly and efficiently to use the authority with which he was clothed to call to him such auxiliary force as he might need." War actually existing and our territory having been invaded, General Taylor, pursuant to authority vested in him by my direction, has called on the governor of Texas for four regiments of State troops, two to be mounted and two to serve on foot, and on the governor of Louisiana for four regiments of infantry to be sent to him as soon as practicable.[23]

Everything was in place for an offensive war. What remained now was to overcome the resistance which he would likely face from the Whigs, the anti-slavery block, and the New England peace advocates. The best way to do that was to have the House leader limit debate on the war resolution and move it on a fast track. Congress approved the declaration of war on May 13, with southern Democrats in strong support. Sixty-seven Whigs voted against the war on a key slavery amendment, but on the final passage, only 14 Whigs in the House voted no, including Rep. John Quincy Adams. Congress declared war on Mexico on May 13, 1846, after only having a few hours to debate. Later, Polk would gleefully write: "We had not gone to war for conquest. But it was clear that in making peace we would, if possible, get California and other parts of Mexico."[24] The Senate voted 40-2 to support Polk's war.

23.   *Ibid.*
24.   Quoted by Sydney Lens, in *The Forging of the American Empire: From the Revolution to*

Ohio Senator Tom Corwin, one of those voting against the war bill, accused Polk of involving the United States in a war of aggression. Senator John C. Calhoun of South Carolina abstained from voting, correctly foreseeing that the war would aggravate sectional strife. Other citizens shared their legislators' concern, particularly those in the Northeast who saw the war as a ploy to extend slavery. The most celebrated was Henry David Thoreau, who refused to pay his Massachusetts poll tax because he believed the war an immoral advancement of slavery.

Many Americans opposed what they called "Mister Polk's War." Whig Party members and Abolitionists in the North believed that slave owners and Southerners in Polk's administration had planned the war. They believed the South wanted to conquer Mexican territory for the purpose of spreading and strengthening slavery. Polk claimed to be sympathetic with the concerns of those who wished to limit the growth of slavery, but said that he considered those who did not support the war to be giving comfort to the enemy and, essentially, no better than traitors. He would include among this latter contingent, not only the loyal Whig opposition, but also a young Illinois congressman by the name of Abraham Lincoln.

Fig. 3. Earliest known representation of Abraham Lincoln. Taken shortly after his election to Congress. Daguerreotype by Nicolas H. Shepherd. Springfield, Illinois 1846. Courtesy of Library of Congress, Daguerreotype Division. 20th century quality image made from a copy of a 19th century negative.

4

THE LOYAL OPPOSITION ARGUES AGAINST
WAR WITH MEXICO

Opposition to the War was mixed. Abolitionists and those who believed that this conflict would create an opening for more slave states were among the most outspoken. The leaders of the Whig party who saw Polk's imperialist tendencies as contrary to America's founding principles were also quick in their response to Polk's war declaration. Peace societies and movements centered mainly in New England were vociferous in their opposition. For the majority of the country, however, the war was seen as a chance to expand into territory that was sparsely populated or settled mostly by Indio or Mestizo people whom they considered inferior. Manifest Destiny was the catchword of the day, from a newspaper editorial of John L. Sullivan. "More, more more!..till our national destiny is fulfilled...and the whole boundless continent is ours."[25] It captured the prevalent belief that the States had the divine right to expand from "sea to shining sea."

There were some obvious impediments to unchecked expansion. As mentioned earlier, the border that the United States claimed for the new state of Texas was in Mexican territory. In addition, California, with its attractive ports of San Francisco and San Diego, was Mexican, as was Santa Fe, the necessary link in

---

25. New York *Morning News*, February 7, 1845.

the overland route. And, while the doctrine of Manifest Destiny allowed for the displacement of Indians, and the Monroe Doctrine could justify sharp dealing with European powers, Mexico was now an independent republic, and one which had thrown off the chains of Spanish colonialism just thirty-five years earlier. How could the US possibly justify an unprovoked attack on a sister republic?

The answer would be twofold. First, that allegiance to the Catholic Church was evidence of the Mexicans' ignorance and degradation. Second, the mixed blood of the people, the large numbers of Indians among them, and their three hundred years of Spanish dominance made them unfit for self-government. It was the US mission to save them from themselves. According to an editorial in the *Boston Times*, the taking of Mexican territory would not be a "conquest" at all in the usual sense of the term, but rather one which:

> ...institutes the reign of law where license has existed for a generation; which provides for the education and elevation of the great mass of people, who have for a period of three hundred years been the helots of an overbearing foreign race, and which causes full freedom and liberty of conscience to prevail where priesthood has long been enabled to prevent all religion save that of its worship,—such a "conquest," stigmatize it as you please, must necessarily be a great blessing to the conquered. It is a work worthy of a great people, a people about to generate the world by asserting the supremacy of humanity over the accidents of birth and fortune.[26]

More poetically, an editor for the *New York Herald* wrote an oft-quoted simile that encompassed both sexism and arrogance. "Like the Sabine virgins, she [Mexico] will soon learn to love her ravisher."[27]

For some American soldiers, this latter quote was taken literally. The Arkansas Cavalry, known as the "Rackensakers," were described as "wild and reckless fellows."[28] Like many volunteers convinced of their racial superiority they had "the firm belief that their own State could whip the world and Mexico in particular."[29] When

26. *Boston Times*, October 27, 1847.
27. *New York Herald*, October 8, 1847.
28. Samuel E. Chamberlain, *My Confession* (New York: Harper & Bros., 1956), 89.
29. *Ibid.*

one of their men was found killed in an ambush, they captured a group of Mexican peasants and raped and killed indiscriminately. As many as thirty men, women, and children had been brutally murdered when a company of Illinois volunteers finally arrived at the scene to restrain them. No one was prosecuted because General Taylor was unable to identify the guilty parties. He initially ordered two companies of the regiment back to the Rio Grande, but changed his mind when the battle of Buena Vista became imminent.[30]

The Texans who entered the war with a sworn hatred for the Mexicans were noted for their indiscriminate acts of murder and vengeance. The Texas Rangers, wrote one American observer, "spare none but shoot down every [Mexican] they meet."[31] General Taylor remarked that the Texans were "too licentious to do much good" but that he was "unsuccessful in [his] attempts to discipline them."[32]

Some degree of dehumanization is to be expected in any war, but the level and intensity of it in the Mexican War was virulent. Perhaps the only comparable contemporary example would be My Lai during the Vietnam War. After the massacre at My Lai was revealed, however, there was moral outrage back home, the offenders were brought to trial, and soul-searching on the part of the nation began. In contrast, the atrocities in Mexico by American volunteers were ongoing and commonplace. They were widely reported in the press and formally documented by the federal officers. Still, they continued. Commanders felt powerless to prevent them and neither the public nor the politicians back home seemed perturbed. As one contemporary put it:

Time, with his scythe and hourglass, had brought another and newer race, to sweep away the mouldered and mouldering institutions of a worn-out people, and replace them with a fresher and more vigorous civilization.[33]

30. *Niles' National Register,* LXXII (April 10, 1847), 89. See also Johannsen, *To the Hall of the Montezumas: The Mexican War in the American Imagination* (New York/Oxford: Oxford University Press, 1985). 37-38.

31. Frank S. Edwards, *A Campaign in New Mexico With Colonel Doniphan* (Philadelphia: Carey and Hart, 1847), 155-156.

32. William H. Samson (ed.) *Letters of Zachary Taylor from the Battlefields of the Mexican War.* (Rochester: The Genesee Press, 1908), 24.

33. Raphael Semmes, *Service Afloat and Ashore During the Mexican War* (Cincinnati: Wm.

Right from the start, there were those who, convinced of An-
glo-Saxon superiority and the compelling mystique of Manifest
Destiny, urged the prosecution of the war and the conquest of
Mexican territory. One of the most vocal was the well-known (and
now much-revered) American poet, Walt Whitman. As soon as
he heard about the bloodshed at the skirmish on the Rio Grande,
Whitman wrote a fiery editorial for the Brooklyn *Daily Eagle* urging
President Polk to declare war.

> Yes, Mexico must be thoroughly chastised. We have reached a point in our
> intercourse with that country, when prompt and effective demonstration of
> force are enjoined upon is by every dictate of right and policy. The news of
> yesterday [i.e. the Thornton Affair] has added the best argument wanted to
> prove the necessity of immediate Declaration of War by our government
> towards its southern neighbors.[34]

Whitman went on to describe the Mexicans as "a race of bravos."
His contempt for the people, for their religion, for their government, and his belief in the "great mission" of Manifest Destiny
would become even clearer in a subsequent editorial.

> What has miserable, inefficient Mexico—with her superstition, her burlesque
> upon freedom, her actual tyranny by the few over the many—what has she
> to do with the great mission of the new world with a noble race. Be it ours,
> to achieve that mission.[35]

Meanwhile, the United States forces under General Taylor, with
their advanced "flying artillery" that was far superior to any the
Mexicans possessed, easily mowed down their larger but un-
der-equipped enemy. Taylor won battles at Resaca de Palma, Palo
Alto, and then Monterrey. By February 1847, the American forces

---

H. Moore 1851), 126. Semmes' commentary on the atrocities of the volunteers was
simply, "Jack would have his frolic." His gratuitous and demeaning remarks on the
qualities of Mexican women, as well as his remarks generally on the people of Mexico,
make for diverting reading. A Captain in the US Navy, he was promoted to Admiral
after the war.

34. Brooklyn *Daily Eagle*, 11 May 1846.
35. *Ibid.*

had their fourth major victory (with many casualties) in the ultimate conflict in Northern Mexico, the Battle of Buena Vista.

Now the President's true colors appeared. He was no longer satisfied with merely negotiating for the outstanding debt he claimed was the cause of the war, or even for indemnities for the cost of the conflict. He initiated a plan to conquer the entire country. He appointed General Winfield Scott as Commander in Chief and ordered him to attack central Mexico with the largest amphibious invasion in history up to that time. The jumping off point would be Veracruz, the eastern seaport of Mexico. His intent was to get Scott to borrow the bulk of Taylor's forces to join his own substantial army, go inland, and conquer the Mexican capital. The task was an ambitious one and would not be as simple as he had planned. Mexican resistance would grow as he approached the capital. His men would also engage in many reprehensible acts and depredations against Mexican civilians; Mexican women would be assaulted; churches and Catholic convents would be bombed and looted.[36]

The invasion of Veracruz was preceded by five days of American bombardment. Approximately 6,700 US artillery shells struck the city, or roughly 1,340 shells every 24 hours.[37] Mexican casualties were estimated at 1,100—at least 500 of them civilians.[38] Despite pleas from the foreign consuls and from the Bishop, no pause in the shelling was granted by Scott so that women, children, and foreign nationals could be evacuated.[39] A contemporary observer, Colonel Ethan Hitchcock, noted:

---

36. See Henry, 314 where Gen. Taylor begs "that no more mounted troops be sent from Texas. They have scarcely made one expedition without unwarrantedly killing civilians." The greater part of Veracruz was reduced to rubble including the Cathedral, the churches of Santa Gertrudis, San José, San Fernando and Santa Bárbara, the convent of Santo Domingo (used as a hospital) and the church of San Francisco (also used as a hospital). As to the rape and robbery of Mexican women, see Hitchcock, 250; also Scott to Marcy, HQ Army Go #20, Feb. 19, 1847, which reports one of several cases resulting in Scott's General Order #20 to try crimes not covered by the Articles of War and provide a more stringent code of conduct for the army.

37. Frías, *Guerra Contra los Gringos*, 101; Bauer, *Mexican War*, 252.

38. Bauer, *op. cit.*, p. 252.

39. See Ex. Doc 1, H.R. 30th Cong. 2nd Sess., pp. 1179-1180. See also Henry, *The Mex-*

I shall never forget the horrible fire of our mortars...going with dreadful
certainty and bursting with sepulchral tones often in the center of private
dwellings—it was awful. I shudder to think of it.[40]

When news of the shelling arrived in the United States and Europe, people were repulsed by the indiscriminate bombing. It was
after reading newspaper accounts of this atrocity that Henry David
Thoreau refused to pay his taxes in Concord, Massachusetts, and
was later to write his famous essay "On Civil Disobedience," which
outlined his philosophy of nonviolent resistance to immoral acts
of a government. It was to give the anti-war movement in New
England an added boost and lead to many editorials of which Santa
Anna was aware, and which would encourage the Mexican leader to
generate broadsides[41] encouraging defections among sympathetic
immigrant soldiers. One example of those who became convinced
they were fighting for the wrong side were the more than two hundred soldiers of the Saint Patrick's Battalion (Los San Patricios),
a group of Irish, Scots, and German Catholics who left the US
Army, and joined the Mexicans.

The American Peace Society that met in Boston was vocal in
its opposition to the war. Charles Beckwith, the Society's director,
published *The Peace Manual: or, War and Its Remedies,* in 1847. The Society's journal, *The Advocates of Peace,* contained stories of American
atrocities, the effects of war on Mexican civilians, and the blatant
injustice of the American invasion and the continued occupation
of Mexico. The journal invoked young men to avoid enlistment in
the armed forces.

---

ican War at 268. "On the 24th, the British, French, Spanish and Prussian consuls in
Veracruz moved by 'the frightful results of the bombardment,' collectively addressed
to Scott an appeal for a suspension of hostilities and a truce for the removal of the
foreign families and the Mexican women and children from the city." This request
was denied.

40. Col. Hitchcock quoted in Bronwyn Mills, *The Mexican War* (New York, Facts on File,
1992), 70.

41. Michael Hogan, *The Irish Soldiers of Mexico* (Guadalajara: Fondo Editorial Universitario,
1997), 168. Most of the broadsides were written by John Riley, the leader of the San
Patricios, at Santa Anna's direction.

Another organization that advocated peace was the New England Non-Resistance Society. This group associated the occupation of Mexico with the concept of expansion of slavery. William Lloyd Garrison, the Abolitionist, was also of this persuasion and saw the war as a blatant attempt to add more slave states to the Union.

Senator Thomas Corwin, the Whig senator from Ohio, was outspoken in his condemnation of the war, on moral grounds. The Republican congressman from Illinois, Abe Lincoln, was equally outspoken.

The peace movement, though vocal, was a minority one. For most of the people in the US, the war with Mexico provided the first opportunity for the expression of national solidarity and patriotism. The growth of newspapers, the creation of the penny press, and the invention of the telegraph, all made the war accessible to large numbers of people. Patriotism, an abstract and relatively meaningless term prior to 1845, now began to resonate with meaning as it became more concrete through vividly written accounts of American clashes with Mexican troops; clashes which, as the press jubilantly reported, the Americans won decisively.

At no time during the war was there any real question that the Americans might retreat from the position held in Mexico. After the invasion of Veracruz by General Scott, there was no doubt that the American goal would be to take the capital and thus tumble the Santa Anna government, bring the nation to its knees, and demand a vast territorial settlement as reparations.

Despite the fact that the anti-war movement was not a reflection of either American policy or the vote in Washington, which would continue to supply the American invasionary forces, misapprehensions about what it meant were current in Mexico and stiffened Mexican resistance, partly accounting for Santa Anna's reluctance to sue for peace.[42] Santa Anna read the anti-war litera-

---

42. Henry, *Mexican War*, 254. Johannsen, *To The Hall of the Montezumas*, 276. While the opposition to the war was vociferous, it was largely ineffectual. Probably it contributed to Mexican resistance and thus, ironically, prolonged the war and added to the number of casualties.

ture and he was aware that the critics of the war were well-placed in American society, and vociferous. His letters, his strategies, his rejections of peace feelers especially in 1847, all reflect this knowledge. What Santa Anna did not understand, however, was that in the Republic to the north, outspoken and even vehement criticism of the government was commonplace. Nor did he comprehend that it was entirely possible for intellectuals, senators and congressmen, ministers and free thinkers, to completely reject their country's foreign policy but continue to support their nation's troops abroad and to vote appropriations to supply and equip them, once those troops had been committed. To most Americans, failure to support the soldiers now that they had been sent to Mexico would be seen as nothing short of treason, regardless of one's personal feelings about the righteousness of the American cause.

Nevertheless, there were some disturbing signs among the troops that all was not well. By as early as March of 1847, over 9,000 men had deserted from the United States Army.[43] Brought low by dysentery and disease, disgruntled by their harsh treatment under martinet West Pointers, many simply returned to their homes at the end of a battle; some were volunteers who simply "un-volunteered," believing that they had done their share. Others headed into California or into Indian Territory where there was rich land for the taking, and the possibility of a new life. A handful, lured by drink or the charms of a Mexican señorita, headed south. Over a dozen of these, mostly Anglo-Americans, asked the British consul in Mexico City for asylum.

Abraham Lincoln Is Elected to Congress

From the beginning, Lincoln was critical of those who advocated adding Texas as a state. He saw it both as an unnecessary provocation to Mexico and a move by slave owners and their democratic representatives in Congress to create another slave state, thus dis-

---

43.   Ex. Doc. 36, 30th Cong, 1st Sess., pp. 6-7.

turbing the very fragile equilibrium between slave and free states in the Union.

Those few historians who even acknowledge Lincoln's criticism of the war with Mexico seem compelled to note that he was silent or even "indifferent" in its early stages as a way of promoting his political career. Nothing could be further from the truth. Lincoln won the Whig nomination to Congress on May 1, 1846. His views on the annexation of Texas, which had taken place the year before, were well-known. It was also clear from those who knew the party platform and voted for the Whigs that he was against creating more slave states, against southwestern expansion, and against provoking a conflict with Mexico. He was elected to Congress in August 1846, but did not take his seat until December of the following year.[44] Within three weeks of taking his seat, however, he delivered one of the most important speeches against the War.

As most freshmen congressmen, Lincoln was thoughtful, took his time to study the issues, and met with party leaders, especially those who were both articulate and shared the same moral ground. One such was Senator Thomas Corwin. Corwin was a good choice for Lincoln as a model. He had been elected to five straight terms to the House of Representatives where he was known as "the terror of the House" for his sharp wit, his devastating command of evidence, and his eloquence. In 1844, he became a US Senator and, as early as May 1846, he spoke often and vehemently against the war. But it was not mere opposition for opposition's sake. His speeches showed a clear understanding of the issues. He pointed out compelling historical connections; he argued persuasively and logically. It is clear that both his character and his legal mind had a powerful effect on the young Lincoln. Moreover, his condemnation of the war as immoral and greedy expansionism that would precipitate a sectional clash over slavery[45] was prescient. It would become the defining issue in Lincoln's career.

---

44. Although Lincoln was elected in 1846, the 30th Congress did not convene until December 6, 1847.
45. Frederick Merk, *Manifest Destiny and Mission in American History* (New York: Random House, 1966), 93.

With the demise of the Whig Party after the War, Corwin would become a Republican and campaign vigorously for Lincoln in the presidential elections of 1860. Lincoln, not only grateful for this support but clearly conscious of Corwin's voice of reason during Polk's warmongering, would appoint him Minister to Mexico (equivalent to the post of ambassador today) from 1861-64. He was one of the most popular Americans ever to hold that position in Mexican history.[46] Not only did he help heal the wounds of the conflict, but helped the US maintain a trusting and supportive relationship during its own Civil War when the United States could ill-afford to have a bitter and resentful neighbor to the south.

In 1847, Corwin faced the fact that the United States was "winning" the war but considered winning the peace something that would be a bit harder to accomplish. In a powerful speech to the Senate he noted:

> You may wrest provinces from Mexico by war—you may hold them by the right of the strongest—you may rob her, but a treaty of peace to that effect with the people of Mexico, legitimately and freely made, you will never have! I thank God that it is so, as well for the sake of the Mexican people as ourselves, for, unlike the senator from Alabama [Mr. Bagby], I do not value the life of a citizen of the United States above the lives of a hundred thousand Mexican women and children—a rather cold sort of philanthropy in my judgment. For the sake of Mexico, then, as well as our own country, I rejoice that it is an impossibility that you can obtain by treaty from her those territories under the existing state of things.[47]

Unlike the majority of Americans who couldn't have identified a single leader of Mexican independence, or found the location of Puebla, or Veracruz, or Churubusco on the map, Senator Corwin knew his history and used it to good effect.

> What is the territory, Mr. President, which you propose to wrest from Mexico? It is consecrated to the heart of the Mexican by many a well-fought battle

---

46.   Jeffrey J. Auer, "Lincoln's Minister to Mexico" in *Ohio State Archeological and Historical Quarterly 57* (1950), 115-128.

47.   Thomas Corwin, *Speech to the United States Senate,* February 11, 1847. http://www.bartleby.com/268/910.html

with his old Castilian master. His Bunker Hills, and Saratogas and Yorktowns are there. The Mexican can say, "There I bled for liberty! And shall I surrender that consecrated home of my affections to the Anglo-Saxon invaders? What do they want with it? They have Texas already. They have possessed themselves of the territory between the Nueces and the Rio Grande. What else do they want?" To what shall I point my children as memorial of that independence which I bequeathed to them when those battlefields shall have passed from my possession?"[48]

Sir, had one come and demanded Bunker Hill of the people of Massachusetts, had England's lion ever showed himself there, is there a man over thirteen and under ninety who would not have been ready to meet him; is there a river on this continent which would not have run red with blood; is there a field but would have been piled high with the unburied bones of slaughtered Americans before these consecrated battlefields of liberty should have been wrested from us? But this same American goes into a sister republic and says to poor, weak Mexico, "Give up your territory—you are unworthy to possess it—I have got one half already—all I ask is that you give up the other!"[49]

Of course for those in Boston, the words rang especially true. As the cradle of liberty, its sons and daughters were opposed to the war. John Quincy Adams was an outspoken opponent; his son was killed in combat in what he considered a disgraceful and unnecessary war. Henry David Thoreau, as mentioned above, wrote his famous essay in response to it. In addition, he refused to pay his poll taxes since he felt that money would go to support an unjust war. His friend, Emerson, is said to have asked him what he was doing inside jail. To which, he replied: "What are you doing *outside* jail, Ralph Waldo." It was his belief that jail was precisely where any American of conscience should be.[50]

Both John Greenleaf Whittier and James Russell Lowell wrote popular poems against it. Lowell's "The Biglow Papers" notes:

Ez fer war, I called it murder,—
There you have it plain and flat.
They may talk of Freedom's airy

48. *Ibid.*
49. *Ibid.*
50. Bauer, *op. cit.*, p. 359.

Tell they're purple in the face, —
It's a grand, gret cemetery
For the barthrights of our race.
They just want this Californy
So's to lug new slave states in
To abuse ye and to scorn ye
And to plunder ye like sin.[51]

Lowell's objection to the war was largely based upon the fear that new territories acquired from Mexico would become slave states.[52] He was not opposed to Manifest Destiny in principle having also written that

> ...it is the manifest destiny of the English race to occupy this whole continent and display there the practical understanding in matters of government and colonization which no other race has given such proof of possessing since the Romans.[53]

How this was to happen was still a matter of grave moral concern to citizens in New England and elsewhere. Many felt that the United States was abandoning the values of liberty and self-determination enshrined in the Declaration of Independence and their Constitution. They were concerned with how the United States would be one day be judged "in the stern tribunal of history." Like Lincoln, Corwin was a practicing attorney and knew criminal law quite well.

---

51.   J. R. Lowell, *The Biglow Papers, A Critical Edition* (DeKalb: Northern Illinois University, 1977), 51-52.

52.   Not only Lowell's objection to the War but that of most Northern Whigs was based on the fear of slavery being extended into any new territories acquired from Mexico. The Wilmot Proviso, an amendment added to an appropriation bill in 1846, made prohibition of slavery in any new territories a condition of the bill. The bill passed in the House and was defeated in the Senate. Nevertheless, the evidence seems clear that while expansion to gather new slave territory was a theme for New England opponents to the War, it was never the motivation of either the legislative branch of the United States nor the President, although some earlier historians so argued. A brief discussion of the earlier view and that now current is in the "Preface" to Henry's *The Story of the Mexican War*, no pp. To my knowledge, no US historian since the publication of Justin Smith's study of the War has maintained that expansion of slave states was a significant factor in prosecuting the War with Mexico.

53.   Quoted in Johannson, *op. cit.* at 218.

He saw the seizure of territory, even if a modest sum was to be paid for it (ultimately far less than was offered before the invasion for a much smaller portion of territory), as nothing less than armed robbery. There would be no difference legally from pointing a gun at a man and compelling him to sell his priceless Michelangelo for a tenth of its value. Noted Corwin:

> Why, says the Chairman of this committee on foreign relations, it is the most reasonable thing in the world! We ought to have the Bay of San Francisco. Why? Because it is the best harbor on the Pacific! It has been my fortune, Mr. President, to have practiced a good deal in criminal courts in the course of my life, but I have never yet heard a thief arraigned for stealing a horse pleased that it was the best horse he could find in the country![54]

Finally, Corwin attacked those who said that America simply needed the territory, the "living room," for its growing population to expand. He noted all the conquerors of history had offered the same argument. He reminded his listeners of "Tamerlane's throne built of seventy thousand human skulls," of "Alexander, the Macedonian madman, who wanted room," of the far-flung expansion of the Roman Empire, of the ravages of Napoleon, of Frederick the Great and his dismemberment of Poland, of the burning of Moscow.

> They too said, as you say, "it is our destiny." They, too, wanted room. Doubtless each of these thought, with his share of Poland, his power was too strong to fear invasion, or even insult. One had his California, another his New Mexico, and the third his Veracruz. Did they remain untouched and incapable of harm? Alas! No—far, very far, from it. Retributive justice must fulfill its destiny, too.[55]

---

54. Corwin, *op. cit.*
55. *Ibid.*

Fig. 4. Twenty-two Day Siege of *Veracruz*, 1847, by William Henry Powell, 1867. Photo courtesy of Library of Congress, Image Reproduction Service.

Fig. 5. Close-up of Abraham Lincoln at the time of his election to Congress. 1846. Courtesy of the Daguerreotype Collection, Library of Congress.

5

ABRAHAM LINCOLN AND THE SPOT RESOLUTIONS

Now we come to Lincoln's magnificent contribution to this protest against an "unjust and unprovoked war." Conventional accounts of Lincoln's life, and most publications on the Mexican War before Howard Zinn's *People's History of the United States*, tended to ignore entirely or, at least, minimize Lincoln's objections to the war. It will be clear in this chapter how significant his voice was at the time, and continued to be in subsequent relations with Mexico and the continuing mutual histories of the United States and its sister republic. It will also become clear how much Lincoln risked both personally and politically by taking this bold stance in Congress, and how consistent it was with his character both as a young lawyer and legislator, and later as president.

President Polk in his message to Congress on May 11, 1846, stated categorically that Mexicans "after a long-continued series of menaces have at last invaded our territory and shed the blood of our fellow citizens on our own soil." Polk went on to insist that "war exists," effectively preempting the congressional authority he was ostensibly requesting, and asking for a rubber stamp approval of his own war declaration. Several senators objected, including John Calhoun and William Archer. The latter observed:

> Does the existence of hostilities on one of the frontiers of the United States necessarily put us in a state of war with any foreign Power? Clearly not.

Suppose we misunderstood the state of things on the Rio Grande, and that the Mexican authorities have acted justifiably under the circumstances: the danger of admitting that a state of war can exist except by the constitutional action of the Government of the United States will then be evident. There can be no question about that. There can be no war till the ascertained facts be submitted to the Congress.

Instead of having the Committee on Foreign Relations investigate the facts, as Senator Archer suggested, and submit a report the following day on the actual situation to Congress, the Democratically-controlled Senate moved on to a discussion of increasing troops on the border by an additional 15,000. The war supply bill was passed by a voice vote since few senators were willing to leave the existing troops unsupported now that hostilities had begun.

In the House of Representatives similar tactics prevailed. Representative Garrett Davis, a Whig leader, when he was briefly allowed to get the floor by the opposition, announced that there was not during the entire session an opportunity for a single Whig to be allowed to say "one word upon it" [the war resolution].

Now, in December of 1847, Lincoln had finally taken his seat in Congress and had an opportunity to take the floor and express his views. There in a lawyerly fashion, he methodically assailed Polk's justification for the war and, in a series of resolutions (which were essentially rhetorical questions), he proceeded to expose the false premises upon which the war was commenced, the unjust and rapacious nature of the president's policies, and the untruths which continued to form the underpinnings for the continuation of the conflict.

Lincoln analyzed three messages from President Polk. These consisted of the original war message cited above, stating that "war existed," and two others which re-affirmed that American blood was shed on American soil. Lincoln quoted these words which appeared on at least three occasions in the President's speeches and then asked a series of questions in order to determine the exact "spot" where this alleged American blood was shed on American soil. Thus, the resolutions came to be known as "the spot resolutions."

It is clear that repetition of "American blood, shed on American soil" was intrinsic to the argument of Polk that the war was justified and that it was constitutional. If Lincoln could show that the blood was **not** shed on American soil, then the war would have been unconstitutional, an over-reaching of presidential power, and also unnecessary and unjust. That is, he would be able to show that Polk, by sending General Taylor's troops from the Rio Nueces to the banks of the Rio Grande at the direction of the Secretary of War, had invaded Mexican territory and preemptively started a war with a neighboring republic. There were eight such resolutions.

Each of the resolutions begins with the word, *whether*. Lincoln's repetition of this word was not merely used as a rhetorical device or a tool of organization, but rather as the lead to a series of practical legal interrogatories. If the answer to any of them were in the affirmative, then the declaration of war was both justified and constitutional. If the answers were negative, then the declaration of war was fatally flawed.

Modern readers might find it difficult to actually visualize the area in contention. Where exactly was the Rio Nueces? Where was the Rio Grande in relation to it? What did the map of the area look like in 1836? With that in mind, I have included such a map here.

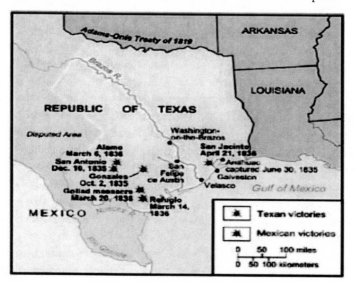

Now, with the map, it is clear that there was a significant area that the American troops had to cross to reach the Rio Grande. Over ninety miles. It was apparent that this was no accident or hapless maneuvering. The march of Taylor's troops from the Rio Nueces to the Rio Grande was an intentional provocation and was fully calculated to be so. On all the maps of this period, the Rio Nueces was the southern boundary of Texas. Anything below that was Mexican territory, listed as "disputed area" here on this US-centric map. It was a disputed region only in the minds of a handful of Texans because Santa Anna, when captured after the Alamo, agreed to move all Mexican troops across the Rio Grande. However, in no way did Santa Anna concede this land to Texas, nor did he have the authority to do so since, like the United States, only his congress in Mexico could approve such a cession of territory. In addition, at no point after Texas became a state, did the American Congress seek to expand the territory of that state to the Rio Grande. The southern border of the State of Texas, like the southern border of the Texas Republic, remained the Rio Nueces. So back to Lincoln's spot resolutions again.

The first two resolutions considered whether the spot on which "American blood was shed" had been within the territory of Spain after 1819 and then a part of Mexico after its War of Independence. If so, it was now clearly Mexican territory. The maps of the period clearly supported Lincoln's contention. So, as was apparent to the young congressman, at that time it was not "our *own soil.*"

The next four resolutions (3, 4, 5, and 6) considered the background of the people living in this territory. Lincoln inquired whether the people there were Mexican or American. If Americans, they would have clearly welcomed Taylor's troops as an army of liberation since they would have been threatened by a "long-continuing series of menaces" from the Mexicans, as Polk alleged. In fact, Lincoln observed, these people "fled before the approach of the United States Army," which indicated clearly that they were unarmed Mexican residents escaping from an invasionary force in their own land.

Lincoln also noted that the Mexican settlement through which the army passed on their way to the Rio Grande had never submitted themselves to the government of the United States or to that of Texas "either by consent or compulsion." He then lists the ways in which one might be considered a permanent resident or citizen of the United States (or, previously, the Republic of Texas) and shows that these people had never been considered such by themselves or by the respective governments. These Mexicans in whose territory blood had been shed were citizens of Mexico and the territory was Mexican.

Moreover, Lincoln goes on to say that these people had to "flee from their homes and growing crops, before blood was shed...." Then he goes on to wonder whether the first blood shed in that war was that of peaceful Mexicans who unarmed and unprotected tried to escape from Taylor's advancing army.

The seventh resolution suggests that the first *American* blood shed was that of those officers and men "sent into that [Mexican] settlement by order of the President through the Secretary of War" and thus not on American soil at all.

Finally, and most damning to Polk's contention that the war was necessary, was resolution #8, which reminded the Congress and all Americans that "General Taylor had more than once intimated to the War Department that, in his opinion, no such movement was necessary for the defense or protection of Texas."

The document is a classic, and what is even more remarkable is that it does not appear in its entirety in any of the major works on Lincoln in the 20th century, or in any college or high school textbooks. Shortly after the preemptive invasion of Iraq under Bush and Cheney in 2003, references to the spot resolutions began to show up in college texts and more recently revised Advanced Placement US History guidelines (2014). The comparisons between Lincoln's concerns and reservations about the Iraq policy were clear, and the issues of preemptive invasion and presidential overreaching were widely discussed in many classrooms. Almost immediately, conservatives roundly condemned the new College Board guidelines as being too critical of the United States.[56]

---

56. Casey Quinlan, "College Board Caves to Conservatives, Changes U.S. History Curriculum, July 30, 2015. http://thinkprogress.org/economy/2015/07/30/3686060/

The month following this address, Lincoln would carefully examine the one piece of "evidence" that Polk submitted in support
of his position: the "Velasco Treaty." His dismissal of this absurd
document before Congress is a classic. This "treaty," like many bits
of history, is often referred to but seldom read or analyzed, despite
Lincoln's lawyerly-like and conclusive dismissal of its worth.

The So-Called Treaty of Velasco

That history is generally written by the winners is a truism (often
attributed to Napoleon) so old that it cannot be accurately traced.
What is more interesting, however, is how historical documents
that can be accessed by diligent research are purposely mislabeled,
misinterpreted, or completely distorted by politicians and by "patriotic" historians to justify a disreputable course of action or a base
motive. Such is the case with the misnamed Velasco Treaty (sometimes referred to as the Velasco Treaties as there were actually two
documents, one public and one private).

There are over 170,000 references on the Google search engine
for "Velasco Treaty" so one would be justified in assuming that
such a treaty actually exists. One would be mistaken. The accord
was simply an armistice in which Santa Anna agreed to withdraw
his troops to the other side of the Rio Grande del Norte (Rio Bravo). The "Texians" for their part agreed not to "come within five
leagues" of that same area. In addition, it was agreed that Santa
Anna who was being held captive by the "Texian" army would be
released and provided transport to Veracruz.[57]

Several things should be clear about this accord:

First, an agreement to suspend hostilities and withdraw troops
is not a treaty.

Second, if one of the parties is a prisoner and acting under
duress, the agreement is not valid.

conservatives-get-major-win-fight-ap-history-classes/

57.   "Treaties of Velasco, 14 May 1836," *Lone Star Junction*. www.lsjunction.com/docs/vel-
      asco.htm

Third, under international law, any treaty proposal must be ratified by the Congress or constituted legislative body or royal authority.

Fourth, that from 1836 to 1846, no one either in the Republic of Texas or in the United States referred to this document as a treaty. The first person to do so was President Polk in his war message so that he could use the justification that American blood had been shed on American soil, that is, at the Rio Grande del Norte.

But lest the reader think that this argument is revisionist history and that President Polk, patriotic historians, and Google all had it right, let us look at Lincoln's speech to Congress on January 12, 1848. According to Lincoln, the claim that the Velasco agreement constituted a treaty was a fraud ("the sheerest deception") perpetrated on the American people and the international community. In Lincoln's words:

> Now I propose to show, that the whole of this—issue and evidence—is from beginning to end, the sheerest deception...Besides the position, so often taken that Santa Anna, while a prisoner of war—a captive—could not bind Mexico by a treaty, which I deem conclusive—beside this I wish to say something in relation to this treaty, so called by the President, with Santa Anna. If any man would like to be amused by a sight of that little thing, which the President calls by that big name, he can have it by turning to Niles' Register volume 50, page 336. And if anyone supposes that Niles' Register is a curious repository of so mighty a document, as a solemn treaty between nations, I can only say that I learned to a tolerable degree of certainty, by inquiry at the State Department, that the President never saw it anywhere else. By the way, I believe I should not err, if I were to declare, that during the first ten years of the existence of that document, it was never, by anybody, called a treaty— that it was never so called, till the President, in his extremity, attempted, by so calling it, to wring something from it in justification of himself in connection with the Mexican War. It has none of the distinguishing features of a treaty. It does not call itself a treaty. Santa Anna does not therein assume to bind Mexico, he only...stipulates that the recent hostilities should cease and that he would not take up arms against Texas during the existence of the war of independence.[58]

---

58.   Roy P. Basler, Ed. *The Collected Works of Abraham Lincoln*, vol 1. (New Brunswick: Rutgers University Press, 1953), 432-34.

Finally, the most damning evidence that this document should never have been cited as a proof of the border of Texas, Lincoln continues:

> He [Santa Anna] did not recognize the independence of Texas…he did not say a single word about the boundary and probably never thought of it. It is stipulated therein that the Mexican forces should evacuate the territory of Texas, passing to the other side of the Rio Grande, and in another article, it is stipulated that to prevent collisions between the armies the Texas army should not approach nearer than within five leagues—of what is not said—but clearly, from the object stated it is—of the Rio Grande. Now, if this is a treaty, recognizing the Rio Grande, as the boundary of Texas, it contains the singular feauture [*sic*] of stipulating that Texas shall not go within five leagues of its boundary.[59]

Not everyone agreed at the time, including William H. Herndon, Lincoln's law partner in Illinois. And this is where Lincoln moves away from consideration of the border issues and examines much broader questions that are still relevant today.

---

59.   *Ibid.* 434-345.

6

LINCOLN WRITES TO HERNDON

What exactly are the limitations of presidential power? What was the underlying purpose for giving the exclusive war-making power to Congress? What is the difference between a republican form of government and a dictatorship or monarchy? As we will see from Lincoln's letters to his law partner, his answers to those questions will give rise to further comments about preemptive attacks, abuse of presidential power, false or misleading intelligence, all of which readers will find relevant to later conflicts such as that of Korea, Vietnam, and more recently, the second Iraq War. He adds, however, that this is not what happened in the case of Polk. Polk's position was that American blood had been shed on American soil. Here are the specifics of what he actually wrote to William Herndon.

WASHINGTON, February 15, 1848.

DEAR WILLIAM,

Your letter of the 29th January was received last night. Being exclusively a constitutional argument, I wish to submit some reflections upon it in the same spirit of kindness that I know actuates you. Let me first state what I understand to be your position. It is that, if it shall become necessary to repel invasion, the President may, without violation of the Constitution, cross the line and invade the territory of another country, and that whether such necessity exists in any given case the President is the sole judge.

Before going further consider well whether this is or is not your position. If it is, it is a position that neither the President himself, nor any friend of his, so far as I know, has ever taken. Their only positions are—first, that the soil was ours when the hostilities commenced; and second, that whether it was rightfully ours or not, Congress had annexed it, and the President for that reason was bound to defend it; both of which are as clearly proved to be false in fact as you can prove that your house is mine. The soil was not ours, and Congress did not annex or attempt to annex it. But to return to your position. Allow the President to invade a neighboring nation whenever he shall deem it necessary to repel an invasion, and you allow him to do so whenever he may choose to say he deems it necessary for such purpose, and you allow him to make war at pleasure. Study to see if you can fix any limit to his power in this respect, after having given him so much as you propose. If today he should choose to say he thinks it necessary to invade Canada to prevent the British from invading us, how could you stop him? You may say to him— "I see no probability of the British invading us"; but he will say to you, "Be silent: I see it, if you don't."

The provision of the Constitution giving the war making power to Congress was dictated, as I understand it, by the following reasons: kings had always been involving and impoverishing their people in wars, pretending generally, if not always, that the good of the people was the object. This our convention understood to be the most oppressive of all kingly oppressions, and they resolved to so frame the Constitution that no one man should hold the power of bringing this oppression upon us. But your view destroys the whole matter, and places our President where kings have always stood. Write soon again.

Yours truly,

A. Lincoln[60]

Here Lincoln argues with his friend about a related question. If the president was seriously concerned that there was a threat to the United States, would he have been justified in "crossing the line" and initiating a pre-emptive invasion of another country? Lincoln says very politely that he is rewording his friend's position here and will respond to him. He adds, however, that this is *not* what hap-

60. Abraham Lincoln to William Herndon. February 15, 1848. *Classic Literature in the Public Domain Library*. Great Britain. http://www.classic-literature.co.uk/american-authors/19th-century/abraham-lincoln/

pened in the case of Polk. Polk's position was that American blood had been shed on American soil.

But, as to his friend's question, what do we find? Lincoln is equally adamant that such an invasion is not justified. It is not constitutional. Lincoln states that the Constitution was created for the express purpose of limiting that "kingly oppression" for getting the people involved in a war. "No one man should hold the power of bringing this oppression upon us."

Yet, even when Lincoln is transparently clear and lucid, it seems that later educators, historians and even keepers of our archives, tend to muddy the waters. When we go to the National Archives site and look at the material released as aids for educators teaching Lincoln, we find the following statement:

> Ironically when Lincoln became president he extended the war powers of the executive, action he criticized as a Congressman. Following the firing on Fort Sumter, he declared a naval blockade on his own authority. The capture and condemnation of four [blockade] runners led to a case that went to the Supreme Court. In 1863, the Court affirmed Lincoln's actions in the Price Cases, 2 Black 635.[61]

How misleading this statement is both to the instructor and to the students to whom the teacher will pass it on with all the authority of the custodian-scholars in charge of the National Archives!

Let's examine the differences between Polk sending troops to Mexico versus Lincoln imposing a blockade at Fort Sumter. First of all, Polk sent troops into another sovereign nation outside the boundaries of the United States. That area was inhabited by people who were not citizens or even residents of the United States and at no time in their history ever bore allegiance to the United States. Lincoln sent troops to South Carolina, which was part of the United States and part of the Republic of which he was the president and had sworn under oath to protect as commander in chief.[62]

Second, Mexico was a peaceful republic which had not initiated hostilities against the United States. South Carolina, on the other

---

61. http//.www.archives.gov/education/lessons/Lincoln-resolutions/
62. United States Constitution, Article II, Sec. 1.

hand, was a secessionist state within the Union that had attacked a federal fortification and had fomented a revolt against the legitimate government of the United States.

Third, Polk lied about his reasons for invading Mexico. First, he said that the Mexicans invaded US territory. A statement he later retracted after Lincoln's numerous queries. Second, he said that they presented a clear and present danger. A statement that was clearly refuted by the fact that the Mexican army did not even react at all when the troops were stationed at Corpus Christi to pressure Mexico into signing over California. They only reacted when American troops had crossed the Rio Nueces and built a fortification (Fort Texas, later renamed Fort Brown) on the Rio Grande. Lincoln, on the other hand, was forthright in his decision to set up a naval blockade after the rebel artillery bombardment and takeover of the US fortification in the South Carolina harbor.

Fourth, a president, according to the Constitution, needs Congressional approval before he can start a war.[63] Polk declared that a war existed before he even had a congressional vote. In addition, he tied his request for this retrograde approval of his actions to an appropriations bill which would provide support to the troops already in the field. It was this and this alone which gave him a majority vote in Congress for the approval of the war bill. Congressmen such as Lincoln were outspoken in their objections to the preamble to the bill which laid the blame for the conflict on Mexico.

President Lincoln, on the other hand, needed no approval from Congress for putting down an insurrection in his own country. It is one of the powers specifically granted to the commander-in-chief.[64]

Finally, Polk's decision resulted in the trespass upon private property in a foreign nation, displaced innocent civilians from their homes, set up a military fort outside the boundaries of the United States, and resulted in the deaths of innocent civilians. President Lincoln was merely engaged in an effort to stop an unlawful insur-

---

63.   United States Constitution, Article I, Sec. 8.
64.   United State Constitution, Article II, Sec. 2.

rection in his own country and preserve the Republic. There is no comparison.

This letter is a key document in American history. It clearly foreshadows that danger of an executive having unchecked war powers from Hitler's invasion of Poland to the "Gulf of Tonkin Resolution" in Vietnam,[65] or Bush's invasion of Iraq to remove the alleged "weapons of mass destruction" based on faulty intelligence.

Many of the problems in Mexican-US relations today stem from this period. Many of my Mexican students believe that a failure to understand the implications of this debate might be responsible for much of the anti-immigrant feeling in the US based on the belief that these "illegals" are violating American law and should be punished. What if people understood that the seizure of *Mexican* territory began with a violation of international law on the part of the Americans? Might this knowledge make Americans more tolerant?

Other students made much of the fact that the movie *Lincoln*, which was such a box office and critical success, was supposedly based on "bold new information on the life of Lincoln" (from a review one of the students found praising the director for his courage in bringing it out). They asked, "Why wasn't there anything about Lincoln's objections to the Mexican War in the movie? This was an example of Lincoln putting his political career on the line. Why wouldn't the director provide his audience with this information about the iconic American president?"

---

65. Although Congress (based on false intelligence) actually gave Johnson the authority to engage US forces in armed attacks, he far exceeded his mandate and escalated the war, including airstrikes in neighboring Cambodia. Even when Congress later learned that the Resolution was based upon false intelligence and sought its repeal, Johnson's successor (Richard Nixon) insisted that he was within his constitutional rights as commander-in-chief to continue the war. The genie, once out of the bottle, is hard to put back in.

7

CONSUMMATE POLITICIAN
OR COURAGEOUS STATESMAN?

It is interesting to see how many textbook editors, popular historians and even serious researchers and admirers of Lincoln choose to cherry-pick his speeches. On the one hand, they praise his courage in standing up for liberty in 1863 with the publication of the Emancipation Proclamation, while at the same time they dismiss or minimize his stance against preventive war generally, and the invasion of Mexico and the slaughter of thousands of its people particularly.

Even after the publication of Zinn's *A People's History of the United States* when mainstream historians in the US began to acknowledge the existence of the spot resolutions, most gave qualifiers, noting that Lincoln had been relatively unconcerned with the admission of Texas as a state in 1845. Others asserted that Lincoln had little interest in the Mexican War at all until he found his cohorts in the House were opposed, and that he was no doubt merely following the party line as a Whig by speaking against Polk's decision to invade Mexico.

It is almost as if these scholars were willing to undermine Lincoln's legacy as a moral leader rather than acknowledge his sympathy for the Mexican people, his repulsion at the "land of the free" invading a neighboring republic for territorial gain, and his determination to set these facts before the American people. Such is the continuous subtext in even "objective" histories of the period that a careful reader might be justified in reasoning that Honest Abe was not so honest after all, just another crafty politician concerned with denigrating the leader of the opposing political party, much like our own politicians today who are no better than they have to be. But was that the truth about Lincoln? Do these naysayers and revisionists have a case?

Two of the lines from Lincoln's early letters are perennially offered to show they do, and that their case is ironclad. In one, he wrote: "If I could save the Union without freeing any slave I would do it." In another, "I never was much interested in the Texas question." But each of these quotes is highly misleading when taken out of context.

As to the quote about freeing the slaves, his thinking was that the greatest danger to the safety of the people of the United States would be the fracturing of the republic. In this, he was surely correct. Imagine if the United States was split along the lines of Korea, Vietnam, or like the Central American states such as Honduras, Guatemala, and El Salvador. Not only would the nation suffer economically, it would be weak militarily, prone to invasion by foreign powers, and crippled by civil wars and border disputes. And, of course, the condition of the slaves would be unchanged. They would simply be slaves in the new Confederate States of America rather than in the United States.

If these speculations seem far-fetched, one has only to look at the histories of countries in which the north-south divide ended in separate republics. Many think the course of history is somehow inevitable. However, in Lincoln's mind, there was nothing inevitable about it at all. The United States was founded on principles which clearly were not being followed: "all men are created equal" and so on. He questions in the Gettysburg Address whether *any nation* conceived with these ideals can survive. He knew that nothing was inevitable except the movement toward chaos, if intelligent leaders did not work together to organize their society (and then reorganize from time to time) in such a way that would best maximize the good of the whole while preserving the rights of the minorities. He also believed that once the heresy of separation became acceptable, then the nation would already be on the path to interminable conflicts that would affect generations to come. The histories of other nations so divided suggest that he was right.

The other half of the quote was "If I could preserve the Union by freeing all the slaves, I would do so." And this is in fact what he did. The Civil War was already in its third year by the time the Emancipation Proclamation was released to the public and it became not only a precursor to the 13th, 14th, and 15th amendments, but also a moral justification for the bloodshed, and an incentive to the forces of the republic to defeat the rebels.

What Lincoln was doing in this letter from which the quote was taken, a letter he wrote in response to an editorial of Horace Greeley, was distinguishing between what he could and would do as president as opposed to what he felt and believed as a private citizen.

I would save the Union. I would save it the shortest way under the Constitution. The sooner the national authority can be restored; the nearer the Union will be "the Union as it was." If there be those who would not save the Union, unless they could at the same time save slavery, I do not agree with them. If there be those who would not save the Union unless they could at the same time destroy slavery, I do not agree with them. My paramount object in this struggle is to save the Union, and is not either to save or to destroy slavery. If I could save the Union without freeing any slave I would do it, and if I could save it by freeing all the slaves I would do it; and if I could save it by freeing some and leaving others alone I would also do that. What I do about slavery, and the colored race, I do because I believe it helps to save the Union; and what I forbear, I forbear because I do not believe it would help to save the Union. I shall do less whenever I shall believe what I am doing hurts the cause, and I shall do more whenever I shall believe doing more will help the cause. I shall try to correct errors when shown to be errors; and I shall adopt new views so fast as they shall appear to be true views.

I have here stated my purpose according to my view of official duty; and I intend no modification of my oft-expressed personal wish that all men everywhere could be free.[66]

66.   Abraham Lincoln. "Letter to Horace Greeley, August 22, 1862. http://www.abraham-lincolnonline.org/lincoln/speeches/greeley.htm

The other quote often taken out of context was his letter to Williamson Durley in which he gave his view of Texas' annexation. This quote is used by contemporary scholars to illustrate that Lincoln never had any strong opinion about the annexation of Texas and that his interest in both Texas and its boundaries began only as a partisan effort to embarrass President Polk once Lincoln had been safely elected to Congress. The extracted quote is as follows: "I perhaps ought to say that individually I never was much interested in the Texas question."[67]

The quote taken out of context is very misleading. What Lincoln was saying in this letter was that the Whigs had strong reservations about the annexation of Texas and saw clearly that it was a dangerous provocation and could lead to war. Henry Clay, the strongest Whig candidate was clearly in this camp and had expressed his views on the subject. However, Clay was himself a slave owner and not sympathetic to the Abolitionist cause. New England Whigs objected to the acquisition of Texas because they saw it as a movement to extend slavery to the newest state. So while they agreed with Clay on the Texas issue, they disagreed on the basis for their agreement and that, coupled with his slave ownership, disinclined them to support his candidacy. This led to a split in the Whig party and the election of the Harrison/Tyler Democratic administration which in turn led to the admission (under Tyler after Harrison's death) of Texas as a state.

Lincoln is merely reiterating the fact that if the Whigs had stuck together and elected Clay this would not be an issue. He also didn't see how the change from the Republic of Texas with slaves—to the State of Texas with slaves—altered anything. In this he was mistaken of course. Not only would it alter the balance of slave states but it would also result in more slaves being bred and sold to Texas land owners and speculators as they developed agriculture in the region.

---

67. Abraham Lincoln. Letter to Williamson Durley, October 3, 1845. From *Collected Works of Abraham Lincoln*, Vol. 1. http://quod.lib.umich.edu/l/lincoln/lincoln1/1:373?rgn=div1;view=fulltext

But the fact that he was mistaken in that view does not mean that he had no interest in the matter or that he was operating opportunistically. Here are Lincoln's exact words:

> If the Whig abolitionists of New York had voted with us last fall, Mr. Clay would now be president, Whig principles in the ascendant, and Texas not annexed; whereas by the division, all that either had at stake in the contest, was lost. And, indeed, it was extremely probable, beforehand, that such would be the result. As I always understood, the Liberty-men deprecated the annexation of Texas extremely; and, this being so, why they should refuse to so cast their votes as to prevent it, even to me, seemed wonderful. What was their process of reasoning, I can only judge from what a single one of them told me. It was this: "We are not to do *evil* that *good* may come." This general proposition is doubtless correct; but did it apply? If by your votes you could have prevented the *extension* of slavery, would it not have been *good* and not *evil* so to have used your votes, even though it involved the casting of them for a slaveholder? By the *fruit* the tree is to be known. An *evil* tree cannot bring forth *good* fruit. If the fruit of electing Mr. Clay would have been to prevent the extension of slavery, could the act of electing have been *evil?*
> But I will not argue farther. I perhaps ought to say that individually I never was much interested in the Texas question. I never could see much good to come of annexation; inasmuch, as they were already a free republican people on our own model; on the other hand, I never could very clearly see how the annexation would augment the evil of slavery. It always seemed to me that slaves would be taken there in about equal numbers, with or without annexation. And if more *were* taken because of annexation, still there would be just so many the fewer left, where they were taken from. It is possibly true, to some extent, that with annexation, some slaves may be sent to Texas and continued in slavery, than otherwise might have been liberated. *To whatever extent this may be true, I think annexation an evil.* [Emphasis supplied][68]

According to almost all the documentary evidence, Lincoln was a man of principle. But even more importantly, he was a man who thought deeply about major issues, he debated them internally, and his opinions evolved as he was exposed to more facts. In other words, he changed his mind on issues when he discovered he was mistaken. As his contemporary Ralph Waldo Emerson once wrote, "A foolish consistency is the hobgoblin of little minds." Lincoln was not an Abolitionist in the 1840s and 1850s. Far from it. He

---

68. *Ibid.*

associated this group with dangerous radicals such as John Brown, who would murder to advance their cause and result in destruction and chaos. He saw no difference initially between Texas as a slave nation in 1844 and Texas as a slave state in 1845. In both cases there were slaves, but he saw no indications that statehood would in any way lead to an increase in the total number of slaves. And, while he was mistaken, he came to understand that as the war with Mexico progressed and it was apparent that even more territory would be wrested from that nation, that even more slave states might be formed. Accordingly, his opinion changed with this new information, as did his acts.

The Wilmot Proviso

David Wilmot (D. Pa.) was a Democrat who originally supported Polk in the Mexican War. However, as Polk began to formulate plans to ask for territorial concessions from Mexico in exchange for peace, he began to realize that the president was playing an even more complex game. The territorial gain would result in more slave states, upset the balance established by the Missouri Compromise, and lead to increased tensions between north and south unless something was done. Wilmot opposed slavery and so the danger of its acquisition in soon-to-be conquered territories. Accordingly, he introduced a "proviso" or amendment to a bill in the 39th Congress which referred to any which the United States might conquer from Mexico.

> *Provided* that, as an express and fundamental condition to the acquisition of any territory from the Republic of Mexico by the United States, by virtue of any treaty which may be negotiated between them, and to the use by the Executive of the moneys herein appropriated, neither slavery nor involuntary servitude shall ever exist in any part of said territory, except for crime, whereof the party shall first be duly convicted. [69]

---

69. Wilmot Proviso, full text. http://www.ushistory.org/us/30a.asp

The Proviso passed in the House but failed in the Senate. The following year it was introduced again, and this time Lincoln was among those who voted for it in the 30th Congress. It was rejected again several times as it was attached to various bills, which appeared regarding the War with Mexico and territorial acquisition from 1846 to 1848. It was also attached to the Treaty of Guadalupe Hidalgo, the formal agreement that marked the end of the War. It failed there as well when the Senate refused to approve it. In Lincoln's words: "In December 1847, the new Congress assembled. I was in the lower house that term. The 'Wilmot Proviso' or the principle of it was constantly coming up in some shape or another, and I think I voted for it at least forty times."[70] That was a bit of hyperbole on his part. In actuality, he voted for it on roll call votes five times. But, if one counts procedural votes and votes as to the wording and so on, it could easily have been several dozen.

So was he playing politics? Was he capable of moral equivocation? Judge David Davis, a contemporary jurist wrote of Lincoln's professional ethics as a lawyer:

> The framework of his mental and moral being was honesty...The ability which some eminent lawyers possess of explaining away the bad points of a cause by ingenious sophistry was denied him. He thought slowly and acted slowly, he must needs [sic] have time to analyze all the facts in a case and bind them into a connected story...Two things were essential to his managing a case: one was time, the other the feeling of justice in the case.[71]

So, no, he did not have a complete view of the Texas Annexation in 1845, nor of the Mexican War in the spring and summer of 1846. But by 1847, it was clear to Lincoln that the president had lied, that Polk had provoked the war, that he intended to continue the war until territorial demands were met, and that there would be a move to make the newly acquired territory slave states. To quote Herndon again:

---

70. Paul Findley, *A. Lincoln, The Crucible of Congress: The Years Which Forged His Greatness* (Fairfield, CA: James Stevenson Publisher, 2004), 129-130.
71. William H. Herndon, *Recollections of Abraham Lincoln, The True Story of a Great Life* (Charleston: CreateSpace, 2014), Kindle loc. 1651.

In order to bring into full activity his great powers it was necessary that he
should be convinced of the right and justice of the cause he advocated.
When convinced, whether the cause was great or small, he was usually successful.[72]

The speech to Congress on the spot resolutions is one example of
this thoughtful and lawyerly exploration of all the evidence and the
painstaking effort to be precise and to explain the line of reasoning
and the moral stance. He built his case methodically, with clarity
and precision. When Lincoln finally seized on a truth he followed it
to its logical end and supported it with evidence. But it would cost
him. He made the speech while the war was still being fought in
earnest, and was accused by Polk in a thinly-veiled address of "giving aid and comfort to the enemy." He was excoriated in the newspapers of the day, and even his close friend and law partner, William Herndon, tried to dissuade him. In his speeches, he had gone
far beyond his party's position, and the Whigs were afraid that his
radical position might hurt the party so badly that the Whigs, like
the Federalists, might cease to exist. His law partner knew that Lincoln himself might have felt he was treading on dangerous ground.

And so he was, for very soon after, murmurs of dissatisfaction began to
run through the party ranks. I could not refrain from apprising him of the
extensive defection from the party ranks, and the injury his course was doing
him. When I listened to the comments of his friends everywhere I felt that
he had made a mistake. I therefore wrote him to that effect, at the same time
giving him my own views....[73]

But as we know, Lincoln remained adamant even though his career
was in jeopardy. And as Herndon himself notes:

He had a keen sense of justice, and struggled for it, throwing aside forms,
methods, and rules, until it appeared pure as a ray of light flashing through a
fog bank. He was not a general reader in any field of knowledge, but when
he had occasion to learn or investigate any subject he was thorough and

---

72.   *Ibid.*, loc. 1632.
73.   *Ibid.*, loc. 905-906

indefatigable in his search. He not only went to the root of the question, but dug up the root, and separated and analyzed every fibre of it.[74]

Although frustrating to his friends, to many young men in his own party and certainly to his constituents, he went where the evidence led him, and he argued as the justice and morality of the situation demanded. So, too with slavery. He felt that it was morally repugnant and never departed from this view. However, he also thought that the immediate elimination of slavery through violence as was advocated by so many Abolitionists was not the way. Nor did he feel that separation from the Union to form a slave-holding nation was the answer. And when the latter became imminent and the South made its intentions clear, he chose the side of the Abolitionists as he himself had once predicted he would.

At the end of his term in the House of Representatives, he introduced a bill for the abolition of slavery within the District of Columbia. It provided for compensation to the masters of the slaves within the District who were released from bondage, and provided that no person born outside the District could be held to slavery once brought into the District of Columbia.[75] It was not as forceful a bill as Abolitionists would have liked to have seen but it was a bill which he hoped would pass. But even this tentative effort at Congressional action for emancipation was doomed to fail at the hands of Southern opponents.

One day, not long after he was rejected for election to the Senate and had returned to his law practice, he was walking with John T. Stuart, a fellow attorney. According to Stuart, "As we were coming down the hill, I said, 'Lincoln, the time is coming when we will all have to be Abolitionists or Democrats.' He thought a moment and then answered ruefully and emphatically, 'When that time comes my mind is made up, for I believe the slavery question can never be compromised.'"[76]

---

74. *Ibid.,* loc. 1632-33.
75. Roy P. Blaster. Ed. *The Collected Works of Abraham Lincoln,* Vol. II (Rockville, MD: Wildside Press, 2008), 20-22.
76. *Ibid.,* loc. 1937.

Lincoln had been cautious and slow to move in that direction because he felt that the Abolitionists were both disruptive and dangerous and that any unilateral decision by the federal government to free the slaves would destroy the tenuous north-south balance of the republic. But as time progressed he saw that there were no options, that compromise did not work, that the Union would be dissolved if he did nothing, and elimination of slavery not only from the new states but from the country as a whole was inevitable. Once on that path, it not only followed that the cause of emancipation would be advanced through the federal government, but that the war would continue to its bloody conclusion. Lincoln's words in his second inaugural would be prophetic.

> Yet if God wills that it [war] continue until all the wealth piled by the bondsman's two hundred and fifty years of unrequited toil shall be sunk, and until every drop of blood drawn by the lash shall be paid by another drawn by the sword, as was said three thousand years ago, so still it must be said, 'The judgments of the Lord are true and righteous altogether.'[77]

It was not long after Lincoln's death that chroniclers had begun to question his views on race relations. They noted that he had made comments about the relative inequality between races in the United States, and that he had expressed reservations about ex-slaves being given the right to vote. But these reservations were shared by many, including women suffrage leaders of the day. They asked how it was possible that a formerly enslaved, abused, and mostly illiterate group could by constitutional amendment suddenly become thoughtful citizens contributing to the republic, while women, many of whom were college graduates, still did not have the right to vote?[78]

As for Lincoln's views on slavery, a much different question than that of the racial bias prevalent in the day, there was no doubt

---

77. *Ibid.*, loc. 1959.
78. "Form letter from E. Cady Stanton, Susan B. Anthony, and Lucy Stone asking friends to send petitions for women's suffrage to their representatives in Congress, 12/26/1865," Records of the US House of Representatives, National Archives and Records Administration, Washington, DC. ARC Identifier 306686.

where Lincoln stood. One could quote from a dozen of Lincoln's speeches and letters to show how his personal opinion never wavered about the right of all people to be free. One can also observe how his willingness to act on those beliefs gradually evolved until he decided that "The day of compromise is over.... Slavery is a great and crying injustice—an enormous national crime."[79]

Notes Herndon, "It is useless to add more evidence—for it could be piled mountain high—showing that from the very outset Mr. Lincoln was sound to the core on the injustice and crime of human slavery."[80] Similarly with the Mexican War.

Once Lincoln had settled into Congress, analyzed the maps, the history, examined the causes of the war and Polk's culpability, he could not avoid speaking of it. In addition, as he read the dispatches of General Taylor recounting the numerous abuses of the army, the depredations and murder of civilians, and then months later read of the horrible destruction of Veracruz by General Scott, he was overwhelmed with disgust, as were many Americans. On hearing that the president intended to acquire as much Mexican territory as possible as "reparations" from the Mexicans for starting the war, he could no longer remain neutral. He told his law partner that he, Herndon, as a man of conscience, if properly apprised of all the facts, would have done the same. So Lincoln delivers a moral critique on his beloved country, and follows it up with letters to his friend defending his position, and another congressional addendum to seal the war in the annals of history as "unnecessary and unconstitutional."

Led into an unjust and unjustifiable invasion of a sister republic, an act as morally repugnant as the propagation of slavery, which he had always spoken against, he could not remain silent. In both cases it was the exercise of the stronger against the weaker; in both cases it involved conflicting beliefs between racial superiority on the one hand and the rights of human beings on the other. In both cases, he came late to the pulpit, but once there argued brilliantly and forcefully like "a ray of light flashing through a fogbank."

---

79. *Ibid.*, loc. 1989-90
80. *Ibid.*, loc. 1991.

Lincoln's views on the war with Mexico are ones that should inform every briefing on border politics, every discussion on illegal immigration, every class engaged in a discussion of the conquest of Mexican land, every polemic about border walls. But they do not. It is no accident that his views had been consigned to the dustbin of history for 150 years, and minimized or disparaged as "political" during the short period in this century that they have come partially into the light.

To take Lincoln seriously would mean that we would have to reexamine all that we have been taught in school, examine the prejudices that we still harbor against Mexicans whom we call "aliens," as they gradually repopulate the territory which a short time ago was theirs. We conveniently forget that the causes that impel northward migration have their origins in the economic stagnation which resulted from the seizure of Mexico's main ports to the West (San Diego, San Francisco, Los Angeles), the loss of the rich silver mines of Nevada, the gold and fertile lands in California, and the mighty rivers and lakes which provide clean water to the entire southwest. Meanwhile, instead of a "good neighbor" policy of mutual cooperation and development, we see enormous growth in border security, surveillance drones, and East Berlin-type walls, which were repugnant to Americans back in Ronald Reagan's day. Even worse, while the Berlin wall was in an urban environment, the American "border wall" crosses rural and wildlife regions, destroys animal habitats, scars the countryside and erodes the land, exacerbates water shortages, and is responsible for the deaths of hundreds of migrants each year who perish of thirst and exposure in the Sonoran and Mohave deserts.

8

PILLORIED IN THE PRESS
FOR PRO-MEXICAN VIEWS

Lincoln's "spot resolutions," and his vote to censure Polk, had caused a bit of consternation back home. Despite his willingness to vote for supplies and replacement troops during the war with Mexico, Lincoln was still tarred as one who had been giving aid and comfort to the enemy. In addition, his vote on an amendment to a bill recognizing the outstanding service of Zachary Taylor (a fellow Whig and hero of the war) added fuel to the criticism. The amendment declared the war against Mexico to be "unnecessary and unconstitutional." His law partner had warned him about the reaction, both from the press and from some of the young men within his own party, and indicated that he had gone too far. Lincoln was chagrined by his partner's disapproval and the division between them that it caused. He wrote:

> I regret this, not because of any fear we shall remain disagreed after you have read this letter, but because if you misunderstand I fear other good friends may also. That vote affirms that the war was unnecessarily and unconstitutionally commenced by the President; and I will stake my life that if you had been in my place you would have voted just as I did. Would you have voted for what you felt and knew to be a lie? I know you would not. Would you have gone out of the House–skulked the vote? I expect not. If you had skulked one vote, you would have had to skulk many more before the end of the session. Richardson's resolutions, introduced before I made any move or gave any vote upon the subject, make the direct question of the justice

of the war; so that no man can be silent if he would. You are compelled to
speak; and your only alternative is to tell the truth or a lie. I cannot doubt
which you would do.[81]

We see clearly Lincoln's decision to make a moral stand regardless
of the consequences. And the consequences were severe. Among
them would be the end of the political career of his former law
partner and friend, Stephen T. Logan, who was a strong candidate
for the Congressional elections of 1849 in Illinois but was defeated
mainly through his association with Lincoln. Meanwhile, Lincoln's
own political fortune had waned and his influence as a political
force was dismissed by most newspapers. The effect it would have
on future campaigns and elections remained to be seen, but the
signs were not favorable. Publicity is one thing but notoriety is quite
another. Many politicians were counted out for considerably less.

Perhaps the most painful criticism came from the newspapers
of his own state of Illinois, where he was called "spotty Lincoln,"
"poor Lincoln," and even "Benedict Arnold." It was devastating.
While Lincoln, as a loyal Whig, did some campaigning for Taylor's
presidential race, and for his friend and former partner, Stephen
Logan who was running for Congress, he probably did neither of
them any good. Taylor won on his sterling war record and on his
apolitical stance throughout the conflict, and after severe provocation from Polk and betrayal by Scott. Taylor was the consummate
military man of his day. He was indifferent to politics except when
they interfered with his job, and in fact, he had never voted in a
national election!

The defeat of Lincoln's former law partner for the Congressional seat, on the other hand, was directly attributed to his association with Lincoln. Noted the *State Register*, "The loss was caused by
'spotty Lincoln' who has given whiggery a bad odor." It went on to
add that: "This gentleman [Lincoln] had a severe attack of 'spotted

---

81.   Lincoln to Herndon, Feb 1, 1848. From Classic Literature in the Public Domain Li-
      brary. Great Britain. http://www.classic-literature.co.uk/american-authors/19th-cen-
      tury/abraham-lincoln/

fever' in Washington not long since...and it is probable the disease died with the patient.... Poor Lincoln."[82]

The implication of the latter quote was that the American people were not only indifferent to the issue raised in the "spot resolutions" now that the War was over and the territory was secured, but that they no longer wished to be reminded of the man who stood up against presidential overreaching and fabrication, and pointed out the lack of justification for the War itself. The Treaty of Guadalupe Hidalgo had been signed. The US had acquired more than a million square kilometers of territory out of which they would carve half a dozen new states. It was time to move on. The discussion was dead. And so, apparently, was the political career of the man who raised the issue in the first place.

Yet in spite of this disastrous effect on his career, in spite of his insistence on taking the high moral ground and defending it earnestly to his friend, as one reads through the Lincoln's biographies, one finds the historical bias that Lincoln was calculating, opportunistic, and political in regard to his stance on the Mexican War. Almost all of these authors ask some variant of the question, *Why didn't he make the war an issue when he was running for office?* Lincoln himself answered this question when he addressed a rally in 1846. Hostilities had begun. Polk declared war existed even before Congress could vote on it. Lincoln said that it was the duty of those who, whether they knew too much or too little about the causes of the war, to remain silent until the conflict was over. That now was the time to support the troops who were currently in battle. Once elected to Congress he voted for every bill to supply the army.

It wasn't until the major battles were over and Polk was considering seizing Mexican lands as "indemnity" for the war, that Lincoln felt free to express his views without being disloyal to his country or failing to support the men in combat. And when he did, his position was clear. The United States had invaded a peaceful country, it had attacked unarmed civilians, and now it was prepared to take land from that nation, as "compensation" for a war the

---

82.   Benjamin P. Thomas, *Abraham Lincoln, A Biography* (Carbondale: Southern Illinois University Press, 2008), Kindle Edition, 120.

United States itself had provoked. If before the Mexican War he might have known too little, it was apparent from his exact and evidence-laden speeches that he now knew more than enough. He was outraged at the injustice of Polk's decision to order the troops into Mexico, as he makes clear several times. It is for this reason that we have included in this book the full text of his remarks in an appendix. Otherwise, one might simply continue to believe that Lincoln, despite his reputation to the contrary, was less than honest in practical matters and was a typical politician.

The problem is not the character of Lincoln. The problem is the unwillingness of biographers and historians to take into account the complexity of his views on Mexico. Yes, he was attacking Polk and there was a political aspect. However, there was also ample evidence that Polk had lied to the American people, and that he had started a war without justification and unconstitutionally. And it is this evidence Lincoln lays out in a very compelling and lawyer-like fashion. It was apparent to Lincoln, and the facts that he presented in his speeches support it, that the whole purpose of the war was not to address wrongs done by the Mexican people or their government, not to resolve boundary issues, not as a preventative first strike, but rather as a planned invasion for the sole purpose of acquiring territory.

Nevertheless, in spite of that evidence, these biographers persist. One mentions that Lincoln had no love for Mexicans. Another that he had used the word "greaser." Even Pulitzer Prize-winning historian David Herbert Donald wrote in his classic work:

> Now that the fighting was over and the peace treaty expected in Washington momentarily, the only purpose Lincoln had for assailing the president's course in beginning the war was political. The object was to hurt the Democrats in the next presidential election.[83]

In his famous "Essay on Self-Reliance" Emerson once wrote, "To be great is to be misunderstood." How true that is of Lincoln. With almost 15,000 books written about his life and his policies, we still

---

83.   Donald, David Herbert, *Lincoln* (New York: Touchstone, 1995), 226.

see this misapprehension. Lincoln the politician is presented as an alter ego of Lincoln the moral leader. The "real" Lincoln, these authors suggest, simply made a miscalculation of the political weather at the time and forfeited (at least in the short term) his chances for political advancement, thus setting his career back a few years. It is what Herndon felt as well. And it is clear from Lincoln's exasperation and his acerbic comments to his law partner that Herndon also completely misunderstood what Lincoln was about.

Lincoln's words were unequivocal and apolitical when, after voting on George Ashmun's resolution declaring the war had been "unnecessarily unconstitutionally begun by the president of the United States," he responded to Herndon's criticism mentioned in the previous chapter. "I will stake my life that if you had been in my place you would have voted just as I did," he swore to his law partner.

These are not the words of a politician who has merely submitted a vote to embarrass a rival party. This is a letter from a thoughtful man of principle who was determined to convince his friend and partner that he had made a moral choice that his friend, if placed in similar circumstances and possessed of similar facts, would have made as well.

As to those historians who note Lincoln's use of language such as "greasers" to suggest otherwise, one might also recollect that he had a store of "Paddy" jokes and "darky" jokes as well, and that such terms and quips were common in his day.[84] But his willingness

---

84.   Lincoln told many stories which touched the race or religion of his contemporaries. But they were not offensive and there was no malice intended or taken. As an Irish-American and a Catholic I could find no animus in any of the recorded Mike and Pat stories. Typical of his ethnic jokes was this one related in Herndon's book cited earlier. "One time Mr. Lincoln told the story of one of those important fellows—not an Irishman— who lived in every town and had the cares of state on their shoulders. This young fellow met an Irishman on the street, and called to him, officiously: 'Oh, Mike, I'm awful glad I met you. We've got to do something to wake up the boys. The campaign is coming on and we've got to get the voters. We've just had a meeting up here, and we're going to have the biggest barbecue that ever was heard of in Illinois. We're going to roast two whole oxen, and we're going to have Douglas and Governor Cass and some one from Kentucky and all the big democratic guns, and we're going to have a great time.

'By dad, that's good!' says the Irishman. "the byes need stirrin' up!'

'Yes, and you're on one of the committees, and you want to hustle around and get

to use what might be considered a racial epithet did not prevent him from taking a stand for justice. A perfect example of this was when he defended the Irish immigrants from the attacks of the Know Nothing Party, wondering how it was that this new political group could be against slavery and yet be so prejudiced against immigrant labor, including Irish and Catholics.

Lincoln demonstrates again and again that his position was one of conscience. He was convinced of the importance of this stance. This is the Lincoln who sent 7,580 copies of his speeches hand-addressed to his constituents. Now he is writing only to his friend. He makes no copies of this letter. He is not apologizing. He says that remaining silent was not an option, and that any man of principle would have done the same. This is not an argument of a man running for office. This is not a document he publicized and printed in newspapers. This is a man privately sharing his true beliefs.

In the past, Lincoln responded readily to criticism in the press. He used his friendship with editors and publishers to have his speeches and letters printed so that his view would be published for all to see. Now he withdrew. He had made his stand. He had presented his best arguments. Those who had supported him in the past withdrew their aid. Even the minor reward of a small sinecure as Land Office Commissioner for his service to the Whig Party in helping get Zachery Taylor elected would be denied him. So be it. He would return to his law practice with renewed energy. He would develop his mind; he would travel, observe, and try to reason out the problems that beset the age. If his clarity of vision and moral purpose should ever be needed by the republic, which now ignored him, he would be ready.

---

them waked up, Mike."

'When is the barbeque to be?' asked Mike

'Friday, two weeks'

'Friday, is it? Well, I'll make a nice committeeman, settin' that barbeque on a day with half the Dimocratic party of Sangomon county can't ate a bite of mate. Go on wid ye.'"

(Alexander K. McClure, *Lincoln's Yarns and Stories: a complete collection of funny and witty anecdotes that made Lincoln famous as America's greatest story teller* (Chicago: The John C. Winston Company, 1901. Public Domain. Kindle Edition. 2012), Loc. 1301-1303).

9

THE MEXICAN REPUBLIC MUCH REDUCED

The United States Army occupied Mexico City from September 1847 to May 1848. During that time, negotiations were being conducted by Nicolas Trist, special envoy of the US State Department, and various officials for the Mexican government. The negotiations were in Mexico City rather than in Washington for US fear that if Mexican ministers went to Washington and concluded a treaty, by the time they returned to Mexico there could be a change in government that would result not only in the rejection of the treaty but in the imprisonment or death of the ministers. The State Department was committed to a large territorial cession from Mexico as a result of the conquest, urged on by both the president who demanded "recompensatory" [*sic*] territory and a land-hungry group called "All Mexico" that wanted the entire country. But as the months passed without a treaty, the Polk administration began to get nervous.

The Mexican ministers for their part were aware of the deep divide in the US between North and South. They hoped that an appeal to northern senators and congressmen, who clearly saw that their states might be slave states and thus upset the precarious balance provided by the Missouri Compromise, might mitigate State Department demands. Meanwhile, Scott's defeat of the Mexican Army was having unintended consequences. In some regions that had been abandoned by the army, peasants attacked the homes and looted the ranches of wealthy land owners. On the Yucatán peninsula, more than 30,000 Indians took to the warpath, burning and pillaging. They were determined, according to the governor of the state, to "exterminate the white race." Back in the States, those who called for "all Mexico" to be joined to the Union were having second thoughts. No one wanted more Indians added to the population. America had its own Indian problems and did not want to import those of Mexico. Indians might be considered "Native Americans" in some semantic circumlocution in a later century, but in the 19th century, they were considered to be a savage and dangerous race to be cleared out to make room for white settlers of the West, not new residents to be added to the Republic, conquest or no conquest.

Polk, upset that Trist was taking so long to get any kind of settlement, made an effort to have him recalled. Another wrinkle was that gold was discovered in Sutter's Creek, California. This information had to be concealed from the Mexican negotiators who, if they found out, would be reluctant to make any settlement at all. But the discovery of a major strike, worth untold millions, was the kind of news that was hard to keep a lid on.

The US Occupation of Mexico

Meanwhile, General Scott's Army of Occupation was not faring well. The Marines had taken over the Castle of Chapultepec, remembered today in the Marine Corps' hymn as "The Halls of Montezuma." It had been defended mostly by teenaged cadets of the Military College, many of whom died heroically in its defense. Most of the US Army regulars now were hunkered down and facing a different kind of enemy. Women and children were using abandoned muskets, homemade explosives, even rocks thrown from buildings to assault the Yankee soldiers occupying the capital. In addition, since the retreat of the Mexican Army, men who had been released from local jails had begun to join the street fighters. These ragtag groups of irregulars created havoc among the Americans. The occupying troops responded by indiscriminately blasting both government and private residences with artillery whenever they encountered resistance. This was only briefly effective since the partisans who survived fled the buildings and began to spread out using guerilla tactics and setting up bases in small towns outside Mexico City. Many of them were joined by Mexican troops who had left the capital after the occupation to continue the fight in the hinterlands and small pueblos.

At one of these small villages called Huamantla, on the road to Puebla, Brigadier General John Lane's force of 1,800 men was met by severe partisan resistance. One of the officers under his command, Captain Samuel Walker of the Texas Rangers,[85] was killed. Lane ordered his men to avenge the death of their fallen officer. According to one army witness, Lt. William D. Wilkins, "Old women and young girls were stripped of their clothes and many others suffered still greater outrages."[86] The soldiers pillaged liquor stores and taverns, got drunk, raped women by the score and burned homes to the ground. Neither Lane nor his men were punished although the incident was well known, not only among the troops stationed in Mexico but even in Washington.

At another village called Atlixco, Lane fired artillery into the most populated area killing civilians and guerillas indiscriminately, resulting in more than 500 casualties. Bragging in his report to Scott that he had destroyed a guerilla base, Lane wrote of the decimated villagers that "so much terror has been impressed upon them, at thus having the war brought to their own homes, that I am inclined to believe they will give us no more trouble."[87]

Scott, who should have cautioned restraint and given appropriate orders to his troops, was instead so exasperated by the resistance of Mexican civilians, that he gave the following order: "No quarter will be given to known murderers or robbers whether called guerrillas or rancheros & whether serving under Mexican commission

---

85. Well known as the co-designer of the Walker Colt revolver, the largest and most pow-erful black powder repeating handgun ever made.
86. Quoted in David A. Clary, *Eagles and Empire* (New York: Bantam Books, 2009), 383.
87. Quoted in Stephen A. Carney, *The Occupation of Mexico May 1846-July 1848* (West Point. US Army Center of Military History, 2015). 16.

or not. They are equally pests to unguarded Mexicans, foreigners, and small parties of Americans, and ought to be exterminated."[88]

These problems were of increasing concern not only to the army but also to Washington and hindered negotiations for peace. The army was having trouble remaining properly provisioned because the supply line from Veracruz to Puebla to Mexico City was constantly being attacked by both bandits and by irregular cavalry. Washington was concerned because peasant revolts in Veracruz and Indian uprisings in the south had drawn resources from the remains of the central government. If irregulars and bandits were fighting the gringos, insurgents and Indians were fighting the landowning gentry. Only a few local militias and armed ranch hands were available to landowners to fend off attacks on local *ranchos* and estates. Without a central government in power, any peace treaty would be meaningless because there would be no one to enforce it.

So, while Polk, Trist, and others in the American government were anxious for a peace treaty, so was most of the Mexican elite who saw it as the only way to keep their hold on power. They could not rebuild their army and secure their hold on power without it. The American government and American business leaders saw the importance of having a peaceful and economically viable Mexico to the south, both as a trading partner to consume its surplus production, but also as a buffer against the incursion of more warlike Indians and savagery.

Finally, the Mexican leaders were brought to the bargaining table by the simple fact that they could not continue a war on three fronts, protect their property, and retain power without an agreement. The American Army was draining Mexican resources every day. The Americans controlled all ports and thus collected all import duties. They also appropriated the ore from silver and gold mines, as well as excise taxes, and other income necessary for the government to survive. The continued ravages on Mexican property by bandits and Indians, and the threat to local governments by peasant uprisings, made the present situation untenable for the Mexican elite.

---

88. *Ibid.*, 18.

Stabilization Plan

While the treaty that ended the war is often spoken of in Mexico as a sellout by the Mexican elite, and highway robbery on the part of the Americans, it did serve the purpose of stabilizing the country. One of the first steps was to provide the Mexican leaders with modern US weapons to aid the government in the reconstruction and rearming of the Mexican military. Many of these weapons were available almost immediately from the supply depot of the American Army. They included modern rifles and carbines, and thousands of cartridges to replace the antiquated Brown Bess muskets the Mexicans had been using. In addition, both sides worked together to stabilize the Veracruz-to-Mexico City route so that merchants were able to ship goods without fear of attacks from bandits. Finally, the American Army provided convoys to escort shipments of precious metals from the mines to the coast.

The two sides met in the village of Guadalupe Hidalgo, today a part of the Federal District of Mexico City, to decide the terms of the peace in late January and early February of 1848, five months after the fall of Mexico City. As we shall see, however, it was not benevolence which motivated the Americans but crafty self-interest. Time was of the essence. Washington had already issued orders for Trist to return if he could not get an agreement.

Treaty of Guadalupe Hidalgo

After weeks of negotiations in which Trist pressed for large territorial concessions, the treaty was signed. Mexico agreed to recognize the Rio Grande as the southern border of Texas, thus adding considerably to the original territory of the Lone Star State. In addition, it agreed to relinquish upper California with the major ports of San Francisco, San Diego, and Los Angeles. Finally, it also surrendered an enormous land mass, which eventually became the states of Nevada, New Mexico, Utah, and Arizona, as well as part of Colorado, Nebraska, Wyoming, and Oklahoma. In return, the US agreed to pay $15,000,000 to the Mexican government and as-

sume $3,500,000 in claims against the government. Notes histori-
an Michael Meyer, "For a total of $18,500,000—less than a year's
budget—Mexico's territory was reduced by half." It also created a
rift in US-Mexico relations that still exists today. As Meyer notes:

> The war reinforced the worst stereotypes that each country held about the
> other, and these stereotypes, in turn, contributed to the development of
> deep-seated prejudices. United States historians rationalized, justified, and
> even commended the decision to wage the war as well as the prosecution of
> it. On grounds ranging from regenerating a backward people to fulfilling a
> preordained destiny, they went so far as to use this war of aggression for the
> purpose of instilling historical pride in generations of American children...
>   It is almost axiomatic that wars nurture the development of xenopho-
> bia, especially on the part of the country that is dismembered. This particular
> war yielded its own particular variety—a virulent, almost pathological, Yan-
> keephobia. The fears and the hatred of the United States ran deep and were
> disseminated and popularized in the traditional Mexico *corrido*, the folk song
> of the common people.[89]

The Price Is Right

Since students have been taught for generations that the United
States "purchased" all this land from Mexico, it might be worth
a bit of clarification. First of all, when you have occupied another country and remain in occupation of their capital, whatever
"agreement" you reach in terms of acquisition of territory is the
result of conquest. Second, the price, less than the Mexican budget
for one year was hardly just compensation for almost 1.9 million
square kilometers of territory, by anyone's calculation. Third, to
reinforce this from the historical point of view, the US offered
Mexico $25,000,000 in 1845 for California alone, which the Mexi-
can government refused! How could an amount considerably less
than that possibly be fair compensation for a territory of a million
square miles? Finally, the US had discovered gold in California, a
fact it kept secret from negotiators for fear it would "complicate"

---

89.   Michael C. Meyer and William KL. Sherman, *The Course of Mexican History* (New York:
      Oxford University Press, 1991), 352.

negotiations. A fact freely admitted. The income from the 1849 Gold Rush in conservative estimates totaled $300,000,000 in 1850 dollars. Howard Zinn in his classic *A People's History of the United States* quotes the *Whig Intelligencia* editorial comment following the ratification of the 1848 treaty: "We take nothing by conquest... thank God." Even at the time that trenchant remark was published, it was considered pure irony by even the least sophisticated of its readers.

Treaty Trickery

If the terms of the treaty were less than honorable, it should come as no surprise that the changes made prior to its ratification by the US Senate were worse, and the actual compliance with terms finally agreed upon was less than what was promised. A number of changes were almost immediate. Article X, which would have honored previous Spanish land grants and Mexican deeds, thus guaranteeing Mexican landowners the security of their property, was deleted from the final document. Article IX, which allowed Mexicans residing in the newly conquered territory to be admitted as citizens of the United States "within one year of the signing of the treaty should they so choose," was amended. When it was apparent that 90 percent would so choose so as to be guaranteed the protection of citizenship, the Senate changed that clause to read "at a future time to be determined by Congress."[90]

An attempt to add the Wilmot Proviso to the treaty declaring that any new US states acquired as a result of the conquest would be free was voted down along sectional lines. An agreement that the United States would patrol its borders and work actively to prevent any incursion of hostile Indians from the United States to Mexico was simply ignored. In fact, the US Army saw little action in the decade after the war, except for the Mormon War of 1856-58, which was merely a series of skirmishes, and the cap-

---

90. The Complete Treaty of Guadalupe Hidalgo, February 2, 1848, as ratified. Treaties and Conventions between the United States of America and Other Powers Since July 4, 1776. (Washington, DC: Government Printing Office, 1871).

ture of the notorious Abolitionist John Brown when he attacked a
federal arsenal and tried to incite a slave revolt. Ironically, it
would be a former Mexican War captain, Robert E. Lee, who
would bring John Brown's radical ambitions to an abrupt end.

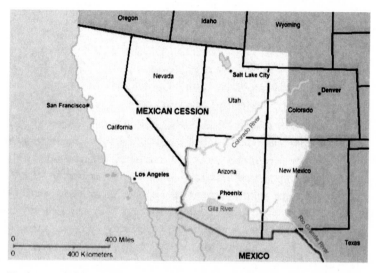

Territory ceded by Mexico to the United States under the Treaty of Guadalupe
Hidalgo, February 2, 1848. Courtesy of the Robinson Library.

Fig. 6. John Brown, 1859. Photo by Black & Batchelder. Library of Congress.

10

THE UNITED STATES INHERITS THE WHIRLWIND

If there is little doubt these days among scholars that the immediate cause of the Civil War was slavery, there should also be agreement that the single major catalyst for that was the conquest of Mexico. The failure of the Wilmot Proviso meant that the former Mexican territories were now up for grabs. Texas was already a slave state and was admitted to the Union as such. Now there was a possibility that a half dozen more would be added.

This was not only an issue of slave labor but also one of political power. According to the Constitution, slaves counted as three-fifths of a whole man when counting population. A larger state population meant a larger presence in the House of Representatives and thus more legislative power. This "Three-Fifths Compromise" of the Founding Fathers was only the beginning in a series of compromises which would make the study of America's struggle to come to terms with its "peculiar institution" so tedious to US students and a genuine perplexity for foreigners.

The Missouri Compromise and Its Aftermath

As the rest of the world did away with slavery, and slave importation had ended in the United States, many people began to call for an end to the institution itself and for the freedom of those presently enslaved. Moreover, as the West opened up, many new settlers feared that white labor would face a challenge from unpaid slave labor should the institution be recognized in the new territories. In 1820, there were twenty-two states, evenly divided between slave and free. When Congress voted in 1820 to admit Maine to the Union as a free state and Missouri as a slave state, they stipulated there would be no slave states admitted to the newly acquired territories north of the 36th parallel in any of the land acquired as a result of the Louisiana Purchase. There had been no slavery in acquired western territories since Northwest Ordinance of 1787, and to continue that policy had been one of Thomas Jefferson's major concerns. Congress would honor that tradition with the exception, of course, of Missouri itself.

So the country continued half slave and half free until the 1840s. Then with Texas (1845) a slave state, as well as Florida (1845), the balance was upset and thus resulted in a country very much divided at the outbreak of the Mexican War, a conflict which many saw clearly as an attempt to garner more slave states. At the end of the war, the balance was somewhat restored with the admission of Minnesota and Wisconsin as free states in 1848. But also with the war's end and the likelihood that several new states would be added from conquered Mexico, the Wilmot Proviso was the only remaining solution to prevent the further spread of slavery. Lincoln had voted for it several times as previously noted. When it was finally proposed as an addendum to the Treaty of Guadalupe-Hidalgo, it again failed in the Senate along divisional lines. Now two years after the end of the Mexican War, Senator Henry Clay proposed the Compromise of 1850 in still another effort to hold the Republic together. It was the most controversial and convoluted compromise yet, and would ultimately lead to a final confrontation when it became the subject of a national debate involving two senatorial candidates: Stephen Douglas and a former congressman from Illinois.

Abraham Lincoln Returns

By 1850, the balance between the states looked to be shifting again. Henry Clay of Kentucky, in an attempt to temper the demands of both North and South, proposed that California be admitted as a free state with Utah and New Mexico allowed to decide for themselves whether to be slave or free. Also, while mollifying Northerners by abolishing the slave trade in Washington, DC, the new law tried to please Southern slave owners by strengthening the Fugitive Slave Act and making it a crime to conceal, transport, or otherwise aid in the separation of a fugitive slave from his owner. In an attempt to please both sides, this Compromise of 1850 satisfied no one. In addition, with the admission of California, free states now outnumbered slave states and things were about to get worse.

In May of 1854, the Kansas-Nebraska Act was passed by Congress. This gave the citizens of these territories the right to choose ("popular sovereignty") whether their respective states would be slave or free. The law, sponsored by Stephen Douglas, satisfied neither side and incited outbreaks of violence as slavery and anti-slavery settlers fought for control of Kansas. These eruptions would also have a butterfly effect on Washington, DC, as the issue heated up on Capitol Hill. In 1856, a South Carolina congressman viciously beat Senator Charles Sumner of Massachusetts with a cane on the Senate floor. Two years later in the House of Representatives, fifty congressmen broke out in a fist-fight over the question of whether slavery should be expanded to the western territories.

Lincoln saw this as the last gasp of slavery in America. All the compromises had failed. This latest effort in Kansas and Nebraska was doomed to failure as well. Only violence remained. Noted Lincoln:

> The people are to decide the question of slavery for themselves; but WHEN they are to decide; or HOW they are to decide; or whether, when the question is once decided, it is to remain so, or is it to be subject to an indefinite succession of new trials, the law does not say, Is it to be decided by the first dozen settlers who arrive there? or is it to await the arrival of a hundred? Is it to be decided by a vote of the people? or a vote of the legislature? or, indeed by a vote of any sort? To these questions, the law gives no answer. There is a mystery about this; for when a member proposed to give the legislature express authority to exclude slavery, it was hooted down by the friends of the bill. This fact is worth remembering. Some Yankees, in the east, are sending emigrants to Nebraska, to exclude slavery from it; and, so far as I can judge, they expect the question to be decided by voting, in some way or other. But

the Missourians are awake too. They are within a stone's throw of the contested ground. They hold meetings, and pass resolutions, in which not the slightest allusion to voting is made. They resolve that slavery already exists in the territory; that more shall go there; that they, remaining in Missouri will protect it; and that abolitionists shall be hung, or driven away. Through all this, bowie-knives and six-shooters are seen plainly enough; but never a glimpse of the ballot-box. And, really, what is to be the result of this? Each party WITHIN, having numerous and determined backers WITHOUT, is it not probable that the contest will come to blows, and bloodshed? Could there be a more apt invention to bring about collision and violence, on the slavery question, than this Nebraska project is? I do not charge, or believe, that such was intended by Congress; but if they had literally formed a ring, and placed champions within it to fight out the controversy, the fight could be no more likely to come off, than it is. And if this fight should begin, is it likely to take a very peaceful, Union-saving turn? Will not the first drop of blood so shed, be the real knell of the Union?

Lincoln's words were prophetic. Violence was coming in a shape that had been most feared by Southern slave owners: an organized attempt to free slaves across the country, wherein they might secure advanced weaponry, and move against their white masters. The new revolt would be led by a man who—even though he would fail in the attempt—would become a folk hero and a catalyst for the war that would ultimately result in the liberation of the enslaved.

John Brown's Body

Born in Torrington, Connecticut, John Brown studied briefly for the ministry before giving up and settling for his father's trade: a tanner. He traveled quite a bit pursuing his work and was very early on a convert to the Abolitionist cause. He had met Frederick Douglass in his travels and was impressed with the eloquence and the passion of the former slave. Brown began to work actively in support of the Underground Railroad ferrying escaped slaves to Canada. In 1848, he moved to a community of free blacks in North Elba, New York. He also founded a group to protect blacks from fugitive slave hunters.

In 1855 following the passage of the Kansas-Nebraska Act, he was one of the "Yankees" mentioned by Lincoln who moved to the area to use violence if need be to see that Kansas would come into the Union as a free state. Brown believed in using force since, for him, slavery itself was conceived and maintained by violence. In 1856, in retaliation for an earlier attack, he and his men killed five pro-slavery settlers at Pottawatomie Creek. In 1858, he freed a group of slaves in Missouri and escorted them to freedom in Canada. Once there, he spoke about forming a free black community in the mountains of Maryland and having them all armed and ready to defend themselves against hostile whites. But the big show was yet to come.

In 1859, Brown masterminded and then led an attack on the federal armory at Harper's Ferry, Virginia. He and his supporters (twenty-one men, including his three sons, and five blacks) took over the arsenal. Their plan was to secure the weapons there (over 100,000 rifles were in storage) and then move down through Virginia and thence to other Southern states, liberating slaves as he went, and forming a great army. However, local militia and a group of Marines led by former Mexican War veteran Col. Robert E. Lee foiled the plan. They raided the facility, killed ten of his followers, and captured most of the remaining. A few escaped including one of his sons. Two others, Watson and Oliver, were dead. Brown was taken into custody and charged with murder, conspiring to get slaves to rebel, and "treason against the Commonwealth of Virginia."[91] Assisting Col. Robert E. Lee in the Brown capture and in attendance at the trial was another veteran, J.E.B. Stuart, who like Lee had an even more interesting fate in store for him.

Brown was found guilty on all three counts and was sentenced to hang by the neck until dead. The sentence was duly carried out in the city of Charles Town (in what is now West Virginia) on December 2, 1859. However, as we all know, it was not the end of the affair but just the beginning. As Brown noted prior to his hanging in a note given to his wife Mary Ann: "I, John Brown, am now quite certain that the crimes of this guilty land will never be purged

---

91. "John Brown's Raid." West Virginia Archives and History. http://www.wvculture.org/history/johnbrown.html

but with blood. I had, as I now think, flattered myself that without much bloodshed it might be done."[92]

Abraham Lincoln was not impressed by Brown's raid or his forecast, at least not publicly. Privately, one might suppose he saw the writing on the wall. However, when Republicans were accused of provoking slaves to revolt, he replied cuttingly:

> You charge that we stir up insurrections among your slaves. We deny it; and what is your proof? Harper's Ferry! John Brown!! John Brown was no Republican; and you have failed to implicate a single Republican in his Harper's Ferry enterprise....John Brown's effort was peculiar. It was not a slave insurrection. It was an attempt by white men to get up a revolt among slaves, in which the slaves refused to participate. In fact, it was so absurd that the slaves, with all their ignorance, saw plainly enough it could not succeed.[93]

At the hanging, Thomas Jackson, a former major in the Mexican-American War[94] (later a Confederate general popularly known as "Stonewall" for his heroic resistance at the Battle of Bull Run) stood with the VMI cadets. In addition to J.E.B. Stuart and Robert E. Lee, John Wilkes Booth also appeared dressed in a borrowed uniform from a Virginia militiaman. They were like wraiths of the future, all foreshadowing the conflict to come. Walt Whitman, who once lusted in print for conquest of the Mexicans, now wrote his firsthand account:

> I would sing how an old man, tall, with white hair, mounted the scaffold in Virginia;
> (I was at hand—silent I stood, with teeth shut close—I watch'd
> I stood very near you, old man, when cool and indifferent, but trembling with age and your

---

92. *Ibid.*
93. Scott J. Hammond, et al., ed. *Classics of American Political Thought,* Vol. 1 (Indianapolis: Hackett Publishing Company, 2007.),1082.
94. Stonewall Jackson would later write in his *Memoirs* that he received two bad orders from commanders while serving in Mexico. The first was to withdraw from his attack on Chapultepec Castle, which he disobeyed because he felt he would lose more men in the retreat than he would by continuing the assault. The second "bad order" was when he was commanded to open fire with artillery on a crowd of civilians in Mexico City when they refused to disperse after the surrender of the capital. He obeyed that order.

Unhealed wounds, you mounted the scaffold); I would sing...[95]

The song would begin in earnest, not Whitman's, but one more popular even today. Shortly after Brown's execution, a popular camp revival tune received new words: "John Brown's body lies a-mouldering in the grave. His soul is marching on!"[96] Before long it would become "The Battle Hymn of the Republic"[97] with additional lyrics penned by Julia Ward Howe,[98] and the "much bloodshed" that Brown sought to avoid would fertilize fields in Pennsylvania, cover the green hills of Maryland, and stain the city streets of Atlanta.

95.   Walt Whitman. "Year of Meteors," public domain. http://
      www.bartleby.com/142/100. html
96.   "John Brown's Body/Battle Hymn of the Republic," Library of Congress.
      www.loc. gov/teachers/lyrical/songs/john_brown.html
97.   Ibid.
98.   The Julia Ward Howe version eliminated John Brown's name, which made it
      acceptable for both Northerners and Southerners to sing, and led to its popularity on
      both sides of the conflict.

11
LINCOLN AND THE BEGINNINGS
OF CIVIL WAR

Shortly after the death of John Brown, a memorial service was held at the Cooper Union in New York praising the Abolitionist for his service to the country. Although Lincoln tended to dismiss Brown's actions and disassociate the Republican Party from their causes and consequences, he nonetheless accepted an invitation to speak at the same locale two weeks later.

There was no question that in the upcoming contest for the presidency, Lincoln would draw most of his support from the North and that the Abolitionists would have a major influence in the election. The day was February 27, 1860. Lincoln had not yet been nominated for the presidency, but this speech would solidify his northern supporters. In it, he cited the Founding Fathers who had agreed not to extend slavery in the territories controlled by the federal government. He noted that while they tolerated slavery in the States where it already existed, they imposed clear limits on its growth. He stated that this was essentially the Republican position, and those southerners who sought to change that policy or to refuse to support a president who would follow the Constitution were no better than thieves.

> But you will not abide the election of a Republican president! In that sup-
> posed event, you say, you will destroy the Union; and then, you say, the great
> crime of having destroyed it will be upon us! That is cool. A highwayman

holds a pistol to my ear, and mutters through his teeth, "Stand and deliver, or
I shall kill you, and then you will be a murderer!" To be sure, what the robber
demanded of me - my money - was my own; and I had a clear right to keep it;
but it was no more my own than my vote is my own; and the threat of death
to me, to extort my money, and the threat of destruction to the Union, to
extort my vote, can scarcely be distinguished in principle.[99]

It is clear that Lincoln already saw the division approaching, and
saw as well that it was not compatible with the Constitution or his
idea of the Union. To him, it was clear that there was no right
to secede. A Republic might, he argued, as a Union, agree to
dissolve and, as Jefferson would have it, "institute a new
government," but no single state would have that right.

Speaking in New York to a crowd that basically supported Lincoln's views on the prohibition of slavery in the territories, and
perhaps went even further and tended to support the eventual end
of slavery itself in the republic, Lincoln was essentially preaching
to the choir. Yet, in those days as mass media was quickly develop-
ing, he also knew that his words would be transmitted by telegraph
to newspapers in the South and that readers there would be parsing
his every word. As a result, his speech is a carefully reasoned and
moderate one. His main argument was that he intended to follow
the Constitution not only in spirit but in letter. And he was equally
firm that, while he would not depart from that principle, neither
would he push the Abolitionist agenda.

Wrong as we think slavery is, we can yet afford to let it alone where it is, because that much is due to the necessity arising from its actual presence in the
nation; but can we, while our votes will prevent it, allow it to spread into the
National Territories, and to overrun us here in these Free States? If our sense
of duty forbids this, then let us stand by our duty, fearlessly and effectively.[100]

He concluded the speech with an affirmation of authority based on
the principles as he understood them, as promulgated by Founding
Fathers in the Constitution and the Northwest Ordinance. In other

---

99.   Abraham Lincoln. Cooper Union Speech. http://www.abrahamlincolnonline.org/lin-
      coln/speeches/cooper.htm
100. *Ibid.*

words, he relied on the precedents that then existed as his guide. He articulated clearly what was right and with his peroration asserted it firmly.

> Neither let us be slandered from our duty by false accusations against us, nor frightened from it by menaces of destruction to the Government nor of dungeons to ourselves. Let us have faith that right makes might, and in that faith, let us, to the end, dare to do our duty as we understand it.[101]

Three months later he was nominated as president by the Republican Party. The turnout of the electorate was enormous. It was the second highest in history with 81.2 percent of the electorate casting their votes.[102] However, most of the support came from the North and the Midwest. Lincoln was not even on the ballot in ten of the Southern states. In Virginia he received only 1,920 votes out of 167,301 actually cast, that is, 1.15% of the popular vote.[103] Events would move swiftly after that. The Southern states would proceed to go their separate ways. By mid-February, 1861, Jefferson Davis, another veteran of the war with Mexico, would become president of the newly-organized Confederate States of America.

Two weeks later, Lincoln arrived in Washington via a secret route to avoid assassination. Already, there was murderous talk in the air. Between the time of his election and the day of his inauguration, seven southern states had seceded and more were soon to follow. He was guarded by a special battalion of soldiers commanded by General Winfield Scott as he ascended the dais and made one final plea to his countrymen to avoid violence.

Once again, he asserted that he would not interfere with slavery in any of those states where it currently existed. He affirmed that the prohibition of the slave trade and the exclusion of slavery from the territories was already law and that he would enforce it. He again affirmed that no State had the right to secede from the

---

101. *Ibid.*
102. *Harper's Weekly*, The Presidential Elections 1860-1912. http://elections.harpweek.com/1860/Overview-1860-2.htm
103. Richmond *Daily Inquirer*, 24 December 1860. 1860 Presidential Returns. http://www.virginiamemory.com/docs/1860_election_returns.pdf

Union. Then he called for national unity in a hopeful last plea to the southerners for the solidarity which made all of the people citizens of the Republic living under the same Constitution.

> In your hands, my dissatisfied fellow-countrymen, and not in mine, is the momentous issue of civil war. The Government will not assail you. You can have no conflict without being yourselves the aggressors. You have no oath registered in heaven to destroy the Government, while I shall have the most solemn one to "preserve, protect, and defend it."

> I am loath to close. We are not enemies, but friends. We must not be enemies. Though passion may have strained it must not break our bonds of affection. The mystic chords of memory, stretching from every battlefield and patriot grave to every living heart and hearthstone all over this broad land, will yet swell the chorus of the Union, when again touched, as surely they will be, by the better angels of our nature.[104]

But the appeal to the "better angels of our nature" was not to prevail. The next month, following Lincoln's attempt to resupply Fort Sumter in South Carolina, one of the last remaining federal outposts in the South, Confederate batteries under General P.G.T. Beauregard opened fire.

The Attack on Fort Sumter

Beauregard was another of the Mexican War veterans. He had served with Robert E. Lee in the Corps of Engineers and many, including Beauregard himself, felt that he was a better engineer than Lee. He resented Lee's rapid promotion to the ranks and he also resented Braxton Bragg, another Mexican War veteran, who had already achieved high rank in the Confederate Army. As a result, he ingratiated himself with Jefferson Davis, former commander of the Mississippi Rifles in Mexico and now President of the Confederate States. Davis, impressed by his qualifications, put him in

---

104. Abraham Lincoln, First Inaugural Address, March 4, 1861. http://avalon.law.yale. edu/19th_century/lincoln1.asp

charge of all the coastal defenses. Not long after, he would become the first general officer in the Confederate Army.

When news arrived in Charleston that ships from the north were on their way to resupply the fort, Davis contacted Beauregard and asked him to demand the surrender of the fort. The commander of the facility was Major Richard Anderson, a former professor of Beauregard at West Point. Beauregard sent a formal request for the surrender, along with a case of whiskey and a box of cigars.[105] Anderson returned the gifts accompanied by a formal apology that he was unable to comply. (This level of politeness between northern and southern officers prevailed for quite a long time despite the slaughters that were to follow). At 4:30 a.m. on the morning of April 12, 1861, Jefferson Davis issued his order to Brigadier General Beauregard to open fire.

The bombardment lasted thirty-four hours. On April 13, 1861, the Stars and Stripes were lowered, and the Stars and Bars raised over Fort Sumter. The War Between the States had begun, although a bit inauspiciously. Despite the lengthy bombardment, there were no Union casualties from combat. The only death was one soldier killed by an exploding cartridge as they were giving a final cannon salute when lowering the flag.[106]

On April 15, President Lincoln called for 75,000 volunteers to serve in the US Army for a period of ninety days. Lincoln believed that the insurrection, now begun by South Carolina, could only be settled by force of arms. Most of Lincoln's advisers and not a few of his generals were preparing for a ninety-day uprising that would be easily suppressed. Another veteran of the Mexican War, William Tecumseh Sherman, felt different. However, he felt that the President had vastly underestimated the number of troops required. He

---

105. John Richard Stephens, *Commanding the Storm: Civil War Battles in the Words of the Generals Who Fought Them* (Guilford, CT: Lyons Press, 2012). https://books.google.com.mx/books?isbn=0762789859

106. Pvt. Daniel Hough died an accidental death when a cannon discharged while he was loading it. This occurred the day after the battle ended, during a surrender ceremony. Another Union soldier was mortally wounded during the surrender ceremony. http://www.nps.gov/fosu/faqs.htm#fatalities

speculated that they would need at least 200,000 volunteers to clear out the rebels in his home state of Kentucky alone![107]

Fig. 7. Pierre G.T. Beauregard, Brigadier General, CSA, 1861. Photo courtesy of the Aztec Club.

107. James Tuttleton, "Lincoln's Generals: Sherman and Grant in Their Memoirs," *The New Criterion*, October, 1990, 4/11. http://newcriterion.com/articles.cfm/Lincolns-gen-erals-Sherman-and-Grant-in-their-memoirs-5278

Fig. 8. Jefferson Davis, President of the Confederate States of America. Photo by Matthew Brady, 1861.

12

FRIENDS OF MEXICO, FRIENDS OF LINCOLN

Several of Lincoln's military leaders, as well as important members of his administration, would be selected from Mexican War veterans and from those who supported his views against the war in Congress. The first of these, whom we mentioned and quoted at some length in an earlier chapter, was Thomas Corwin. A well-known Whig senator whose speeches we have quoted earlier, and whom Lincoln admired enormously, he was opposed to Texas annexation and to the invasion of Mexico a year later. He went on to become Lincoln's ambassador to Mexico.

Caleb Smith was another Whig congressman and former associate of Lincoln. His objections to the war with Mexico were so forceful and eloquent that the editor of the Richmond *Jeffersonian* angrily suggested that his speech criticizing Polk's decision to invade "would have been very creditable to him had it been delivered before a Mexican Congress. It partakes of the wordy, windy character of Mexican proclamations, speeches, etc."[108] A grateful Lincoln would appoint him Secretary of the Interior.

Still another choice which Lincoln made from among the notables who sided with his opinion on the war with Mexico was William H. Seward. A lifelong opponent of human trafficking, he

---

108. Richmond, Indiana, *Jeffersonian.* January 13, 1847.

clearly saw the implications of the war for the creation of more slave states. Seward had also been opposed to the acquisition of Texas. He, like Lincoln, was consistently against the war. In his brief legal career as a defense attorney in Auburn, NY, Seward was vilified for his defense of a black man accused of murder. Seward was considered an Abolitionist and quite a bit more passionate for the cause than Lincoln. While governor of New York, he also protected black sailors who were arrested on a confiscated vessel, and refused to return them to the south under the Fugitive Slave Act.

Seward ran against Lincoln for the presidential nomination and was somewhat bitter that he did not win. Despite the fact that they had been political rivals, Lincoln chose him to be his Secretary of State. They gradually became best of friends with Seward encouraging Lincoln to dress more carefully, and present himself more presidentially. Lincoln for his part began to trust Seward on almost every matter including many issues outside the usual responsibilities of the State Department. They remained close confidants throughout his terms in office.

Seward was Lincoln's only Secretary of State; he stayed with him in his second term and, after Lincoln's assassination, continued on in that post under President Andrew Johnson. Although he is far better known today for his purchase of Alaska ("Seward's Folly"), his special interest in Mexico would bear fruit after the Civil War ended and he was able to bring diplomatic pressure to help terminate another occupation, and eliminate the French presence in the Americas.

There were other friends of Lincoln's, however, who thought Seward was doing too little to help Mexico as a new crisis developed in the 1860s: among them were Charles Sumner, William Dennison, and James Speed.

Sumner was a Radical Republican, an Abolitionist who was against the Texas accession and the Mexican War, which he saw as an attempt by the South to gain more slave states. He had been viciously attacked in the Senate after giving an anti-slavery speech in 1856. As head of the Senate Foreign Relations Committee, he would be a force to resist French interference during the Civil War, and would have many meetings with Mexico's special envoy on strategies to assist that country as it faced a new enemy. Mrs. Lincoln, writing about him in her later years, noted that Sumner and her husband were great friends, even though the senator had more radical views than the president. "They were like boys during his last days," she remembered fondly.[109]

William Dennison was the Governor of Ohio and not only an Abolitionist but one of the first state governors to pass an anti-discrimination statute. In addition, he raised one of the first regiments at the outbreak of the Civil War, and was instrumental in the creation of West Virginia as a free state. When he did not get reelected as governor, Lincoln appointed him to be Postmaster General. The position might seem a minor one, but Dennison used his influence as a businessman and financier to encourage the Mexican envoy to the United States in his efforts to raise funds to support the government in exile and ultimately overthrow the French. Writing about him in 1865, the Mexican envoy noted: "The acquisition of Dennison's sympathy and friendship is a great gain for our cause. He is a man of talent, of very good reputation in the United States, and on very good terms with the president."[110]

At the time of the Mexican-American War, James Speed was a legislator in Kentucky. He was highly vocal in his anti-slavery views. He not only objected to the Mexican War as a conquest which would lead to more slave states but later protested the Compromise of 1850 and the Kansas-Nebraska Act. When the Civil War broke out, he was active in organizing Union forces from Kentucky and even introduced a bill to confiscate Confederate property (including slaves—which would be equivalent to freeing them). Perhaps even more important to Lincoln was the fact that he was the brother of Joshua Speed, a fellow Kentuckian who had relocated to Springfield, Illinois, had built a successful business there and also edited the local newspaper. He and Lincoln would be friends throughout his life. It was Speed who provided Lincoln with a room

109. Douglas L. Wilson and Rodney O. David, eds. *Herndon's Informants* (Chicago: University of Illinois Press, 1998), 358.
110. Thomas D. Schoonover, ed., *Mexican Lobby: Matías Romero in Washington 1861-1867* (Lexington: The University of Kentucky Press), 1986, 95-96.

and furnishings when he first arrived in Springfield as a struggling young lawyer. Speed who lent him books. Speed who helped him overcome his shyness and meet people.

When Lincoln became president, he offered him a position in his cabinet but Speed declined, feeling he could be of more service as an influential citizen and businessman. And so he was. It was Joshua Speed who used his connections as a businessman to get rifles shipped to Sherman at a crucial time in the Civil War—one of the many times in which he used his influence to aid the Union cause.

When Speed's brother James was not reelected to the Kentucky Senate because of his radical Republican views, Lincoln chose him to be Attorney General of the United States. James Speed would often meet with the minister from the Mexican government-in-exile to discuss legal ways in which they could raise funds in the US to support the overthrow of the French.

Perhaps the most notable appointment, however, would be that of Lt. General Ulysses S. Grant, as General of the Armies. Grant in his memoirs noted that the war with Mexico was "the most unjust ever waged by a stronger nation against weaker."[111] Although Grant believed that the American invasion of Mexico was an unjust and unethical use of force, he did his duty in the field and was praised by his commanders for his resourcefulness and his bravery. Grant served with both Zachary Taylor and with Winfield Scott's invasion forces.

Most significant, however, was his independence of action and his decisiveness. Once he made a decision he did not hesitate; he followed through regardless of the odds of the consequences. These were qualities that would serve him and his country well in the Civil War and also, when that conflict ended, would impel him to provide (often in an unofficial capacity significant encouragement and assistance to Mexico in her struggle against foreign occupation.

Sorry that he had ever enlisted during the War with Mexico in 1846, and unhappy with the invasion (at one point he thought

---

111. Ulysses S. Grant, *Personal Memoirs*, 53

he might resign his commission), he nevertheless crossed the Rio Grande with his troops under General Taylor after the bombardment of Matamoros. Acting as regimental quartermaster at the Battle of Monterrey, he volunteered to bring ammunition to beleaguered troops under fire. The streets of Monterrey were filled with Mexican troops cutting off the Americans from their supply base. With one foot in the stirrup and his body slung to the side of his horse opposite the enemy, he sped through the streets on his mission, saddle bags loaded with cartridges. For an officer to volunteer for such a mission was unheard of, and it clearly impressed Taylor and the other officers under his command. Bold and inventive, this Indian-style run not only got the ammunition to the soldiers under fire but endeared him to all the troops who witnessed his courage.

Later, serving under Scott in 1847, he worked his way toward the capital from Veracruz with the main body of troops participating in skirmishes along the way. Finally, in Mexico City after the fall of Chapultepec, he ordered the dismantling of a field howitzer, had it brought by a pulley to a secure position in the belfry of a church, and took control of the Mexican troops below.

Not only was he a good general (his contemporary, General Sherman, judged him the best of all time) but he was a careful and astute observer. Since most of his rival generals also served in the Mexican War this gave him a decided advantage. As Grant wrote in his *Memoirs*:

> Graduating in 1843, I was at the military academy from one to four years with all the cadets who graduated between 1840 and 1846—seven classes. These classes embraced more than fifty officers who later become generals on one side or another in the rebellion, many of them holding commands. All the older officers who became conspicuous in the rebellion, I had also served with in Mexico: Lee, J.E. Johnson, Holmes, Herbert, and a number of others…The acquaintances thus formed were of immense service to me in the war of the rebellion—I mean what I learned of the characters of those to whom I was afterwards opposed.[112]

112. Grant's *Personal Memoirs* quoted in Tuttleton, *op. cit.* at 4/11.

While many saw Robert E. Lee, the brilliant commander and tactician, as a general who could not be defeated and who had uncanny abilities of the highest order, Grant had a more down-to-earth opinion. "I had known him personally, and knew that he was mortal; and it was just as well that I felt this."[113]

Grant's associate-in-arms in the Civil War, General William Tecumseh Sherman, had served in an artillery unit in the Mexican War. However, he was not engaged in any combat activities due to delays in transport of him and his troops. Nevertheless, his evaluation of the need for more troops at the start of the war, and his rejection of the general consensus that it would be a short war, and his clear assessments of important issues, mirrored those of Grant. Both were pilloried in the press, both were underestimated. Grant was called a drunk, and Sherman was called "insane" by more than one newspaper, and suffered from severe depression. He, too, was admired and respected by Lincoln and referred to as a friend.

Although he would later prove a disappointment to Lincoln, General George McClellan was given the command of the Union Armies in the early days of the Civil War. He graduated from West Point just as the war with Mexico began and was one of the most enthusiastic young lieutenants. Unlike Grant who had his reservations, McClellan saw the war with Mexico as the road to advancement in his military career. Although his early letters home were full of enthusiasm the feeling soon faded as disease, tropical heat, and the perils of combat wore him down. At the Battle of Contreras, he had two horses shot out underneath him and came close to his end when canister fire struck the hilt of his sword. When he finally arrived in Mexico City, he wrote in clear relief, "Here we are. The deed is done. No one can say 'poor Mac' over me."[114] It may have been precisely this experience in Mexico which made him a bit too cautious and resulted in his ultimate replacement as a Union commander.

---

113. Gary W. Gallagher, ed. *The Spotsylvania Campaign* (Chapel Hill: University of North Carolina Press, 1998), 242

114. Michael J. McHugh, *George B. McClellan: The Disposable Patriot* (Arlington Heights, IL: Christian Liberty Press, 1998), 22.

Perhaps the most important general, after Grant and Sherman, was one who graduated too late from West Point to serve in Mexico. This was the diminutive Irish-American, Philip Sheridan. Born in Albany, NY, Sheridan earned his nickname of Little Phil because of his five-feet-five-inch stature. In 1848, he received his appointment to the US Military Academy. At first, he was disqualified because of a poor grade in the math exam and, even after his admission, it was still touch and go. He was involved in a fight with a classmate and threatened to kill him with a bayonet. He was therefore suspended from the Academy for the full year. He graduated in 1853, thirty-fourth in his class of fifty-two cadets.[115]

After the Civil War broke out, he was appointed to serve under Grant as a commissary officer, and his organizational skills and his ability to make tactical decisions under pressure soon endeared him to his superior. He would soon be the youngest major general in the army. By the end of the war, he would be Grant's most trusted commander. When General Sherman was sent to the western territories to guard the settlers and the expanding railroad against hostiles, it was "Little Phil" who would be charged with the responsibility of helping Mexico throw off its latest invader.

115. http://www.historynet.com/philip-sheridan

Fig. 9. "Sheridan" by Alex Gardner - File from *The Photographic History of The Civil War in Ten Volumes: Volume Four, The Cavalry.* The Review of Reviews Co., New York. 1911. p. 268. Licensed under Public Domain via Commons.

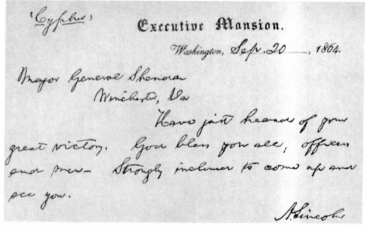

Fig. 10. Congratulatory 1864 letter of Lincoln's pasted in Sheridan's *Memoirs.* Public domain. Philip H. Sheridan, *Personal Memoirs of P.H. Sheridan, General, United States Army.* New York: Charles Webster, 1888.

13

THE FRENCH EMPIRE IN MEXICO

Eduardo Galeano once wrote, "History never really says *goodbye*. History says, *see you later*."[116] This seems to be true whether one is speaking about Iraq in the twenty-first century or Mexico in the nineteenth. When an invading force destroys a country's army, eliminates the central government, neutralizes the national police, and occupies the capital, a major problem occurs when it finally decides to pull out. And it makes little difference whether the invaders have rearmed a new military force and left useful equipment behind. Untrained in the new weaponry, without proper leadership, understaffed and assailed by civil conflict, the defeated country is vulnerable to outside invaders as well as internal division and civil strife.

When the US Army of Occupation commanded by General Winfield Scott left Mexico in the spring of 1848, it left behind a power vacuum. The country had no strong central government. There were Comanche and Apache attacks at the northern border, and to the south there were uprisings of both peasants and indigenous people. The capital was politically divided between Church-supported conservatives and reform-minded liberals. It

---

116. Eduardo Galeano, Una entrevista en el 2013 con periodista Gary Young, "La historia nunca dice adiós. La historia dice hasta luego." http://www.masde131.com/2015/04/el-arte-de-la-memoria-indomita-para-recordar-a-eduardo-galeano/

was also divided economically and socially with a handful of elites managing the details of the transition, with less concern for the Republic of Mexico than for feathering their own nests and making alliances with American business interests.

The Failed Invasion of William Walker

Attacks from the outside would occur swiftly. One of the first and most colorful invasions was that of William Walker. A lawyer from New Orleans with delusions of grandeur, Walker wished to establish a slave republic in Northern Mexico. He began recruiting colonists and ex-soldiers to go to Mexico to establish a colony. He tried to convince the Mexican government that his group would also form a buffer state protecting Mexico from border raids of hostile Indians. The Mexicans, who made that mistake once with Texas, were not about to do it again. He was rebuffed by the government of Santa Anna, who had just returned from exile.

Undismayed, and knowing that the Mexican Army would be preoccupied with defending the capital and putting down peasant uprisings in the south, Walker invaded Baja California with a small contingent of men in the summer of 1853. He "conquered" the small fishing village of La Paz. To his surprise, the Mexican government responded quickly and he was forced to retreat to Ensenada. There he set up his headquarters and he declared himself President of the Republic of Sonora.[117] A brief skirmish with Mexican troops led by Manuel Márquez de León forced him to retreat. He escaped with his life back to the safety of the United States.[118]

When he returned to San Francisco, he was put on trial for violation of the Neutrality Act and for starting an illegal war. However, his adventures were praised in the newspapers of the

---

117. Although Ensenada is in the present State of Baja California, at that time there was no such state, but simply a Mexican territory. Walker proposed to incorporate all of that territory into the Republic of Sonora.

118. Christopher Minster, "The Biography of William Walker: The Ultimate Yankee Imperialist." http://latinamericanhistory.about.com/od/historyofcentralamerica/a/wwalker.htm.

South and he was considered a folk hero by many in those halcyon days of Manifest Destiny. The jury took only eight minutes to acquit him of all the charges.[119]

Meanwhile, back in Mexico, Santa Anna was strapped for cash. He had barely enough money to pay the troops that he had sent north, and little left in the Treasury, or from day to day receipts of taxes and import duties, to pay for the maintenance of the government. James Gadsden, a former railroad executive and now ambassador to Mexico proposed a solution. Sell off a portion of the northern section of Sonora (now a strip of southern Arizona and New Mexico) and he could have the operating funds necessary to run his country.[120]

Santa Anna was suspicious. With the acquittal of William Walker, Santa Anna suspected that the US government, Ambassador Gadsden, and the railroad interests had planned the whole takeover of Sonora. Indeed, Gadsden *was* in collusion with railroad executives to build a transcontinental railroad across the southern part of the US to offset the stupendous growth of railroads in the North. When Santa Anna could not find a neutral party to intercede in the negotiations (Great Britain refused), the Mexican president finally agreed to sell the land for $15 million with the provision that the US would fortify the area and protect the Mexican border against Apache attacks that had ravaged Mexican villages in the region.[121] Gadsden agreed. However, when he brought the treaty back to the US, the Senate reduced the amount to $10 million and omitted the clause about the Apaches.[122] Santa Anna, desperate, signed it anyway. The Gadsden Purchase would be the final straw for his countrymen.

119. *Ibid.*
120. US Department of States. Office of the Historian. "Gadsden Purchase." https://history.state.gov/milestones/1830-1860/gadsden-purchase
121. *Ibid.*
122. Statutes of the United States. Gadsden Purchase. Yale Law School. http://avalon.law.yale.edu/19th_century/mx1853.asp

The Rise of Benito Juárez

Benito Juárez, a young lawyer and former governor of Oaxaca whom General Santa Anna had forced into exile when he refused to support the military dictatorship, now drafted the Plan of Ayutla calling for Santa Anna's deposition to explain his actions and for a new constitutional convention. Abandoned by the conservatives who supported him in the past and condemned by the liberals who saw him selling off the country bit by bit, Santa Anna resigned in 1855.

The Liberal Party now formed a provisional government with Juárez as head of the Supreme Court and Ignacio Comonfort as President. The new government eliminated ecclesiastical courts, prohibited clerics from taking part in politics and in the press, restricted the power of the military, and restricted the Church's right to own vast tracts of property, thus freeing up land for the peasants.[123] However, the Liberals underestimated the power of the Church, the fear of the conservatives in any land divestiture scheme, and the influence of both landowners and the Church on the peasants. The new change in the laws was called "La Reforma." Noted one Mexican critic in a classic run-on sentence fragment:

> The clergy, deprived even of their rights as citizens, the Church whose property is that of the poor, the army destroyed as a class and prostituted by the entrance into the ranks of notorious bandits and jailbirds, the proprietor whose possessions are unprotected by an unbridled government, and the artisan, humiliated by the presence in the capital of the republic of the filthy, insolent, and immoral horde which the weakness of a few men has vomited upon Mexico out of the mountains of the south, and which threaten the lives and honor of our wives and daughters.[124]

The Conservatives launched a revolt that was to be known as La Guerra de La Reforma. The rebels, under General Félix Maria Zuloaga, demanded the resignation of Comonfort and imposed a

---

123. Michael C. Meyer and William L Sherman, *The Course of Mexican History*, 4th ed., New York: Oxford University Press, 1991, 378-379
124. Manuel Doblado quoted by Kristen Arias in "Ley Juárez ." http://historicaltextarchive.com/print.php?action=section&artid=572.

military dictatorship with Zuloaga as head of state. However, under terms of the new constitution, Juárez as head of the Supreme Court became the legal interim president after the resignation of Comonfort. With General Zuloaga's troops already occupying Mexico City, Juárez was forced to retreat. He made his capital in Veracruz and used the customs receipts from that port to fund the resistance. The government of the US under President Buchanan recognized Juárez as the legitimate leader, and that recognition brought many more supporters to his side and enabled him to retake Mexico City on January 1, 1861. In March 1861 (the same month and year that Abraham Lincoln took office), he was finally inaugurated as president of Mexico under the new constitution. While Lincoln was six foot four inches and his counterpart in Mexico only four foot six inches, they would both rise to mythic stature in their respective countries and would ironically be inextricably intertwined with each other's wars, policies, and friendships.

Romero and Lincoln

President Juárez assumed leadership of the country that was not only devastated by civil strife but one whose treasury was seriously depleted by the depredations of Santa Anna and the Reform War. He realized that if he was going to maintain any semblance of order in the country, he would need to suspend payments on foreign debts for at least two years so that he could repair the infrastructure, pay his army, and keep the country afloat. William Seward as Secretary of State offered one solution where Mexico would provide major mining concessions in exchange for American loans. However, it carried the proviso that if Mexico defaulted for any reason, it would give up Baja California and other territory in compensation. This was too drastic an agreement for the liberal president.[125] Not only did it reek of the conservative sellouts of previous administrations (Santa Anna and the Gadsden Purchase for one), but it was

---

125. US Department of State. Office of the Historian. https://history.state.gov/milestones/1861-1865/french-intervention

politically unsound and a poor business move. The mines were the geese in Mexico that laid the golden (and silver) eggs.

In March of 1861, shortly after his inauguration, President Lincoln appointed his good friend, Senator Thomas Corwin, as "Envoy Extraordinary and Minister Plenipotentiary" in Mexico.[126] Corwin, sympathetic to the Mexican cause since the days in 1846-47 when he castigated Polk and railed against the warmongers, proposed a more palatable solution. On behalf of the Lincoln Administration, he negotiated a treaty with Mexican Representative Manuel Maria Zamacona that would provide funds to the Mexicans on more liberal terms.

Matías Romero, the Mexican Chargé d'Affaires[127] in the US, was in Washington to ensure that everything would go through without a hitch. He had an exclusive interview with Lincoln shortly after his election and visited Lincoln at his home in Springfield, Illinois, shortly after his election and before his move to the White House. The President-elect took to him immediately and promised that his administration would treat Mexico fairly.[128] Romero, who knew of Lincoln's anti-expansionist views, promised in turn that Juárez would pursue liberal policies and be friendly to American investments.

Romero, in his voluminous notes and correspondence (now part of the archives of Banco Nacional de México), was the first to note the similarities between Lincoln and Juárez, and Lincoln for his part found the young Mexican envoy particularly gracious. Af-ter they both went to Washington, Lincoln befriended the twenty-four-year-old diplomat and their friendship would last his lifetime. What particularly endeared the American President to Romero was that he escorted Mrs. Lincoln on her frequent shopping

---

126. Debra J. Allen. *Historical Dictionary of U.S. Diplomacy from the Revolution to Secession* (Lanham, MD: Scarecrow Press, 2012), 70.

127. Romero will be variously referred to as Chargé d'Affaires, ambassador and consul. He held all of those titles at one time or another.

128. Matías Romero, "Communication to the Minister of Foreign Relations," Chicago, January 23, 1861. Reservada, Numero 17. Archivo de Relaciones Exteriores, Mexico, D.F.

trips in the capital with good-natured grace. It was a duty which Lincoln was happy to relinquish.[129]

Romero also became friends with Ulysses S. Grant, another individual who supported his country, enjoyed Mexican cuisine, and admired President Juárez. Grant, for his part, enjoyed the company of the young ambassador who gave him a chance to practice his Spanish.

Despite these good intentions on both sides, however, the Senate did not ratify the proposed treaty. By the time it came before the Congress, the Civil War had already begun and it was considered unwise to divert funds from the Union war effort. Mexico was on her own, wounded and vulnerable, and the vultures were circling.

Enter Napoleon III, Empress Eugenia, Maximilian, and Carlota

European countries that had extended Mexico credit were unwilling to wait two years for payments to be resumed. Napoleon III suggested that France, Spain, and England—the three European countries that were major creditors—come together and negotiate an occupation of Veracruz, the main port of Mexico, until the debts were paid in full. There they could collect port fees and customs fees until the debts had been satisfied. England and Spain agreed and believed that France was acting in good faith.

The three countries signed the Treaty of London at the end of October 1861. On December 8th, the feast of the Immaculate Conception, the Spanish fleets arrived at the port city with the British and French troop ships behind. The three powers invaded Veracruz and set up their military commands.

Unfortunately, Napoleon III had much grander designs in mind. He had no intention of merely collecting the debts and then withdrawing French troops. His plan was to move troops inland and seize the silver mines in Puebla, Taxco, and eventually Zacate-

---

129. Richard Grabman, *Gods, Gachupines and Gringos, A People's History of Mexico* (Mazatlán: Editorial Mazatlán, 2008), 175-176.

cas. He also intended to occupy the major cities of Mexico City and Guadalajara, seize estate lands, bring French settlers in, and make Mexico a colonial French possession.

His wife, Eugenia, was a devout Catholic who was outraged at what the Liberal government had done under Juárez with his reform laws. Not only had the Church lands been seized and sold, but the Church was relieved of its fees for marriage and birth certificates, death registration fees, and even adoption papers. The Department of Health took over operation of the burial sites, which traditionally had been the *campos santos,* or churchyard places of interment, exclusive to the institutionalized Church. All burial permits must now be issued by the government.[130]

Empress Eugenia was appalled, and suggested to the Mexican conservative leaders who had been exiled by Juárez that a strong monarchy in Mexico might be the answer. The exiled Mexican archbishop was a willing and vocal ally who was outraged that the Church had been effectively removed from Mexico politics. He saw a monarchy as a way not only to return to Mexico with his fellow conservatives, but a restoration of his clerical privileges and the financial growth of the Church in Mexico.

It also seemed like a workable idea to Napoleon and to Pope Pius IX. Napoleon clearly understood what the republican revolution of 1789 and the subsequent Reign of Terror had done to France with its bloodshed, class war, and attacks against the Church until his ancestor finally restored the Empire. The pope also saw clear similarities in Mexico, which under the new republican government had become anti-clerical, anti-Church, and anti-elitist. They both saw a restored monarchy as the answer. Mexico had briefly been a monarchy under Emperor Iturbide before Santa Anna came to power. And this time, the monarch would be imported from one of the oldest royal families in Europe. What could go wrong?

Meanwhile in Austria, Emperor Franz Josef was looking for a way to get his brother Maximilian from underfoot. His extravagant expenditures had created a drain on the treasury, and his marriage to Charlotte, the daughter of the King of Belgium, was trouble-

---

130. *Ibid.* 178-180.

some. She was clearly dissatisfied with being merely the sister-in-law of an emperor. This was common knowledge. The solution to everyone–conservative Mexicans in exile, the Pope, the Mexican archbishop, Napoleon III, and Empress Eugenia–was obvious. Make Maximilian von Hapsburg emperor of Mexico and install him in the Castle of Chapultepec with the French Army and the returned conservatives to support him.

The French Invade!

The combined fleets bombarded Veracruz on December 16, 1861. They captured San Juan de Ulúa, the main fort in the harbor and, subsequently, the city itself. Two months later, the city of Campeche was captured by the French. When the French allies discovered that it was the intention of the French to conquer the entire country, they withdrew and, by the end of April 1862, the Spanish and English fleets and their troops had left Mexico. The French now faced Mexican resistance, which they, and most of the world, had severely underestimated.

Emboldened by the withdrawal of the English and Spanish, the Mexicans scored a signal victory when the French Army moved to the fortified city of Puebla on May 5, 1862. There General Ignacio Zaragoza and his Liberal Army (hereinafter referred to as "Republican Army" since they were defending the country against the French Empire defeated the superior French forces. After a heavy artillery barrage on the city's fortifications in which the French expended all their shells, the Mexicans counterattacked using both frontal cavalry assaults as well as irregulars fighting guerrilla-style hidden behind rocks and bushes along the road to the city. A series of torrential downpours turned the battlefield into a swamp trapping the more delicate French horses, while the Mexican ponies were unaffected.

The cavalry charges were led by a young officer by the name of Porfirio Diaz, who became a general as a result of his boldness and clarity of purpose under fire. He would be wounded twice in battles to come, would defeat the French on nine different occasions, and would emerge as the hero of the war and as a presidential candidate.

The quick retreat of the French prevented the defeat from becoming a complete disaster, but the battle was a clear victory for the Mexicans. At the end of the day, only eighty-three Mexicans had fallen. The French lost well over four hundred soldiers and their confidence was shattered. It was a signal victory. Zaragoza sent a message to Juárez, declaring, "The national arms have covered themselves in glory."[131]

Later that week, Benito Juárez declared that this unprecedented victory over the superior French force would be a national holiday—Cinco de Mayo—to be celebrated throughout the Americas as the defeat of monarchist and mercenary troops at the hands of the free people of a Republic.

There is a Mexican *dicho*, or popular saying, which might have been created after this proclamation. *Mejor no festejar antes de la victoria inal.* In other words, "Don't celebrate until the victory is final." One is reminded of President Bush on the aircraft carrier, bragging "Mission accomplished!" after the initial Iraq invasion. In both instances, the worst was yet to come.

Napoleon, aware that he had miscalculated, would send additional troops, ships and cannon to Mexico to reinforce his army, as well as tons of ammunition and supplies. A year later, the Imperial Army would lay siege to the city of Puebla. An attempt to relieve the siege by the Republican forces of General Comonfort would fail, and the French would retake the city on May 17, 1863. By June, the French would occupy Mexico City and force Juárez to abandon the capital.

A military junta then proclaimed Mexico a Catholic Empire, and the crown was presented to Maximilian the First by his conservative Mexican supporters. His wife, Charlotte of Belgium, became Empress Carlota of Mexico. The regime was not recognized by the Lincoln Administration despite diplomatic pressure from France. Lincoln considered it a puppet government and instead recognized Juárez as the legitimate leader of the Mexican people with his pres-

---

131. *Las armas nacionales se han cubierto de Gloria.*

ent capital on the Texas border in El Paso del Norte (now Ciudad Juárez in the State of Chihuahua), where it would remain until his triumphant return to Mexico City in 1867.[132]

So it was only the Juárez government that had representatives in Washington and, despite the pressures of the Civil War, it was one with which Lincoln and Grant would stay in touch. They also gave Ambassador Romero and his agents great freedom to raise money in the United States to support the Republican cause in Mexico. It was this arrangement which kept the Mexican cause well in the forefront of the United States both diplomatically and militarily even after Lincoln's death, as Grant and Sheridan, sometimes with–but more often without–the reluctant help of President Johnson, would support Juárez and his troops to bring about the final victory over the French invaders.

Seward's View and Sheridan's

Secretary of State Seward made a diplomatic protest to the French occupation early in 1862, but he was careful not to further antagonize Napoleon and risk French intervention on the part of the Confederacy. So, this hands-off policy prevailed for quite some time. However, Matías Romero worked assiduously on Mexico's behalf in Washington telling everyone who would listen that the Civil War and the French invasion were the same cause. If the French succeeded in Mexico, he maintained, it would be no problem at all for them to help the Confederacy to bring about the fall of the Union. It was only the armed resistance of Juárez's Republican troops which kept that from happening. Grant and others agreed. With Lincoln's sympathies for the Mexican cause growing, another solution presented itself. Slaves in the territories under rebellion were considered contraband when found by the federal army or

132. Juárez had no official standing. It was Romero now, whose *carte de visite* title claimed he was "Special Envoy of Mexico to the United States," who maintained the ties with the Lincoln Administration. He relied on a letter which Lincoln wrote shortly before his inauguration as his credential. See Appendix. Lincoln to Romero, January 21, 1861.

if they escaped across Union lines. They were thus given the protection of the US Army and not returned to their owners. This practice initiated by Major General Butler[133] early on in the war was formalized by the Congress with the Confiscation Act of 1861.

In July of 1862, Lincoln had written a draft of the Emancipation Proclamation which he shared with Seward. He felt that it would have two major and almost immediate results. First, it would liberate the slaves who were taken as contraband from the Southern forces or those who escaped captivity, thus removing over three million from service with the Confederacy. With no one to harvest their crops, manage their households, care for their livestock, or cook their meals, the Confederates would be in trouble. Second, it would prevent the involvement of France or England in the war as supporters of the Confederacy. Both countries had considered it, but this document would completely alter the way Europeans would perceive the war, and support of slave states would be considered both immoral and unwise since all of Europe had banned the institution of slavery. Finally, as Lincoln wrote:

> And I further decree and make known that such persons of suitable condition, will be received into the armed service of the United States to garrison forts, positions, stations and other places, and to man vessels in all sorts in said service.[134]

With this new moral imperative, the war was no longer about "preserving the Union" versus "state rights," it was clearly about ending slavery. It was also, as Lincoln would note in his brief speech at

---

133. In the early days of the war, Major General Butler of the Union Army encountered three escaped slaves who had made their way to Fort Monroe, which was under his command. They had been working on a Confederate construction project reenforcing defenses across from Hampton Roads, Virginia. When the owners, supported by Major John Cary, CSA, sought their return under the Fugitive Slave Act of 1850, General Butler refused. He asserted that the owner had no claim under that Act, since it was a federal law and was not applicable to states which had seceded from the Union. Later there would be a "Butler medal" which was awarded to black soldiers who served with distinction.

134. Abraham Lincoln, The Emancipation Proclamation, January 1, 1863. http://www. archives.gov/exhibits/featured_documents/emancipation_proclamation/transcript. html

Gettysburg, "a new birth of freedom;" one that had been promised "four score and seven years ago" and never delivered.

Lincoln also stated in the Proclamation that his decision was "founded upon military necessity,"[135] which clearly showed his intent that these former slaves would not only be free men but free men who would advance the cause of freedom by participating actively in the defeat of their former owners.

As with so many documents which are part of the American canon, the Emancipation Proclamation has not been closely analyzed when it comes to the subsidiary clauses. To most Americans it is simply seen as a document that freed the slaves, or, at least, those slaves in states that were in rebellion. Few see it as the beginning of active participation by blacks in the defense of the Republic, an act of citizenship before they were even recognized as citizens. Few see it as the beginning of their own fight for freedom, which was not handed to them by the Proclamation; it merely opened the way for them to fight for it.

Writing about Thoreau's *Walden*, Kathryn Schultz once noted: "Like many canonized works, it is more revered than read. So it exists for most people only as a dim impression retained from adolescence...or as the source of a few famous lines."[136] With the exception of the Gettysburg Address (which has been analyzed ad infinitum), this is true of most of Lincoln's speeches, which is why the full texts appear in an appendix to this book.

There are many who love to quote Lincoln's remark that, if he could save the Union by freeing no slaves he would do so. Likewise, if he could save the union by freeing all the slaves he would do so. The implication being that he was indifferent to the issue. In fact, this statement was written a month after he had already composed the Emancipation Proclamation! That document freeing the slaves was on his desk. The statement was from an open letter to Horace Greeley, editor of the influential *New York Daily Tribune*, and was intended as a reminder to Southerners that they had brought this

---

135. *Ibid.*
136. Kathryn Schultz, "American Chronicles: Henry David Thoreau's Moral Myopia," *The New Yorker*, October 19, 2015, 40.

on themselves. There was a time when Lincoln saw the president's constitutional duty to support the Compromise of 1850, which meant respecting the "property" of Southern plantation owners and the Fugitive Slave Act, and merely arguing against the extension of slavery to new territories. Now, he was reminding the rebel states of what could have been, not what he would do in the future. He was also saying what he had seen as his official duty, and not his personal wishes or his beliefs. He was sworn to "preserve, protect and defend the Constitution of the United States."

The always-cautious Seward advised Lincoln to table the Proclamation until the North had a significant victory. That would come with the Battle of Antietam when the Confederates were forced to withdraw from Maryland.[137] While most military historians saw that battle as more of an impasse, it was enough for Lincoln. On January 1, 1863, the Proclamation went into effect. The response from blacks wishing to join the US Army would be impressive. Over 175 black regiments would be formed with a force of over 178,000 men determined to fight to the death to maintain their freedom. They would be formidable. Despite critics and naysayers, they would perform with great courage under fire and several would be decorated with their country's highest award, the Congressional Medal of Honor.

Meanwhile in Mexico, the French continued to have military victories against the Republicans, as Maximilian presided over the new Imperial government. Surprisingly, he turned out to be a liberal emperor supporting education reforms, child labor laws, ingratiating himself with the indigenous people, and bringing Enlightenment ideas to Mexico. This, of course, was not what the Church or the conservatives expected or desired from the Austrian monarch. With no liberal support in the country and now losing the backing of the conservatives, the Emperor began to feel isolated. When he declared a guarantee of freedom of religion for all Mexicans, he antagonized Rome, the last of his allies. The papal nuncio withdrew his support and left the country. His generals had lost respect for him and were not following his advice. Carlota may have been

---

137. http://www.civilwar.org/education/history/emancipation-150/10facts/html

on the verge of a nervous breakdown. There were rumors that he had taken a mistress, which may have been unfounded. Financial backing from Napoleon III was drying up. The last straw was his adoption of the grandson of former Mexican Emperor Iturbide, a bizarre act[138] that alienated Victoria of England, who also withdrew her support.

138. Maximilian believed that if he had a child born in Mexico, his regime would be accepted by the people. So he "adopted" the grandson of former Mexican Emperor Iturbide. However, the child's mother and father were both very much alive. Maximilian actually bought the child from his aunt who had custody at the time. Moreover, the young boy whose mother was an American, was also a US citizen. The ensuing scandal brought public opinion down on Maximilian from all over the world. American women were outraged. British women picketed Buckingham Palace and Victoria had little choice but to withdraw her support from this erratic head of state. An interesting book on the subject is C.M. Mayo's *The Last Prince of the Mexican Empire*, Denver, CO: Unbridled Books, 2009.

Fig. 11. Matías Romero, Special Mexican Envoy to the US *Carte de visite*, 1863. Age 26. Photographer unknown. Provided by the Republic of Mexico. Public domain.

14

FOUR FOR FREEDOM: GRANT AND SHERIDAN, ROMERO AND JUÁREZ

The spring of 1865 was a turning point for both the United States and Mexico. In the US on April 9th, Robert E. Lee surrendered to General Grant at Appomattox Court House. By April 11th in Mexico, the Republican Army had successfully engaged the Imperial forces in several battles. Still, there were clouds on the horizon. On April 14th, President Lincoln was shot by John Wilkes Booth and lay in a coma for nine hours. He died from the injuries the next day. Emperor Maximilian, in an attempt to undermine the Republican forces, issued the "Black Decree" on October 3rd that threatened immediate execution for anyone involved in the war who was captured.

In neither country were the hostilities ended. Lee had merely surrendered the army of Northern Virginia. Resistance would continue in various other regions of the country up until November of 1865. Among the major battles would be a two-day bloodbath in Texas. In fact, it would not be until August 20, 1866, that President Andrew Johnson would finally declare that the war had officially ended.

The defeat of the Confederates in three of the major states of the Eastern Front in April and May of 1865 enabled General Grant to free up troops and send them to the Texas-Mexico border. There were two concerns on the part of Grant. First, a strong rebel force in Texas was still operational. Second, demobilized soldiers from other parts of the Confederacy could join up with either their fellow rebels in Texas or the Imperial forces in Mexico. Either one would be disastrous for the United States and prolong the war indefinitely. Romero had warned Lincoln that the French occupation of Mexico was inextricably bound up with the US Civil War. Now that became abundantly clear to Grant as intelligence revealed an active effort on the part of Maximilian's government to recruit former Confederate soldiers to the French imperial banner.

Accordingly, Grant sent 50,000 men to the Texas border under the command of General Philip Sheridan. About twenty thousand of these troops were from regiments of the United States Colored Troops (USCT), first recruited back in 1863. They now constituted ten percent of the American Army. In addition to service in Texas, many of them would stay on to fight in the Indian wars where they would receive the nickname "Buffalo Soldiers." Sheridan hoped that their presence on the border would put pressure on the French to withdraw, and also help the Liberal Army in Mexico by cutting off any supplies which they might receive at the border from Texas merchants and Confederate sympathizers.

With the death of President Lincoln, Johnson relied heavily on his Secretary of State, William Seward, to resolve the Franco-Mexican problem. Although Seward was sympathetic to the Mexican cause, he disapproved the use of US military resources against the French in Mexico because he did not want to alienate France as a future ally, nor did he want to continue to see American troops in the field after four years of bloody warfare. Grant disagreed with this decision as did General Sheridan and most US military advisors. Johnson, who may have had his own reservations, chose not to oppose his Secretary of State, who had just lost his best friend through assassination and his wife through a fatal carriage accident and was himself recovering from injuries.[139] In addition, he would come to see Grant as a contender for the presidency and as such someone whose policies could be questioned and even undermined

---

139. Seward received a broken arm in this accident. While lying in bed recuperating, he was
     attacked and seriously injured by John Wilkes Booth's co-conspirators.

should they in some way tend to promote Grant's heroic image among the American electorate that might consider him a better choice than Johnson for the presidency.

Grant strongly suggested that Johnson, at least, supply arms to the Republican Army in Mexico. His argument was that if Juárez's forces could have more field successes, then the French would be more inclined to withdraw. While this was being debated, Grant encouraged Sheridan to give the Republican generals logistical advice and share intelligence about the movement of Imperial forces near the border. Meanwhile, Sheridan was making full use of his black troops, many of whom were working as scouts within Mexican territory.

Moreover, Grant suggested, now that the Union Army had more rifles and munitions than it needed as the war in the East ended, perhaps Sheridan might "lose" 30,000 rifles near the border in El Paso del Norte so that the Juarist troops could retrieve them. As Sheridan would later write in his *Memoirs*:

> Thus countenanced and stimulated, and largely supplied with arms and ammunition which we left at convenient places on our side of the river to fall into their hands—the Liberals under General Escobedo—a man of force and character—were enabled in Northern Mexico to place the affairs of the Republic on a substantial basis.[140]

Over the next few months, Sheridan would leave an increasing number of supplies, weapons, and ammunition, including Sharps rifles and carbines, Colt revolvers, and even rifled cannon which would have a devastating effect on the French. The diminutive Irishman, who barely made it out of West Point, had not only been one of the prime instruments in the destruction of the South, he would also be a one-man terror against the European imperialist forces in their last deadly foray in the Americas.

Ultimately, the Mexican consul, Matías Romero, was able to obtain a clandestine meeting with President Johnson during which Johnson stipulated that the United States through private mer-

---

140. Philip H. Sheridan, *Personal Memoirs of P.H. Sheridan, General, United States Army* (New York: Charles Webster, 1888. Kindle edition. Vol II), 290

chants would supply weapons to the Republican government in exile. This so infuriated Secretary Seward, who was afraid of direct intervention, that he issued a directive prohibiting any foreign envoy from having direct access to the president.[141]

General Sheridan, who had been providing Juárez with intelligence regarding movements of French troops near the border, was ordered by the State Department to cease and desist and to preserve a strict neutrality. Despite the fact that the activities of the French were in clear violation of the Monroe Doctrine, despite the fact that the recent policy of forbearance went far beyond what Lincoln would have countenanced and clearly what Grant wanted, Seward pushed his slow diplomatic agenda. Sheridan was more than a little annoyed. As he wrote in his *Memoirs*:

> We were again debarred from active sympathy. After this it required the patience of Job to abide the slow and pokey methods of the State Department and in truth it was often very difficult to restrain officers and men from crossing the Rio Grande with hostile purposes. Seward was also seriously injured in an attack by John Wilkes Booth's co-conspirators which made Johnson even less reluctant to oppose him.[142]

Both Grant and Sheridan encouraged men who were being discharged at the end of the war to enlist in the Mexican Republican Army to help drive off the French. Many of the colored troops[143] took advantage of this, as did white soldiers who saw an opportunity to receive pay for a cause with which they also agreed. In the end, more than three thousand Americans would participate in the final battles of the Franco-Mexican War. And it all began with a congressman—later president—who cared for Mexico, a young Mexican envoy who helped a first lady, a reluctant general haunted by conscience and determined to make amends for the wrongs of the Mexican War, and a young Irish-American general who imple-

---

141. Walter Stahr, *Seward: Lincoln's Indispensable Man* (New York: Simon and Schuster, 2012), 464.

142. *Ibid.*, 411-12

143. For those who find the term offensive, it should be noted that it is the correct military term in use at the time. The group was designated U.S.C.T., the United States Colored Troops.

mented all of their wishes. As Sheridan would write toward the end
of his *Memoir* in 1865:

> Within two years Imperialism had received its death blow. I doubt very much
> whether such results could have been obtained without the presence of an
> American Army on the Rio Grande, which, be it remembered, was sent there
> because, in General Grant's words, the French invasion was so clearly related
> to the rebellion as to be essentially a part of it.[144]

One might remember that these were the same words that Romero
had used back in 1863 when he met with President Lincoln and
tried to convince him that the French taking advantage of the
Southern secession was itself a clear support of the rebellion. By
1865, with Lincoln's death, it was also clear to his best and brightest
military commanders, that after the long and bitter agonies of the
Civil War, if nothing was done, the United States would be involved
in another war with France at their border, and this time weakened
by four years of combat and with a country reluctant to engage in
another prolonged conflict. Grant and Sheridan did more to save
the Mexican Republic than anyone has heretofore credited. The
military assistance they gave to the Army of Juárez not only helped
preserve the Republic and drive off the last European power from
the Americas, it also freed the United States from prolonged military conflict and allowed the country to concentrate its resources
on rebuilding and repairing the damage done by four long years of
civil war.

Even Seward agreed at the end that it was, in fact, the threat
of US involvement that pushed the French to make their initial
troop withdrawal and withhold further support from Maximilian
in 1867. He had sent Thomas Campbell, the new US Ambassador
to the Mexican government, along with General Sherman to Paris
to negotiate. When the discussion bogged down and the French
seemed to be reluctant, he used the new international telegraph,
not a private communiqué, to his ambassador to inquire "as to
whether US forces would be useful in favoring the restoration of

---

144. Sheridan, *op. cit.* 412.

law, under a republican government in Mexico."[145] The French finally got the message.

Fig. 12. Company E, 4th US Colored Infantry. Washington, D.C. Photo by William Morris Smith. Courtesy of Library of Congress.

---

145. Stahr, *op. cit.*, 465.

15

US COLORED TROOPS AND AMERICAN
LEGION OF HONOR

In the papers of Matías Romero in 1865, we find the following notation:

> This morning I went to inform Grant…but found him with other people so I had to limit myself to generalities. He showed me great cordiality. He reiterated what he had said on other occasions that although he was tired of wars, his major desire is to fight in Mexico against the French, that the Monroe Doctrine had to be defended at any price, and that France ought to have left Mexico before the United States demanded it imperatively. He was glad to know, he also told me, that one of Lincoln's last acts had been to sign an exequatur recognizing José A. Godoy as Mexican Consul in San Francisco.[146]

With the end of the Civil War, more and more citizens were unnerved by the presence of French troops so close to the border of the United States. In addition, there had been several incidents where the French had raided small border towns to secure food and supplies. The French presence was a clear violation as well of the Monroe Doctrine that, although ignored in the main because of the Civil War, was now considered an outrage. A number of groups were formed in the United States to raise both money and

---

146. Thomas D. Schoonover, ed.. *Mexican Lobby: Matías Romero in Washington 1861-1867* (Lexington: The University of Kentucky Press), 1986, 58.

troops to assist the Mexican Republicans in their efforts to oust the French Imperialists. Some of the largest of these groups were centered in San Francisco, so the appointment of José A. Godoy by Lincoln just before his death was indeed a signal that Lincoln had intended these civic groups to flourish and to put an end to French occupation.

The Monroe League of San Francisco had a number of activities designed to raise funds, and men to fight for the Juarist cause. They held fund-raising dinners, had torchlight parades, and printed recruitment posters designed to get demobilized soldiers to join the Mexican Army. In addition to the group in San Francisco, there were also the Defenders of the Monroe Doctrine in New Orleans, Louisiana, and most notably in Brownsville, Texas, which had seen the depredations of the French troops close at hand. In Indiana, former general Lew Wallace[147] was not only the head of the Mexican Aid Society, raising large amounts of money for the effort and helping to sell Mexican bonds, but he was also preparing to raise a force of men with himself in command.

Romero continued his work as well with the cooperation of Grant and Sheridan. Noted Sheridan:

> During the winter and spring of 1866 we continued covertly supplying arms and ammunition to the Liberals—sending as many as 30,000 muskets from the Baton Rouge Arsenal alone—and by mid-summer Juárez having organized a pretty good sized army, was in possession of the whole line of the Rio Grande.[148]

At nearby Fort Bliss, Juárez received ten new cannons with rifled barrels after being cordially received by the American commander

---

147. General Lew Wallace Study and Museum, http://www.ben-hur.com/meet-lew-wallace/soldier/. In March of 1864, President Lincoln had Wallace appointed as Commander of the 8th Army Corps at Baltimore. There he was credited with preventing a Confederate attack on Washington. He spent the early months of 1865 on a secret mission in Mexico trying to stop the flow of goods across the border into the Confederacy. After Lincoln's death he was appointed by Secretary of War Stanton to serve as one of the two presiding judges at the military trials of the conspirators. This is also the famed author of the best-selling novel *Ben Hur*.

148. Sheridan, *op.cit.* II, 226.

there. Meanwhile, over 3,000 American veterans of the Civil War had mustered out and joined Juárez. The troops raised by Lew Wallace were no longer necessary.

The hard cash raised by Mexican bond issues was also impressive. Notes John Mason Hart in his excellent work, *Empire and Revolution*:

> The amount of financial power supplied by the American supporters of the Mexican Liberal cause testifies to the success of Romero in stimulating the interest of Sturm and Tifft [arms merchants] in converting that support into arms. The Mexican agents developed an impressive list of investors and suppliers, whom they often repaid with concessions. Arms merchants and financiers composed the widest network of American elites involved in Mexican affairs. Banker Eugene Kelly, of Kelly and Company, held one of the largest blocks, some $500,000 of the Mexican issue.[149]

In total, there were over 30-million dollars' worth of bonds issued with actual sales totaling about $18 million. Among the investors were J.P. Morgan, Cornelius Vanderbilt, Charles Stillman (perhaps the richest man in Texas), William Dodge of the Phelps Dodge Corporation, and John Jacob Astor of the National City Bank of New York.[150]

As a result, by mid-1866, the US volunteers and most of the Mexican cavalry, as well as a significant portion of infantry were better armed than their imperialist foes. They had Sharps and Remington carbines. According to military historian, René Chartrand:

> Of special note were the units attached to the Army of the North, armed with 16-shot American breech-loading rifles. These were Henry rifles, a thousand of which had been sold to the Republic in 1866. The lever action repeating .44 caliber rifle held 15 rimfire cartridges in its tubular magazine and a sixteenth round in the chamber. US army tests had shown that 120 rounds could be fired in 340 seconds, including reloading time—less than three seconds per shot.[151]

149. John Mason Hart, *Empire and Revolution: The Americans in Mexico Since the Civil War* (Berkeley: University of California Press, 2002,), 14-15.
150. *Ibid.*, 16.
151. René Chartrand, *The Mexican Adventure 1861-67* (Men-At-War Series) (Oxford: Osprey Publishing Co. 1994), 13.

The Mexican Army also had American Parrot rifled cannon,[152] the latest in artillery produced in the United States. At least ten of these were used to devastating effect at the siege of Querétaro, the last of the major battles with the Imperialists where the Mexicans and their American allies took back the city from the French and proceeded to a final siege of the capital.

The United States Colored Troops (USCT)

While most readers are aware there were black troopers in the Civil War, few know of their broad participation. Most assume that they were relegated to menial jobs within the service or, if used in combat, were ineffective, or easily defeated by superior Confederate troops. The movie *Glory* depicting the noble but disastrous Battle of Fort Wagner in South Carolina appears to show the latter example. There, the 54th Massachusetts, a black unit commanded by Robert Gould Shaw, assaulted a strong fortification and were repulsed with heavy casualties. So many were killed, in fact, that they were buried in a mass grave. The event is depicted as emblematic of the sacrifice of black troops in the war, and a statue on the Boston Commons memorializes this regiment's service. The bronze relief created by the famed artist August Saint-Gaudens depicts a section of the 54th Infantry Regiment marching along beside Colonel Shaw on horseback. The inscription reads:

> The White Officers taking life and honor in their hands cast in their lot with men of a despised race unproven in war and risked death as inciters of servile insurrection if taken prisoners besides encountering all the common perils of camp march and battle. The Black rank and file volunteered when disaster clouded the Union Cause. Served without pay for eighteen months till given that of white troops. Faced threatened enslavement if captured. Were brave in action. Patient under heavy and dangerous labors. And cheerful amid hardships and privations. Together they gave to the Nation and the World undying proof that Americans of African descent possess the pride, courage and devotion of the patriot soldier. One hundred and eighty thou-

---

152. *Ibid.*

sand such Americans enlisted under the Union Flag in MDCCCLXIII-MD-CCCLXV.[153]

Colonel Shaw died along with his men in this gory battle along with a general and three other colonels. Shaw's body reportedly had seven bullet wounds, which indicates a certain amount of vindictiveness on the part of the enemy. His colored sergeant, who survived, received the Congressional Medal of Honor. The battle was more a monument to poor strategy and waste of life than of military necessity but it proved to the Confederate command and to the world that black soldiers were brave, were capable of cohesiveness under fire, and were a serious element to be considered in the remainder of the war.

But there were other more successful battles in which the various black regiments were employed. In addition to foot soldiers, there were also cavalry regiments that saw battle. Many of these such as the 5th Massachusetts Volunteer Regiment and three other regiments (including Colonel Shaw's men) were composed of free blacks rather than liberated slaves. Four regiments of Louisiana Guards, the Corps d'Afrique, were also incorporated into the USCT, and one of them was a cavalry regiment as well. Out of 178,000 black soldiers who served in the Civil War, there were twenty-five who received the Congressional Medal of Honor for bravery. Eighteen were soldiers and seven were in the US Navy.

A few of the citations for the medal are worth noting here since they show not only courage under fire but effective leadership on the part of the black soldiers. For example, Sergeant Robert Pinn, a first sergeant with the USCT, "took command of his company, all the officers having been killed or wounded, and gallantly led it in battle."[154] That was at the Battle of Chapin's Farm, close to Appomattox on the 6th of April in 1865. Another was Corporal James Miles who, "having his arm mutilated, making immediate

---

153. Robert   Gould   Shaw   Memorial.   http://ctmonuments.net/2010/05/robert-gould-shaw-memorial-boston/.

154. Civil-War, African American Medal of Honor Recipients. http://www.buffalosoldier.net/CIVILWARAFRICAN-AMERICANMEDALOFHONORRECIPIENTS.htm

amputation necessary, he loaded and discharged his piece with one hand and urged his men forward, this within 30 yards of the enemy's works." Still another, Sergeant Kelly Alexander, who, "gallantly seized the colors, which had fallen near enemy lines, raised them and rallied the men at a time of confusion and in a place of the greatest danger." And, lest we neglect the black sailors' contributions to the US Navy, we have John Lawson whose citation for the Medal of Honor reads as follows:

> On board the flagship *USS Hartford* during successful attacks against Fort Morgan rebel gunboats and the ram *Tennessee* in Mobile Bay on 5 August 1864. Wounded in the leg and thrown violently against the side of the ship when an enemy shell wounded or killed most of his 10-man crew as the shell whipped on the berth deck, upon regaining his composure, remained steadfast at his post, and directed fire against the enemy.[155]

The naval action in Mobile Bay was quite significant. It resulted in the surrender of the prize rebel ram Tennessee, the sinking of Confederate gunboats, and in the destruction of the batteries at Fort Morgan.

One of the major land battles in which the black regiments' participation was significant was the Battle of Nashville. There on December 15 and 16, 1864, General John Bell Hood's Confederate Army was effectively destroyed and Hood himself resigned as commander. It is one of the most important battles of the Civil War but barely commemorated. Efforts made to make the area where it occurred a National Battlefield Park, much like Gettysburg, have failed due to lack of civil support for a battle which the South resoundingly lost.

Finally, it is worth noting how many of the Medal of Honor citations speak about how the black soldier being recognized "led the men" after the officers had been killed, and how many of the blacks who received the citation were sergeants, playing a leadership role in the regiment.

---

155. *Ibid.*

After the War, the USCT was disbanded. However, many of those demobilized black freemen, finding little work at home and much prejudice, joined the Americans fighting in Mexico as part of the American Legion of Honor recruited in late 1865 and early 1866. They saw action in the last battles of the Franco-Mexican War including the Battle of Zacatecas, the final siege at Querétaro, and triumphal march to Mexico City. In 1867, the Army established two new regiments of black cavalry (the 9th and 10th Colored Calvaries), who became a bit better known than their forebears as the Buffalo Soldiers, and four regiments of black infantry.

The American Legion of Honor

The American Legion of Honor consisted of approximately 3,000 men who served in Mexico from late 1865 through the final siege of Mexico in 1867. There is a gravesite in Mexico City where those who fell in this conflict are interred. Many, however, survived and went on to settle in Mexico and have families, others returned to the United States and served in the military there or returned to civilian life. They had, in the vernacular of the day, "seen the elephant." The officer corps of the Legion was composed of Union veterans. Most significant among them were Colonel George Green and Colonel Harvey Lake. Green had been active in recruiting in San Francisco since 1865 and had known Mexico very well. He had spent time there in the decade before the Civil War as a traveling photographer and also worked as a military advisor to the Mexican Army. One of his brothers was also active selling a $10-million bond issue to raise money for arms to send to Juárez after the French Occupation.

Colonel Harvey Lake was a former captain in the Union army and was teaching military tactics at a local armory and held the rank of colonel in the California Militia in 1866. He had been actively recruited by General Plácido Vega, and later General Gaspar Sánchez Ochoa. He was deeply committed to the Republican cause in Mexico. Lake and the men he recruited were backed by a San Francisco banker who saw that they were equipped with uniforms, horses, Henry repeating rifles, Colt revolvers, as well as medical equipment. Another weapon that many of the American cavalrymen were armed with was the Spencer carbine. This was an awesome weapon, and one which the French had no knowledge of. It made even a small American mounted force extremely effective against any other cavalry.

Introduced in limited numbers to the Union Army in 1862, it found its first major use by Colonel John Wilder's Indiana mounted forces at Hoover's Gap during the Tullahoma Campaign in the summer of 1863. The firepower and speed of this brigade overwhelmed the Confederate cavalry and allowed George H. Thomas's 14th Infantry Corps to place itself on the flank of the Confederate General Hardee. According to one military historian:

> This sudden development misled Hardee into thinking he had been out-flanked by the entire Union Army of the Cumberland, and he retreated without orders back to Tullahoma, 15 miles in his rear. Wilder then spearheaded the turning movement to the east of Tullahoma, and this, in turn, undermined Bragg's entire defensive line, and he had to pull back into Chattanooga. At the price of about 500 casualties the Union Army advanced 100 miles and made military history.[156]

As the American volunteers arrived in Mexico, their numbers were small in relation to the enemy and in relation to the Mexican Army. They usually accounted for about 500-1000 in forces of 4,000 or more. However, their cohesiveness, their battle experience, their outstanding leadership, and finally their superior firepower made them a fearsome force. Major General James H. Wilson, who was instrumental in crushing Hood at Nashville and defeated Forrest at Selma, wrote the following about the American cavalrymen armed with this weapon:

> Our best officers estimate one man armed with it [the Spencer carbine] equivalent to three with any other arm. I have never seen anything else like the confidence inspired by it in the regiments or brigades which have it. A

---

156. Signal Corps Association, Weaponry of 1860-1965. http://www.civilwarsignals.org/pages/signal/signalpages/weapons.html

common belief amongst them is if their flanks are covered they can go any-where. I have seen a large number of dismounted charges made with them against cavalry, infantry, and breast-works, and never knew one to fail.[157]

The Last Hurrah of the Confederacy

In August 1865, the officers and men of the former Missouri Cavalry division went into battle as a unit down in Mexico. Unwilling to surrender to the Union at the end of the war, Confederate General Joseph Orville "Jo" Shelby took his troops south of the border in June of that year. There he intended to help Maximilian score major victories against the Republicans, and eventually reinvade the United States from the South. It was an ambitious but foolish plan. Their first (and last) clash was with Republican forces at a small and unimportant town called Matehuala. In the words of a contemporary:

> Matehuala is north of San Luis Potosí and was a city of 20,000 at that time. It was being held precariously by 500 Frenchmen of the 82nd Regiment of the line under a Major Pierron. A weak detachment with an exposed post...[158]

This small group of Frenchmen, now reinforced by Shelby's "Iron Brigade" of 1,000 ex-Confederates, was able to attack the Republican forces from the rear and allow the Imperialists to break out. From there they headed south to Mexico City. There they met with Maximilian and offered him their services. The Emperor was greatly disturbed by their presence and regretted that they had interfered in the Matehuala siege. He was fearful, lest word of their action get back to the United States and Johnson's government might actually see grounds for direct intervention of the United States. He refused Shelby's assistance. However, to mollify the Confederate general and to keep his men under his watchful eye, Maximilian granted him a large parcel of land near Veracruz where he and his men could settle, bring their

---

157. *Ibid.*
158. Daniel O'Flaherty, *General Jo Shelby. Undefeated Rebel* (Chapel Hill: University of North Carolina Press, 1954), 282-283.

families, and live comfortably as ranchers. The grant was to be retracted by the Mexican government after the fall of Maximilian, however, and while some of Shelby's men settled in Mexico, most found their way back to their home in the reconstructed South.[159]

This last ditch effort by the Confederacy would be memorialized in song, in literature, and in a John Wayne film, *The Undefeated.* As for the irrepressible Shelby, he would become a US Marshall and would later testify on behalf of his fellow Confederate diehard, Frank James, brother of the notorious Jesse James, in a bank robbery trial. He would be instrumental in James' acquittal. Both ex-Confederates died peacefully of old age.

While there would be scattered groups of ex-Confederates who would find their way south to settle, or even join the Imperial forces, there were no cohesive units after Shelby's, and none that had any significant impact on the future of Maximilian's slowly crumbling empire.

---

159. *Ibid.* 282-283.

16
IMPERIALIST FORCES FALTER

Believing that Benito Juárez and his forces were gaining more power and more popular support for the Republican cause, Maximilian took a fatal step. He decided to use state terror to intimidate the Republican leadership, as well as to intimidate both the military forces and the civilians who might give them aid. In the fall of 1865, he ordered the execution of all Republicans then under arms should they be captured. This proclamation was famously known as *Bando Negro* or the Black Decree. In addition, he ordered severe penalties be applied to anyone giving them aid and support, which by that time was more than half of the population. The decree read as follows:

Mexico, October 2, 1865.

Maximilian, Emperor of Mexico:

The government, strong in its power, will henceforth be inflexible in meting out punishment when the laws of civilization, humanity, or morality demand it. Our Council of Ministers and our Council of State having been heard, we decree:

Article I. All individuals forming a part of armed bands or bodies existing without legal authority, whether or not proclaiming a political pretext, whatever the number of those forming such band, or its organization, character, and denomination, shall be judged militarily by the courts martial. If found guilty, even though only of the fact of belonging to an armed band, they shall be condemned to capital punishment, and the sentence shall be executed within twenty-four hours.

Article II. Those who, forming part of the bands mentioned in the above article, shall have been taken prisoners in combat shall be judged by the officer commanding the force into the power of which they have fallen. It shall become the duty of said officer within the twenty-four hours following to institute an inquest, hearing the accused in his own behalf. Upon this inquest a report shall be drawn and sentence shall be passed. The pain of death shall be pronounced against offenders even if only found guilty of belonging to an armed band. The chief shall have the sentence carried into execution within twenty-four hours,—being careful to secure to the condemned spiritual aid,—after which he will address the report to the Minister of War....

Article V. There shall be judged and sentenced under the terms of Article I of the present law:

I.   All individuals who voluntarily have procured money or any other succor to guerrilleros.
II. Those who have given them advice, news, or counsel.
III. Those who voluntarily and with knowledge of the position of said guerrilleros have sold them or procured for them arms, horses, ammunition, provisions, or any other materials of war.

Article VI. There shall be judged and sentenced in accordance with Article I:

I.   Those who have entertained with guerrilleros relations constituting the fact of connivance.
II. Those who of their own free will and knowingly have given them shelter in their houses or on their estate.
III. Those who have spread orally or in writing false or alarming news calculated to disturb order, or who have made any demonstration against the public peace.
IV. The owners or agents of rural property who have not at once given notice to the nearest authority of the passage of a band upon their estate.[160]

The following day he ordered the execution of two Republican generals, four colonels, and several field officers. In all, it is estimated that over 11,000 officers, men and supporters of Juárez were either shot out of hand when captured, or taken before military tribunals and given the death sentence. The Black Decree was a desperate act and it would have unexpected consequences for the

160. Sara York Stevenson, *Maximilian in Mexico: A Woman's Reminiscences of the French Intervention* (New York: Century, 1899). http://www.executedtoday.com/tag/carlos-fuentes/

man who issued it. Carlos Fuentes would write a hundred years later that Maximilian would be signing his own death warrant.[161] As the war progressed, it would be apparent that Juárez considered Mexican lives just as important as French lives and, as his generals were given no quarter, neither could Maximilian expect any should he be captured. Mexican laws could prove to be as inflexible as French law and just as merciless.

Several key factors were all having their effect as well: The presence of General Sheridan's troops on the border, the stern warning issued by Secretary of State Seward to the French government, the refusal of Queen Victoria of England to support Napoleon's occupation of Mexico, and the growth of pro-Mexico groups throughout the US. An earlier resolution by Congress was being republished in many quarters and printed as a handbill by the Friends of Mexico clubs, Mexican Aid societies, and Defenders of the Monroe Doctrine groups. It read:

> That the Congress of the United States are [sic] unwilling, by silence, to leave the nations of the world under the impression that they are indifferent spectators of the deplorable events now transpiring in the Republic of Mexico; and that they therefore think it fit to declare that it does not accord with the policy of the United States to acknowledge a monarchical government, erected on the ruins of any republican government in America, under the auspices of any European power.[162]

It was clear that Maximilian's Black Decree was ill-timed. Faced with all of the opposition and unwilling to risk a military engagement with the United States, especially one not supported by the other nations in Europe, Napoleon decided to stop financial support of Maximilian and begin the withdrawal of French troops from the Americas. Maximilian, meanwhile, was convinced that the Conservative troops under Olvera, Miramón, Méjia, and Márquez, accompanied by the Belgian and Austrian troops to whom he would offer

---

161. Carlos Fuentes, *The Buried Mirror: Reflections on Spain and the New World, 1862-1867* (Boston: Houghton Mifflin), 1992.

162. Francis N. Thorpe, *The Civil War: The National View* (Charleston, SC: Nabu Press), 2010), 373.

promotion and salary increases in his redesigned Imperial Army, would be more than sufficient to defeat the Republicans. He underestimated both the leadership of General Porfirio Díaz with his well-armed forces backed by the Legion of Honor and their superior weaponry, and that of General Mariano Escobedo, so admired by General Sheridan and now supported by the Colored Troops with American Sharps carbines. He would also overestimate the loyalty of his generals, two of whom would betray him.

In January 1866, the Republicans under General Escobedo, supported by the Legion of Honor and a troop of "American Negro Regulars," took the town of Bagdad, the southern port for Matamoros (the northern portion is now known as Brownsville) and the chief facility for transporting cotton from the Confederate states. Maximilian, who understood the importance of this trade, sent Austrian troops and ships to protect the port as well as ships. General Sheridan and his officers understood well the significance of this, and that is why he had troops stationed in the region along with naval vessels as the Civil war ended. It should come as no surprise that many of his biracial troops would join Juárez's forces to retake this area. It was a critical interruption in the flow of income to Maximilian, a blow the Emperor could ill afford now that Napoleon III had withdrawn financial support.

By late spring of 1866, the Republican forces had taken Matamoros, then moved on and had reinvested Chihuahua, then Guadalajara, and, by July, Acapulco, and Tampico. By the end of November, the French had abandoned Monterrey, parts of Zacatecas, Oaxaca, Sonora, and San Luis Potosí. Defeat of the Imperialist Army was still far from a sure thing, however. Resistance was considerable and the Conservatives had several victories supported by Austrian and Belgian troops. By December, over 4,000 Austrians and Belgians disbanded and headed for the coast along with the withdrawing French. None had been paid for several months, and French ships were in Veracruz to transport them back to Europe. Still, over 1,500 of them stayed with the Conservatives, attracted by offers of advancement and payment in silver promised by Maximilian.

In March, a relief column including many of these Austrians was attacked by the Liberal forces, which included many Legion of Honor soldiers. They had intended to head north to protect Maximilian and the capital. Maximilian, for his part, saw the writing on the wall but hoped by continued resistance to force the Republicans to the bargaining table or even for the US to intercede and help him set up a Liberal government of his own. Neither of these scenarios was logical. However, with Carlota no longer around to give him practical advice, the Emperor was distracted. The Republicans for their part would accept only the unconditional surrender of the Imperial/Conservative forces, and the death of Maximilian himself, along with his traitorous Mexican generals.

On January 27, one of those generals, Miguel Miramón, forced his way past the stronghold of Republican General Aranda in the key city of Zacatecas. President Juárez, unfortunately, was in residence in that city and was almost captured by the enemy. Miramón's troops, including French gendarmes and Austrian cavalry, outnumbered the Republicans four to one. They surrounded the president and his escort as he was fleeing the city and it appeared he would be captured. Just then, Colonel George Church, assigned by Grant to be military advisor to Juárez, broke through with his own fast stallion. He gave his own horse to Juárez so that he could make his escape. Church, risking his own life, took the president's slower mount and remained with the Legion of Honor to engage the superior force of the enemy and cover the escape. He would be awarded the Medal of Valor by President Juárez in Mexico City at the end of the war for his courage at this critical point.[163]

It was later discovered that Maximilian had given Miramón the order that in the event Juárez were captured, he should be "brought before a tribunal and the sentence would be directly imposed by his royal majesty."[164] Given the Black Decree, it is likely that death would be forthcoming regardless of procedure. However, it is

---

163. William Lawrence Adams, *Pennsylvania's Amazon Princess Railroad* (Bloomington: AuthorHouse, 2012), 242.

164. David R. Stephens, *Sin Perdón: Acquiescence with Murder, The Wholesale Betrayal of Maximilian*, Vol. II (Bloomington, IL: AuthorHouse), 2008, 246.

doubtful that, if he were captured, Generals Miramón or Márquez would have wasted time returning Juárez to Mexico City. Far more likely he would be executed on the spot. Church undoubtedly saved the Mexican president's life and changed the course of history.

Forgotten Hero

George Earl Church was one of the most fascinating characters in the War of the French Intervention. He was born in 1835 to a prominent New England family who could trace their American lineage to the Mayflower. He grew up in Providence, Rhode Island, and was trained as a civil engineer. He worked on several projects in the US including the construction of the Boston and Main Railroad, and the Hoosac tunnel. He was later chief engineer of the Argentine Great Northern Railroad in Buenos Aires. With the outbreak of the Civil War, he returned to the US and joined the 7th Rhode Island Infantry as a lieutenant colonel, and then with the 11th Rhode Island where he was promoted as full colonel and commanding officer until 1863. Shortly thereafter, he went to Mexico where he served as chief military advisor to Benito Juárez at the behest of General Grant. Colonel Church's stated position was "foreign correspondent for the *New York Herald*." And he did supply occasional articles and reports from Mexico as a correspondent during that time in addition to his other, more perilous duties with Juárez.

While Church's major function seems to have been advising Juárez's Minister of War, and he was never in actual command of the Legion of Honor, he nevertheless fought alongside them and, as noted earlier, was instrumental in effecting the rescue of the Mexican president. Several observers of that incident credit the Legion of Honor and Church, not only with the rescue of Juárez but with enabling the successful retreat of the outnumbered Republican Army. According to one naval officer, Lieutenant Seaton Schroeder, whose ship was then anchored off the coast, "the republican army was saved from pursuit and annihilation only by the brave stand of the Legion of Honor at the defile of Bufa near the city.[165] After the capture of Maximilian by the Republican forces, Church attempted to intercede with Juárez and obtain the Emperor's release and return to Europe. But the die had been cast.

In later years, Church helped build railroads in countries as diverse in topography as Brazil and Canada. He wrote extensively on Latin American affairs as well as the natural history of regions such as Costa Rica, Bolivia, and Argentina. He moved to London, became a Fellow of the London Geographical Society,[166] and a highly respected author and lecturer. He left all his documents, letters, and manuscripts to Brown University, where they are currently stored in the John Hay Library.[167] John Hay, the reader will recall, was President Lincoln's private secretary. Both his papers (which include many Lincoln letters and notes) and Church's are archived at Brown. Much to the loss of Harvard University, which had the first choice but declined.

165. Seaton Schroeder, *The Fall of Maximilian's Empire as Seen from a United States Gunboat* (New York: n/p, 1887), 57.

166. Obituary, Colonel George Earl Church, JSTOR, 35: 303-205. http://www.jstor.org/stable/1777010

167. Lewis Hanke, "A Note on the Life and Publications of Colonel George Earl Church" (Providence: Transportation Engineers, 1965), 1-33.

17

THE MARCH TO MEXICO CITY

A month after the near disaster at Zacatecas, the Republicans got their revenge. General Escobedo's forces intercepted Miramón's troops and defeated them near San Jacinto. Over five hundred prisoners were captured including Austrians, Belgians, and French grenadiers. The 139 captured Frenchmen, who had earlier been given the opportunity to leave the country but refused, were executed. The Austrian and Belgians joined the Republican army and headed south.

Meanwhile, in Mexico City, Maximilian and the last of the French troops decided to leave the city to reinforce the Imperial/Conservative troops in Querétaro, a fortified city of 40,000 inhabitants and about 8,000 defenders with sufficient heavy artillery to hold off four times their number. On March 5, 1867, the siege of the city began. It would be a fight to the death. The defenders were seriously outnumbered but resistance was total. With well-placed artillery, the Imperial troops were able to withstand several frontal attacks and even attempt breakouts. None of the latter was successful, though. By mid-March, most of the Legion of Honor had arrived and the Mexican Army commanded by Porfirio Díaz now numbered about 25,000. Over four thousand defenders were dead and it was about to get worse.

According to an account by Dr. Samuel Basch, an Austrian medical doctor, who was both confidant and personal physician to Maximilian and had accompanied him to the city:

> The enemy's next move was to cut off the city's supplies, both of water and provisions, hoping to subdue it by starvation. The only water now obtainable was that of the Rio Blanco, while meat soon grew so scarce that many of the cavalry horses had to be sacrificed. Juárez himself joined the republican camp for a time, but, being unable to endure the smell of powder, soon returned to Potosi. On the fourteenth of March, the Juarists made their first general attack on the town, assaults being made on three sides at once, under cover of the batteries. The main struggle, however, took place at La Cruz. After a hot fight they succeeded in capturing the Pantheon, but were afterward driven out by a body of Austrians. During the attack Maximilian remained in the great square before the convent, exposed to the hottest fire, yet quite calm and apparently unconscious of the deadly hail of bullets all about him. Once a shell burst only a few paces in front of him, but fortunately no one was injured, though an adjutant had his sword bent and his clothes burned by a flying splinter. Prince Salm, always conspicuous for bravery, made a brilliant sortie and succeeded in capturing the first guns from the enemy.[168]

General Márquez broke out of the city in the middle of the night on March 22nd with 1200 men and headed to Mexico City. He had promised Maximilian that he would go to the garrison there and return with more troops to help relieve Querétaro. The combined Republican forces had now swollen to well over 35,000. However, instead of returning to relieve the city, anxious perhaps for a more likely chance of victory and some personal glory, he proceeded with his reinforced troops to attack the lesser target of Porfirio Díaz's army at Puebla. But he was unsuccessful and his forces were defeated in a bloody battle. The emperor was devastated when he learned of this betrayal by Márquez. Noted the physician:

> But what of Márquez while all Querétaro watched so anxiously for his return? Where was he and what was he doing? He had arrived safely at the capital on the twenty-seventh of March with few losses, and, finding the city

168. George P. Upton, "Siege of Querétaro," *Maximilian in Mexico* (Chicago: A.C. McClurg & Co., 1911).

"Siege of Querétaro," http://www.heritage-history.com/

of Puebla hard pressed by the Juarist, Porfirio Díaz, determined to go to its relief. Though well aware of the urgency of the situation in Queretaro, and the need of haste in executing his mission, he seems to have troubled himself little concerning it, and to have taken no steps toward sending the promised aid. The relief of Puebla he did indeed undertake, but here as in Querétaro he made so many blunders that the attempt ended in utter failure and involved the needless sacrifice of many of Maximilian's brave Austrians.[169]

Weeks went by, and by May 15th, Maximilian attempted to escape through enemy lines. However, the plan was sabotaged by one of his own trusted officers, Colonel Miguel López, who was bribed by the Republicans to open a gate and let the enemy within. A Hussar cavalry brigade aiding in the escape was captured along with the Emperor the following day.

At the gates they found one of the enemy's guards stationed, and standing nearby were Colonel López, and Colonel José Rincon Gallardo. The latter, to whom the Emperor was well known, said to the guard: "Let them pass, they are civilians," and Maximilian and his companions walked out unmolested. From La Cruz they made their way to Miramón's headquarters on the Cerro de la Campana, several other officers joining them on the way. The lines everywhere were already in the possession of the enemy and even the small body of cavalry they found assembled at the foot of the hill soon melted away, going over to the enemy little by little as their fears overcame them. Turning to Mejía, the Emperor asked if there was no possibility of breaking through with a few faithful followers, but Mejía sadly replied in the negative, saying any such attempt would be useless. Resigning himself to his fate, therefore, Maximilian ordered the white flag hoisted and a few moments later surrendered his sword to a republican officer who galloped up. The Emperor was a prisoner.[170]

He had surrendered to General Escobedo, and he was tried the following month by a military tribunal and sentenced to death. A plan was made by his good friend Felix Salm-Salm and his wife to help his escape. However, it would be necessary for Maximilian to shave his beard and disguise himself as a peasant. Maximilian felt that this would be beneath his dignity and refused.

169. *Ibid.*
170. "Death of Maximilian." http://www.heritage-history.com/

Despite pleas for leniency by the crowned heads of Europe, as well as Victor Hugo, Giuseppe Garibaldi, and others, Juárez ordered that the death sentence be imposed. He felt that it was necessary to send a message to the world that Mexico would not tolerate any foreign power in its territory. Maximilian, as well as general Miramón and Mejía, was shot by firing squad in the Cerro de Campanas on the morning of June 19, 1867. Maximilian gave his executioners some gold coins with a request not to shoot him in the head, so that his mother could see his face.

After his execution, his body was embalmed and then was displayed for several months at the Castle of Chapultepec, the same castle that the young students of the military academy had died to protect during the late American invasion. In 1868, it was taken back to Austria where it can be viewed today in the Imperial crypt in Vienna.

The Siege of the Capital

Mexico City was well-fortified and defended by four hundred cannons, as well as French gendarmes, Austrian cavalry, and conservative infantry and artillery. The city had approximately 200,000 civilian inhabitants in addition to the troops, as well as their support personnel and camp followers. General Porfirio Díaz had effectively cut off all supplies going into the city.[171] While thousands of citizens attempted to abandon the capital, most had neither the means or the funds to do so since it would involve bribing soldiers who guarded the gates and the barricades. Hundreds died from starvation or dehydration each day. Desperate mobs raided private residences and public buildings where they believed foodstuffs were being hoarded. One such place was the National Theater (Teatro Iturbide) which was robbed and looted of stored grain. As the mob

---

171. "Mexican Affairs. Particulars of the Siege of Mexico City. Seventy-nine days of Heroic Endurance." *The New York Times.* July 12, 1867. These and other specific details which follow are taken from this lengthy contemporary account. New York Times, pdf.

moved on to the central market, the Austrian cavalry was ordered to enforce order and it moved in and dispersed the crowd. To appease the mob, a house-to-house search for food was conducted, and all stores found were distributed to the people.

Meanwhile, on the 19th of June, the foreign troops were informed of the capture of Maximilian. They had kept up the fight in the belief that the Emperor was still with his army and would be returning from Querétaro with reinforcements. This news gave them nothing left to fight for. They put down their weapons and went to the National Palace to await a cease fire and negotiations for surrender. That evening General Márquez and a few of his cohorts, along with the remains of the National Treasury, sneaked out of the city under cover of darkness and fled to Veracruz, where he secured passage on a merchant ship headed south.

Meanwhile, the American Legion of Honor was supporting General Díaz's troops and keeping them well supplied by distributing confiscated foodstuffs captured before they could come into the city. The Legion, which had already proved its worth to the Mexicans in small but significant ways, from the rescue of Juárez at Zacatecas to the furnishing of repeating rifles to the Republican forces at Querétaro, also had trained quartermasters in its ranks who transported ammunition and materiel from the north.[172]

Leadership of the Imperialist/Conservative forces now passed to General Ramon Tabera, who surrendered the city to Porfirio Díaz on June 20, 1867. Díaz immediately appointed a Chief of Police, had the opposition leaders and rebellious generals arrested, and turned three public buildings into temporary prisons. He ordered all weapons to be surrendered to the occupying troops to prevent robbery and assault. According to one member of the American Legion of Honor who accompanied General Díaz:

> When the victorious Republicans entered the city, it was found that the inhabitants had subsisted almost wholly on horse and mule meat for weeks, and, more horrible to relate, the dead bodies of men and women lying in the

---

172. Lawrence Douglas Taylor Hanson, "Voluntarios Extranjeros en los Ejércitos Liberales Mexicanos, 1854-1867," *Historia México*, XXXVII, 1987. 226-227.

streets had been gnawed by the inhabitants. Flour was $300 a sack, and bread $2.50 a loaf, while very few had the means to purchase even a single meal.[173]

Díaz ordered fresh food supplies distributed to all the civilians in an orderly way. He notified hospitals to treat the wounded prisoners, and gave permission for family and friends of the prisoners to visit. He ordered all public administrators to present themselves so that he could take steps to ensure a transition government in which the needs of the people were met. Historians differ as to whether he ordered the execution of the certain captured generals, whether they were tried by a military court, or whether Juárez had ordered it. What is certain is that on the previous day, Maximilian, along with generals Miramón and Mejía, had been executed after being tried by a military tribunal and refused leniency by Juárez, who felt that he needed, "to demonstrate to the world that Mexico's existence as an independent nation would not be left to chance or to the goodwill of foreign heads of state."[174] What is equally clear is that both Juárez and Díaz wanted to bring peace to the country as quickly as possible and reduce the animosity that had existed prior to the occupation.

On July 21st, President Juárez made a triumphal entrance into the city accompanied by bands, flags, and ceremonial troops. Joining him in the Zócalo, or central square of the capital, were Porfirio Díaz and the other major leaders of the Republican forces, as well as Colonel Green of the American Legion of Honor whose troops played a pivotal role in the final battle of the war. Although their number was insignificant in military terms, the Legion gave a significant morale boost to the Republican forces. In addition, the repeating rifles and the rifled cannon added significantly to the Mexican firepower as did the efficiency of transport, which American highly-trained volunteers brought to the field.

One such Legionnaire was Thomas Carter, a former quartermaster sergeant from Company F, Second Cavalry of the Union Army. When he mustered out at the end of the Civil War, he joined

---

173. *Daily Alta California* [San Francisco], September 15, 1867; 1:1.
174. Meyer, *op. cit.* 400.

the Mexican Army and was commissioned as a second lieutenant
in the American Legion of Honor. He was instrumental in logistics
planning and in supplying ammunition and supplies to the Republican forces at Querétaro, and participated in the final siege of Mexico City. He, along with several of his countrymen, was honored
by President Juárez for his bravery and his service to Mexico. The
president noted that:

> ...for Mexicans to fight for Mexico was natural; but for foreigners who had
> no other ties except the love of liberty and a desire to assist a brave people
> who were struggling against fearful odds, to make every sacrifice and to suf-
> fer every privation for the republic, was a spirit so noble that it could not be
> put into language.[175]

After the war, Lieutenant Carter made his home in his
adopted country. He died at the age of fifty-one from dysentery
on November 29, 1879, and was interred in the American
Cemetery in Mexico City where his grave marker can be seen
today.

After the defeat of the French, the execution of Maximilian
and his top generals, Juárez felt that he had made his point. He
had shown the world that interference in Mexican affairs by
foreign powers would not be tolerated and that those who
betrayed the cause of Mexico would forfeit their lives. Now
was the time for coming together and building bridges for the
future. He declared a general amnesty to all prisoners and
allowed the Europeans to return home unmolested. He courted
former civilian leaders of the opposition, and encouraged capable
bureaucrats to remain in government. He emptied the prisons of
all political detainees.

Only one person was not included in the amnesty, that
was General Leonardo Márquez, who had fled to Veracruz and
from there headed south on a merchant ship. Márquez had fought
against the Liberal forces, joined up with the French, enforced

---

175. John Sobieski, *The Life Story and Personal Reminiscences of Col. John Sobieski* (Lineal Descendant of King John III of Poland), Miami: Hard Press, 2014. (Reproduction
of 1907 original), 141.

Maximilian's Black Decree and killed hundreds, if not thousands, of prisoners. In the end, he betrayed the Emperor as well. He abandoned his own troops in the capital, and absconded with the remains of the Mexican treasury. His punishment must rest with the odium of history, however, since he lived a peaceful life in exile and died quietly at his villa in Havana, Cuba in 1913 at the ripe old age of ninety-three.

The war was over and now the rebuilding would begin. Mexico had suffered a great deal. Once again the treasury was empty; once again the task of rebuilding the nation was commenced. But what was different this time was that a new sense of national purpose was afoot. Ordinary Mexicans began to feel a sense of solidarity, a sense of being citizens of a republic, not merely peons or functionaries in an autocracy of ranchos and estates. National education would begin, private investment would increase, and railroads would crisscross the country bringing manufactured goods, ideas, and news of the outside world to isolated pueblos. The modern era had come to the country, and Juárez–the Lincoln of Mexico–had accomplished his mission in spite of overwhelming odds. There was still a long way to go, but the ground had been tilled and the seeds planted for a progressive nation which would assume its rightful place in the world.

18

LINCOLN'S LEGACY, MEXICO'S PRIDE

Lincoln's impact on the Mexican people and the history of Mexico is considerable. It is due in no small part to his stance during the Mexican-American War of 1846-48, his providing military experience and a sense of mission to newly-freed slaves, and his later encouragement and support of Romero, Grant, and Sheridan, that we have a neighbor to the south that is friendly despite the conquest of territory in the past and the racist ranting of some US politicians in the present. Thanks to Lincoln and men and women like him we have a Mexico that is not hostile to Americans despite the construction of border fences and walls, and the blatant racism of the Minute Men, and other self-appointed militants and anti-immigrant apologists. Mexicans understand that most Americans, who know even a bit of the history of both countries, are decent men and women–like Lincoln–who wish for a peaceful and prosperous relationship between our two countries.

This book uses an approach to historiography that neither affirms the "great man" theory, nor the "people's history" theory. It attempts to show that ordinary men and women are sometimes called to greatness. If they are blessed by fate and a few good friends, the alliances they make can help modify the errors of the past and forge a new future. Both Lincoln and Juárez managed to rescue their republics from the brink of destruction, but they could not have accomplished what they did without the goodwill and enormous sacrifices of those who walked beside them. Lincoln and Juárez have often been favorably compared. In Mexico today, Lincoln is one of three favorite US presidents. And Juárez himself is sometimes called "the Lincoln of Mexico."[176]

Despite the differences in their statures (one tall and gangly, the other short and stocky), they both supported liberal causes (although both used the term "Republican"), and they both worked for the freedom of oppressed people. Lincoln helped blacks remove the chains of slavery and gave them the opportunity to fight for their freedom; Juárez helped raise Mexican workers out of agricultural peonage and give them dignity.

Both were born of humble beginnings, struggled for their education, became lawyers, and ultimately reached the highest political office of their countries. Both brought their respective nations into a new economic realm, from a feudal era in the southern US and most of Mexico to a modern one. Both began a process of uniting their far-flung states with an extensive system of railroads and encouraged economic growth and investment. Finally, both brought about the end to colonial occupation and oppression in the Americas.

Lincoln, by staying true to his values, preserved the Union, set the slaves free, and honored his commitment to Mexico. Even after his death, his wishes were followed by able (and loyal) leaders who ensured that trained soldiers, materiel, supplies and modern armaments were made available at a time when Mexico needed them most. Also by providing an opportunity to newly freed slaves to join the army, Lincoln not only gave the blacks a chance to fight for their own freedom but also provided them with the opportunity after the war to join the Mexicans in their fight to overcome a foreign oppressor.

On March 27, 2006, the two-hundredth anniversary of the birth of Benito Juárez, a special event was held in Chicago. Carlos M. Seda, the Consul General, and Mexican Senator Emilia Patricia Gomez, presented a cast metal sculpture of Benito Juárez to the

---

176. Jim Tuck, "Mexico's Lincoln: The Ecstasy and Agony of Benito Juárez," MexConnect. http://www.mexconnect.com/articles/274-mexico-s-lincoln-the-ecstasy-and-agony-of-benito-juarez

Lincoln Presidential Library. Tom Schwartz, then interim Director of the Abraham Lincoln Presidential Library, made these observations as he accepted the bust of Benito Juárez:

> Abraham Lincoln and Benito Juárez represented the right to rise and the importance of law in democratic societies. Both men were war presidents with Lincoln preserving the Union and Juárez defeating foreign oppressors. Ultimately, both leaders laid the foundations for modern democratic societies.[177]

However, even more significant are the people who shared the ideals of both Lincoln and Juárez and who acted in good faith to put their tentative, often awkward, thoughts into action. Without Romero taking the lead and getting an appointment to see Lincoln immediately after his inauguration, without his persuasiveness, his friendliness, his willingness to help the often-difficult Mrs. Lincoln on her shopping expeditions, it is unlikely that he would have had such an influence in the Lincoln Administration. And without Romero knowing his history, and how Lincoln defended the Mexican cause back in 1847, it would be unlikely he would have had the confidence to persist. When looked at in this light, it was Mexican intelligence, Mexican diplomacy, Mexican graciousness, and Mexican persistence that turned the tide against the French.

It was Romero's friendship with Lincoln that enabled him to meet Grant and for them to become friends. And, of course, it was Grant's friendship with the diminutive Irishman Phil Sheridan that really carried the day. It was General Sheridan who left the arms at the border and defied his own Secretary of State. It was Sheridan who saw that the Colored Troops would be available. What is even more remarkable, at a time of blatant racism in the Army, was the acceptance, encouragement, and promotion of black troopers in the ranks that made this possible. Sheridan even defended his black troops against civilians in Texas when they were involved in a brawl. He encouraged the *esprit de corps* among the troops and created non-commissioned officers in the USCT, which gave them

---

177. Carl and Roberta Volkmann, Benito Juárez Bust. Springfield's Sculpture, Monuments and Plaques. http://springfieldsculptures.net/Juarez.html

a combat leadership advantage against the French in Mexico. Both Sheridan and Grant helped to ensure that the promise of freedom that Lincoln offered to the freed slaves became a reality. They both helped to ensure that the promise he gave to Romero and Juárez was realized in practical terms.

It was Grant and Sheridan who also encouraged the officers and men of other regiments and even state militias to join the Republicans at the end of the Civil War. It was Seward's missives to France, which were excerpted by newspaper editors and read by citizens in San Francisco and in other cities, that led them to join the bandwagon of the Monroe Doctrine and Friends of Mexico Society. It was those societies that helped raise money and, with the leadership of men like George Church, Harvey Lake, and George Green, enlisted volunteers to go south with the Legion of Honor, and aid the Mexican Republic in their struggle for freedom against Napoleon's Imperial Army, one of the most powerful in the world.

The late Robert Ryal Miller writing about the Americans who fought for Mexico at Zacatecas, Querétaro, and Mexico City noted:

> ...the Legionnaires joining the Juaristas at the nadir of their power and at a critical time boosted the morale as well as the fire power of the Republicans. How can one calculate the psychological and strategic value of American Civil War veterans who served in the Mexican army, who initiated battle plans, serviced artillery pieces, and fought alongside Mexican soldiers? In the engagements they participated in, the Americans made a good showing... That the American Legion of Honor has been forgotten may be due to its limited accomplishments or it may be that Mexico, with a plethora of military heroes, would naturally refrain from giving credit...[178]

Perhaps this is precisely the problem with much of recorded history as written by Mexican and American historians. They either look at the major leaders or at the people *en masse*, with only occasional domestic examples for local color. They omit what is in between, and what is always right before our eyes: the facilitators, the men and women who actually come together to

---

178. Robert Ryal Miller, "American Legion of Honor in Mexico," *Pacific Historical Review*, Vol. 30, No. 3 (Aug, 1961), 241

see that things get done properly. There is no bust for Matías Romero; his figure does not sit in a rotunda in Washington, or in a garden in Mexico City.

But at the same time, all of this—the colored troops at the border, the Legion of Honor, the ex-Union colonel who joined the Juarist cause and worked as military advisor, the repeating rifles, the deadly carbines—none of it would have been forthcoming were it not for a young Mexican man of twenty-four who learned English, went to Washington, and was gracious enough to help the first lady, and be a friend to a busy executive and to a beleaguered general. Similarly, the Legion and all its men would not have been so effective without an ex-quartermaster sergeant from Pennsylvania by the name of Thomas Carter, who after being honorably discharged from the Union forces, wore lieutenant's bars in the Mexican Army and ensured that they had the supplies they needed to carry on against the French invaders.

In 1947, one hundred years after the Occupation of Mexico City, President Harry Truman went to Mexico to lay a wreath on the graves of the Niños Heroes at the Castle of Chapultepec and apologize for the invasion of their country. He was the first American president to travel to Mexico, and the comments he made then are worth returning to today.

> International relations have traditionally been compared to a chess game in which each nation tries to outwit and checkmate the other. I cannot accept that comparison with respect to the relations between your country and mine, Mr. President. The United States and Mexico are working together for the mutual benefit of their peoples and the peace of the world. You have made me feel, what I could not have doubted in any case, that I stand here, in the midst of the great people of Mexico, as a trusted friend and a welcome guest. To you and to the people of Mexico I bring a message of friendship and trust from the people of the United States. Though the road be long and wearisome that leads to a good neighborhood as wide as the world, we shall travel it together. Our two countries will not fail each other.[179]

179. Harry Truman, "Address in Mexico," The Presidency Project. http://www.presidency. ucsb.edu/ws/?pid=12841

This re-visioning of Lincoln as an international figure has been a gift to my Mexican students who have admired him and said so in my classes over the past twenty-five years of teaching in this country. I hope by looking at Lincoln from this broader point of view their admiration will be undiminished, and that they will see that their own great gifts for friendship, for openness, for service, and for persistence in spite of lesser spirits, as exemplified by Matías Romero, are what make the world work. I hope that Mexican historians will also see that the great victories of Mexico over the Imperialist Armies of France and Austria are in no way diminished by acknowledging the aid of the volunteers, black, white, and Native American, who crossed the border and fought by the side of their Mexican brothers-in-arms in the final battles.

Finally, it is my belief that the clarity of re-visioning history can connect both countries and make of our mutual lands the "good neighborhood" that Truman envisioned, one in which their children and my grandchildren will grow and prosper. In these times of xenophobia and polemics, this belief is not a vain one but a reality that is already beginning in classrooms on both sides of the border as students search out the truth of the past.

APPENDIX: A SELECTION OF ORIGINAL DOCUMENTS IN THEIR COMPLETE, UNEDITED FORMAT

Note: *Some original quoted material and archival documents contain spellings, sentence construction, capitalization, and punctuation that might appear to be typos. The author has chosen to retain the original material without modification.*

DOCUMENT 1
TO WILLIAMSON DURLEY

Friend Durley: Springfield, Octr. 3. 1845

When I saw you at home, it was agreed that I should write to you and your brother Madison. Until I then saw you, I was not aware of your being what is generally called an abolitionist, or, as you call yourself, a Liberty-man; though I well knew there were many such in your county. I was glad to hear you say that you intend to attempt to bring about, at the next election in Putnam, a union of the whigs proper, and such of the liberty men, as are whigs in principle on all questions save only that of slavery. So far as I can perceive, by such union, neither party need yield any thing, on *the* point in difference between them. If the whig abolitionists of New York had voted with us last fall, Mr. Clay would now be president, whig principles in the ascendent, and Texas not annexed; whereas by the division, all that either had at stake in the contest, was lost. And, indeed, it was extremely probable, beforehand, that such would be the result. As I always understood, the Liberty-men deprecated the annexation of Texas extremely; and, this being so, why they should refuse to so cast their votes as to prevent it, even to me, seemed wonderful. What was their process of reasoning, I can only judge from what a single one of them told me. It was this: "We are not to do *evil* that *good* may come." This general proposition is doubtless correct; but did it apply? If by your votes you could have prevented the *extention*, &c. of slavery, would it not have been *good* and not *evil* so to have used your votes, even though it involved the casting of them for a slaveholder? By the *fruit* the tree is to be known. An *evil* tree can not bring forth *good* fruit. If the fruit of electing Mr. Clay would have been to prevent the extension of slavery, could the act of electing have been *evil*?

But I will not argue farther. I perhaps ought to say that individually I never was much interested in the Texas question. I never could see much good to come of annexation; inasmuch, as they were already a free republican people on our own model; on the other hand, I never could very clearly see how the annexation would augment the evil of slavery. It always seemed to me that slaves would be taken there in about equal numbers, with or without annexation. And if more *were* taken because of annexation, still there would be just so many the fewer left, where they were taken from. It is possibly true, to some extent, that with annexation, some slaves may be sent to Texas and continued in slavery, that otherwise might have been liberated. To whatever extent this may be true, I think annexation an evil. I hold it to be a paramount duty of us in the free states, due to the Union of the states, and perhaps to liberty itself (paradox though it may seem) to let the slavery of the other states alone; while, on the other hand, I hold it to be equally clear, that we should never knowingly lend ourselves directly or indirectly, to prevent that slavery from dying a natural death—to find new places for it to live in, when it can no longer exist in the old. Of course I am not now considering what would be our duty, in cases of insurrection among the slaves.

To recur to the Texas question, I understand the Liberty men to have viewed annexation as a much greater evil than I ever did; and I, would like to convince you if I could, that they could have prevented it, without violation of principle, if they had chosen.

I intend this letter for you and Madison together; and if you and he or either shall think fit to drop me a line, I shall be pleased.

Yours with respect A. LINCOLN

Abraham Lincoln. Letter to Williamson Durley. October 3, 1845. From *Collected Works of Abraham Lincoln*, Vol. 1. http://quod. lib.umich.edu/l/lincoln/lincoln1/1:373?rgn=div1;view=fulltext

DOCUMENT 2
AGREEMENT OF VELASCO

May 14, 1846. Puerto de Velasco

NOTE: *This document, sometimes referred to by US historians as the "Treaty of Velasco," was never referred to as such until ten years later when President Polk was using it as a justification of his invasion of Mexico. As Abraham Lincoln made clear in his speech to the US Congress on January 12, 1848, having never been formally ratified, the document has no legal standing as a treaty. It was simply an agreement for the withdrawal of troops following the capture of Gen. Santa Anna. It was never approved by the Mexican Congress, and the provisions were violated by both sides.*

Articles of an agreement entered into, between His Excellency David G. Burnet, President of the Republic of Texas, of the one part, and His Excellency General Antonio Lopez de Santa Anna, President General in Chief of the Mexican Army, of the other part.	*Articulos de un convenio celebrado entre S. E. el Gral. en Gefe del Ejercito de operaciones Presidente de la Republica Mejicana D. Ant. Lopez de Santa Anna por una parte, y S. E. el Presidente de la Republica de Tejas D. David G. Burnet por la otra parte.*
Article 1st	Articulo 1o
General Antonio Lopez de Santa Anna agrees that he will not take up arms, nor will he exercise his influence to cause them to be taken up against the people of Texas, during the present war of Independence.	El Gral. Ant. Lopez de Santa Anna se conviene en no tomar las armas ni influir en que se tomen contra el Pueblo de Tejas durante la actual contienda de Independencia.
Article 2nd	Articulo 2o
All hostilities between the mexican and texian troops will cease immediately both on land and water.	Cesaran inmediatamente las hostilidades por mar y tierra entre las tropas Mejicanas y Tejanas.
Article 3rd	Articulo 3o
The mexican troops will evacuate the Territory of Texas, passing to the other side of the Rio Grande del Norte.	Las tropas Mejicanas evacuaran el territorio de Tejas, pasando al otro lado del Rio Grande del Norte.
4th	Articulo 4o
The mexican Army in its retreat shall not take the property of any person without his consent and just indemnification, using only such articles as may be necessary for its subsistence, in cases when the owner may not be present, and remitting to the commander of the army of Texas or to the commissioner to be appointed for the adjustment of such matters, an account of the value of the property consumed—the place where taken, and the name of the owner, if it can be ascertained.	El Ejercito Mejicano en su retirada, no usara de las propiedades de ninguna persona sin su consentimiento y justa indemnizacion, tomando solamente los articulos precisos para su subsistencia no hayandose presente los duenos y remitiendo al Gral. del Ejercito tejano o a los comisionados para el arreglo de tales negocios, la nota del valor de la propiedad consumida, el lugar donde se tomo, y el nombre del dueno si se supiere.

Articles of an agreement entered into, between His Excellency David G. Burnet, President of the Republic of Texas, of the one part, and His Excellency General Antonio Lopez de Santa Anna, President General in Chief of the Mexican Army, of the other part.	*Articulos de un convenio celebrado entre S. E. el Gral. en Gefe del Ejercito de operaciones Presidente de la Republica Mejicana D. Ant. Lopez de Santa Anna por una parte, y S. E. el Presidente de la Republica de Tejas D. David G. Burnet por la otra parte.*

5th	Articulo 5o
That all private property including cattle, horses, negro slaves or indentured persons of whatever denomination, that may have been captured by any portion of the mexican army or may have taken refuge in the said army since the commencement of the late invasion, shall be restored to the Commander of the Texian army, or to such other persons as may be appointed by the Government of Texas to receive them.	Que toda propiedad particular incluyendo ganados, caballos, negros esclavos, o gente contratada de cualquier denominacion q. haya sido aprehendida por una parte del Ejercito Mejicano, o que se hubiere refugiado en dicho Ejercito desde el principio de la ultima invacion, sera devuelta al Comandante de las fuerzas Tejanas, o a las personas que fueren nombradas por el Gobierno de Tejas para recibirlas.

6th	Articulo 6o
The troops of both armies will refrain from coming into contact with each other, and to this end the Commander of the army of Texas will be careful not to approach within a shorter distance of the mexican army than five leagues.	Las tropas de ambos Ejercitos beligerantes no se pondran en contacto, y a este fin el Gral. Tejano cuidara q. entre los dos campos medie una distancia de cinco leguas por lo menos.

7th	Articulo 7o
The mexican army shall not make any other delay on its march, than that which is necessary to take up their hospitals, baggage [---] and to cross the rivers–any delay not necessary to these purposes to be considered an infraction of this agreement.	El Ejercito Mejicano no tendra mas demora en su marcha, q. la precisa para lebantar sus hospitales, trenes, etc. y pasar los rios, considerandose como una infraccion de este convenio la demora q. sin justo motivo se notare.

Articles of an agreement entered into, between His Excellency David G. Burnet, President of the Republic of Texas, of the one part, and His Excellency General Antonio Lopez de Santa Anna, President General in Chief of the Mexican Army, of the other part.	*Articulos de un convenio celebrado entre S. E. el Gral. en Gefe del Ejercito de operaciones Presidente de la Republica Mejicana D. Ant. Lopez de Santa Anna por una parte, y S. E. el Presidente de la Republica de Tejas D. David G. Burnet por la otra parte.*
8th	Articulo 8o
By express to be immediately dispatched, this agreement shall be sent to General Filisola and to General T. J. Rusk, commander of the texian Army, in order that they may be apprised of its stipulations, and to this and they will exchange engagements to comply with the same.	Se remitira por expreso violento este convenio al Gral. de Division Vicente Filisola y al Gral. T. J. Rusk, Comte del Ejercito de Tejas, para q. queden obligados a cuanto les pertenece y q. poniendose de acuerdo convengan en la pronta y debida ejecucion de lo estipulado.
9th	Articulo 9o
That all texian prisoners now in possession of the mexican Army or its authorities be forthwith released and furnished with free passports to return to their homes, in consideration of which a corresponding number of Mexican prisoners, rank and file, now in possession of the Government of Texas shall be immediately released. The remainder of the mexican prisoners that continue in possession of the Government of Texas to be treated with due humanity – any extraordinary comforts that may be furnished them to be at the charge of the Government of Mexico.	Que todos los prisioneros tejanos q. hoy se hayan en poder del Ejercito mejicano, o en el de alguna de las autoridades del Gobno. de Mejico, sean inmediatamente puestos en livertad y se les den pasaportes para regresar a sus casas, debiendose tambien poner en libertad por parte del Gobno. de Tejas, un numero correspondiente de prisioneros Mejicanos del mismo rango y graduacion y tratando al resto de dichos prisioneros Mejicanos q. queden en poder del Gobno. de Tejas con toda la debida humanidad, haciendose cargo al Gobno. de Mejico por los gastos q. se hicieren en obsequio de aquellos, cuando se les proporcione alguna comodidad extraordinaria.

Articles of an agreement entered into, between His Excellency David G. Burnet, President of the Republic of Texas, of the one part, and His Excellency General Antonio Lopez de Santa Anna, President General in Chief of the Mexican Army, of the other part.	*Articulos de un convenio celebrado entre S. E. el Gral. en Gefe del Ejercito de operaciones Presidente de la Republica Mejicana D. Ant. Lopez de Santa Anna por una parte, y S. E. el Presidente de la Republica de Tejas D. David G. Burnet por la otra parte.*
10th	Articulo 10
General Antonio Lopez de Santa Anna will be sent to Veracruz as soon as it shall be deemed proper.	El Gral. Ant. Lopez de Santa Anna sera enviado a Veracruz tan luego como se crea conveniente.
The contracting parties sign this Instrument for the above mentioned purposes, by duplicate, at the Port of Velasco this fourteenth day of May 1836.	Y para la constancia y efectos consiguientes, lo firman por duplicado las partes contratantes en el Puerto de Velasco a 14 de Mayo de 1836.

DOCUMENT 3
JAMES K. POLK, PRESIDENT OF THE UNITED STATES AT WASHINGTON, D.C., TO THE CONGRESS OF THE UNITED STATES. A SPECIAL MESSAGE CALLING FOR A DECLARATION OF WAR AGAINST MEXICO

Washington, May 11, 1846.

To the Senate and the House of Representatives:

The existing state of the relations between the United States and Mexico renders it proper that I should bring the subject to the consideration of Congress. In my message at the commencement of your present session, the state of these relations, the causes which led to the suspension of diplomatic intercourse between the two countries in March, 1845, and the long-continued and unredressed wrongs and injuries committed by the Mexican Government on citizens of the United States in their persons and property were briefly set forth.

As the facts and opinions which were then laid before you were carefully considered, I cannot better express my present convictions of the condition of affairs up to that time than by referring you to that communication.

The strong desire to establish peace with Mexico on liberal and honorable terms, and the readiness of this Government to regulate and adjust our boundary and other causes of difference with that power on such fair and equitable principles as would lead to permanent relations of the most friendly nature, induced me in September last to seek the reopening of diplomatic relations between the two countries. Every measure adopted on our part had for its object the furtherance of these desired results. In communicating to Congress a succinct statement of the injuries which we had suffered from Mexico, and which have been accumulating during a period of more than twenty years, every expression that could tend to inflame the people of Mexico or defeat or delay a pacific result was carefully avoided. An envoy of the United States repaired to Mexico with full powers to adjust every existing difference. But though present on Mexican soil by agreement between the two Governments, invested with full powers, and bearing evidence of the most friendly dispositions, his mission has been unavailing. The Mexican Government not only refused to receive him or listen to his propositions, but after a long-continued series of menaces have at last invaded our territory and shed the blood of our fellow-citizens on our own soil.

It now becomes my duty to state more in detail the origin, progress, and failure of that mission. In pursuance of the instructions given in September last, an inquiry was made on the 13th of October, 1845, in the most friendly terms, through our consul in Mexico, of the minister for foreign affairs, whether the Mexican Government "would receive an envoy from the United States intrusted with full powers to adjust all the questions in dispute between the two Government, " with the assurance that "should the answer be in the affirmative such an envoy would be immediately dispatched to Mexico. The Mexican minister on the 15th of October gave an affirmative answer to this inquiry, requesting at the same time that our naval force at Vera Cruz might be withdrawn, lest its continued presence might assume the appearance of menace and coercion pending the negotiations. This force was immediately withdrawn. On the 10th of November, 1845, Mr. John Slidell, of Louisiana, was commissioned by me as envoy extraordinary and minister plenipotentiary of the United States to Mexico, and was entrusted with full powers to adjust both the questions of the Texas boundary and of indemnification to our citizens. The redress of wrongs of our citizens naturally and inseparably blended itself with the question of boundary. The settlement of the one question in any correct view of the subject involves that of the other.

I could not for a moment entertain the idea that the claims of our much-injured and long-suffering citizens, many of which had existed for more than twenty years, should be postponed or separated from the settlement of the boundary question.

Mr. Slidell arrived at Vera Cruz on the 30th of November and was courteously received by the authorities of that city. But the Government of General Herrera was then tottering to its fall. The revolutionary party had seized upon the Texas question to effect or hasten its overthrow. Its determination to restore friendly relations with the United States, and to receive our minister to negotiate for the settlement of this question, was violently assailed, and was made the great theme of denunciation against it. The Government of General Herrera, there is good reason to believe, was sincerely desirous to receive our minister; but it yielded to the storm raised by its enemies, and on the 21st of December refused to accredit Mr. Slidell upon the most frivolous pretexts. These are so fully and ably exposed in the note of Mr. Slidell of the 24th of December last to the Mexican minister of foreign relations, herewith transmitted, that I deem it unnecessary to enter into further detail on this portion of the subject.

Five days after the date of Mr. Slidell's note General Herrera yielded the Government to General Paredes without a struggle, and on the 30th of December resigned the Presidency. This revolution was accomplished solely by the army, the people having taken little part in the contest; and thus the supreme power in Mexico passed into the hands of a military leader.

Determined to leave no effort untried to effect an amicable adjustment with Mexico, I directed Mr. Slidell to present his credentials to the Government of General Paredes and ask to be officially received by him. There would have been less ground for taking this step had General Paredes come into power by a regular constitutional succession. In that event his administration would have been considered but a mere constitutional continuance of the Government of General Herrera, and the refusal of the latter to receive our minister would have been deemed conclusive unless an intimation had been given by General Paredes of his desire to reverse the decision of his predecessor. But the Government of General Paredes owes its existence to a military revolution, by which the subsisting constitutional authorities had been subverted. The form of government was entirely changed, as well as all the high functionaries by whom it was administered.

Under these circumstances, Mr. Slidell, in obedience to my direction, addressed a note to the Mexican minister of foreign relations, under date of the 1st of March last, asking to be received by that Government in the diplomatic character to which he had been appointed. This minister in his reply, under date of the 12th of March, reiterated the arguments of his predecessor, and in terms that may be considered as giving just grounds of offense to the Government and people of the United States denied the application of Mr. Slidell. Nothing therefore remained for our envoy but to demand his passports and return to his own country.

Thus the Government of Mexico, though solemnly pledged by official acts in October last to receive and accredit an American envoy, violated their plighted faith and refused the offer of a peaceful adjustment of our difficulties. Not only was the offer rejected, but the indignity of its rejection was enhanced by the manifest breach of faith in refusing to admit the envoy who came because they had bound themselves to receive him. Nor can it be said that the offer was fruitless from want of opportunity of discussing it; our envoy was present on their own soil. Nor can it be ascribed to a want of sufficient powers; our envoy had full powers to adjust every question of difference. Nor was there room for complaint that our propositions for settlement were unreasonable; permission was not even given our envoy to make any proposition whatever. Nor can it be objected that we, on our part, would not listen to any reasonable terms of their suggestion; the Mexican Government refused all negotiation, and have made no proposition of any kind.

In my message at the commencement of the present session I informed you that upon the earnest appeal both of the Congress and convention of Texas I had ordered an efficient military force to take a position "between the Nueces and Del Norte." This had become necessary to meet a threatened invasion of Texas by the Mexican forces, for which extensive military preparations had been made. The invasion was threatened solely because Texas had deter-

mined, in accordance with a solemn resolution of the Congress of
the United States, to annex herself to our Union, and under these
circumstances it was plainly our duty to extend our protection over
her citizens and soil.

This force was concentrated at Corpus Christi, and remained
there until after I had received such information from Mexico as
rendered it probable, if not certain, that the Mexican Government
would refuse to receive our envoy.

Meantime Texas, by the final act of our Congress, had become
an integral part of our Union. The Congress of Texas, by its act
of December 19, 1836, had declared the Rio del Norte to be the
boundary of that Republic. Its jurisdiction had been extended and
exercised beyond the Nueces. The country between that river and
the Del Norte had been represented in the Congress and in the
convention of Texas, had thus taken part in the act of annexation
itself, and is now included within one of our Congressional districts. Our own Congress had, moreover, with great unanimity, by
the act approved December 31, 1845, recognized the country beyond the Nueces as a part of our territory by including it within our
own revenue system, and a revenue officer to reside within that district had been appointed by and with the advice and consent of the
Senate. It became, therefore, of urgent necessity to provide for the
defense of that portion of our country. Accordingly, on the 13th
of January last instructions were issued to the general in command
of these troops to occupy the north bank of the Del Norte. This
river, which is the southwestern boundary of the State of Texas,
is an expose frontier. From this quarter invasion was threatened;
upon it and in its immediate vicinity, in the judgement of high military experience, are the proper stations for the protecting forces
of the Government. In addition to this important consideration,
several others occurred to induce this movement. Among these
are the facilities afforded by the ports at Brazos Santiago and the
mouth of the Del Norte for the reception of supplies by sea, the
stronger and more healthy military positions, the convenience for
obtaining a ready and a more abundant supply of provisions, water,
fuel, and forage, and the advantages which are afforded by the Del

Norte in forwarding supplies to such posts as may be established in the interior and upon the Indian frontier.

The movement of the troops to the Del Norte was made by the commanding general under positive instructions to abstain from all aggressive acts toward Mexico or Mexican citizens and to regard the relations between that Republic and the United States as peaceful unless she should declare war or commit acts of hostility indicative of a state of war. He was specially directed to protect private property and respect personal rights.

The Army moved from Corpus Christi on the 11th of March, and on the 28th of that month arrived on the north bank of the Del Norte opposite to Matamoras, where it encamped on a commanding position, which since been strengthened by the erection of fieldworks. A depot has also been established at Point Isabel, near the Brazos Santiago, 30 miles in rear of the encampment. The selection of his position was necessarily confided to the judgment of the general in command.

The Mexican forces at Matamoras assumed a belligerent attitude, and on the 12th of April General Ampudia, then in command, notified General Taylor to break up his camp within twenty-four hours and to retire beyond the Nueces River, and in the event of this failure to comply with these demands announced that arms, and arms alone, must decide the question. But no open act of hostility was committed until the 24th of April. On that day General Arista, who had succeeded to the command of the Mexican forces, communicated to General Taylor that "he considered hostilities commenced and should prosecute them." A party of dragoons of 63 men and officers were on the same day dispatched from the American camp up the Rio del Norte, on its north bank, to ascertain whether the Mexican troops had crossed or were preparing to cross the river, "became engaged with a large body of these troops, and after a short affair, in which some 16 were killed and wounded, appear to have been surrounded and compelled to surrender.

The grievous wrongs perpetrated by Mexico upon our citizens throughout a long period of years remain unredressed, and solemn treaties pledging her public faith for this redress have been disregarded. A government either unable or unwilling to enforce the execution of such treaties fails to perform one of its plainest duties.

Our commerce with Mexico has been almost annihilated. It was formerly highly beneficial to both nations, but our merchants have been deterred from prosecuting it by the system of outrage and extortion which the Mexican authorities have pursued against them, whilst their appeals through their own Government for indemnity have been made in vain. Our forbearance has gone to such an extreme as to be mistaken in its character. Had we acted with vigor in repelling the insults and redressing the injuries inflicted by Mexico at the commencement, we should doubtless have escaped all the difficulties in which we are now involved.

Instead of this, however, we have been exerting our best efforts to propitiate her good will. Upon the pretext that Texas, a nation as independent as herself, thought proper to unite its destinies with our own, she has affected to believe that we have severed her rightful territory, and in official proclamations and manifestoes has repeatedly threatened to make war upon us for the purpose of reconquering Texas. In the meantime we have tried every effort at reconciliation. The cup of forbearance had been exhausted even before the recent information from the frontier of the Del Norte. But now, after reiterated menaces, Mexico has passed the boundary of the United States, has invaded our territory and shed American blood upon the American soil. She has proclaimed that hostilities have commenced, and that the two nations are now at war.

As war exists, and, notwithstanding all our efforts to avoid it, exists by the act of Mexico herself, we are called upon by every consideration of duty and patriotism to vindicate with decision the honor, the rights, and the interests of our country.

Anticipating the possibility of a crisis like that which has arrived, instructions were given in August last, "as a precautionary measure" against invasion or threatened invasion, authorizing General Taylor, if the emergency required it, to accept volunteers, not from Texas only, but from the States of Louisiana, Alabama, Mississippi, Tennessee, and Kentucky, and corresponding letters were addressed to the respective governors of those States. These instructions were repeated, and in January last, soon after the incorporation of "Texas into our Union of States," General Taylor was further "authorized by the President to make a requisition upon the executive of that State for such of its militia force as may be needed to repel invasion or to secure the country against apprehended invasion." On the 2d day of March he was again reminded, "in the event of the approach of any considerable Mexican force, promptly and efficiently to use the authority with which he was clothed to call to him such auxiliary force as he might need." War actually existing and our territory having been invaded, General Taylor, pursuant to authority vested in him by my direction, has called on the governor of Texas for four regiments of State troops, two to be mounted and two to serve on foot, and on the governor of Louisiana for four regiments of infantry to be sent to him as soon as practicable.

In further vindication of our rights and defense of our territory, I invoke the prompt action of Congress to recognize the existence of the war, and to place at the disposition of the Executive the means of prosecuting the war with vigor, and thus hastening the restoration of peace. To this end I recommend that authority should be given to call into the public service a large body of volunteers to serve for not less than six or twelve months unless sooner discharged. A volunteer force is beyond question more efficient than any other description of citizen soldiers, and it is not to be doubted that a number far beyond that required would readily rush to the field upon the call of their country. I further recommend that a liberal provision be made for sustaining our entire military force and furnishing it with supplies and munitions of war.

The most energetic and prompt measures and the immediate appearance in arms or a large and overpowering force are recommended to Congress as the most certain and efficient means of bringing the existing collision with Mexico to a speedy and successful termination.

In making these recommendations I deem it proper to declare that it is my anxious desire not only to terminate hostilities speedily, but to bring all matters in dispute between this Government and Mexico to an early and amicable adjustment; and in this view I shall be prepared to renew negotiations whenever Mexico shall be ready to receive propositions or to propositions of her own.

I transmit herewith a copy of the correspondence between our envoy to Mexico and the Mexican minister for foreign affairs, and so much of the correspondence between that envoy and the Secretary of State and between the Secretary of War and the general in command on the Del Norte as is necessary to a full understanding of the subject.

Citation: James K. Polk: "Special Message to Congress on Mexican Relations," May 11, 1846. Online by Gerhard Peters and John T. Woolley, *The American Presidency Project.* http://www.presidency. ucsb.edu/ws/?pid=67907.

DOCUMENT 4
JAMES K. POLK, SECOND ANNUAL MESSAGE
TO CONGRESS. DECEMBER 8, 1846

Fellow-Citizens of the Senate and of the House of Representatives:

In resuming your labors in the service of the people it is a subject of congratulation that there has been no period in our past history when all the elements of national prosperity have been so fully developed. Since your last session no afflicting dispensation has visited our country. General good health has prevailed, abundance has crowned the toil of the husbandman, and labor in all its branches is receiving an ample reward, while education, science, and the arts are rapidly enlarging the means of social happiness. The progress of our country in her career of greatness, not only in the vast extension of our territorial limits and the rapid increase of our population, but in resources and wealth and in the happy condition of our people, is without an example in the history of nations.

As the wisdom, strength, and beneficence of our free institutions are unfolded, every day adds fresh motives to contentment and fresh incentives to patriotism.

Our devout and sincere acknowledgments are due to the gracious Giver of All Good for the numberless blessings which our beloved country enjoys.

It is a source of high satisfaction to know that the relations of the United States with all other nations, with a single exception, are of the most amicable character. Sincerely attached to the policy of peace early adopted and steadily pursued by this Government, I have anxiously desired to cultivate and cherish friendship and commerce with every foreign power. The spirit and habits of the American people are favorable to the maintenance of such international harmony. In adhering to this wise policy, a preliminary and paramount duty obviously consists in the protection of our national interests from encroachment or sacrifice and our national honor from reproach. These must be maintained at any hazard. They admit of no compromise or neglect, and must be scrupulously and constantly guarded. In their vigilant vindication collision and conflict with foreign powers may sometimes become unavoidable. Such has been our scrupulous adherence to the dictates of justice in all our foreign intercourse that, though steadily and rapidly advancing in prosperity and power, we have given no just cause of complaint to any nation and have enjoyed the blessings of peace for more than thirty years. From a policy so sacred to humanity and so salutary in its effects upon our political system we should never be induced voluntarily to depart.

The existing war with Mexico was neither desired nor provoked by the United States. On the contrary, all honorable means were resorted to to avert it. After years of endurance of aggravated and unredressed wrongs on our part, Mexico, in violation of solemn treaty stipulations and of every principle of justice recognized by civilized nations, commenced hostilities, and thus by her own act forced the war upon us. Long before the advance of our Army to the north bank of the Rio Grande we had ample cause of war against Mexico, and had the United States resorted to this extremity we might have appealed to the whole civilized world for the justice of our cause. I deem it to be my duty to present to you on the present occasion a condensed review of the injuries we had sustained, of the causes which led to the war, and of its progress since its commencement. This is rendered the more necessary because of the misapprehensions which have to some extent prevailed as to its origin and true character. The war has been represented as unjust and unnecessary and as one of aggression on our part upon a weak and injured enemy. Such erroneous views, though entertained by but few, have been widely and extensively circulated, not only at home, but have been spread throughout Mexico and the whole world. A more effectual means could not have been devised to encourage the enemy and protract the war than to advocate and adhere to their cause, and thus give them "aid and comfort." It is a source of national pride and exultation that the great body of our people have thrown no such obstacles in the way of the Government in prosecuting the war successfully, but have shown themselves to be eminently patriotic and ready to vindicate their country's honor and interests at any sacrifice. The alacrity and promptness with which our volunteer forces rushed to the field on their country's call prove not only their patriotism, but their deep conviction that our cause is just.

The wrongs which we have suffered from Mexico almost ever since she became an independent power and the patient endurance with which we have borne them are without a parallel in the history of modern civilized nations. There is reason to believe that if these wrongs had been resented and resisted in the first instance the present war might have been avoided. One outrage, however, permitted to pass with impunity almost necessarily encouraged the perpetration of another, until at last Mexico seemed to attribute to weakness and indecision on our part a forbearance which was the offspring of magnanimity and of a sincere desire to preserve friendly relations with a sister republic.

Scarcely had Mexico achieved her independence, which the United States were the first among the nations to acknowledge, when she commenced the system of insult and spoliation which she has ever since pursued. Our citizens engaged in lawful commerce were imprisoned, their vessels seized, and our flag insulted in her ports. If money was wanted, the lawless seizure and confiscation of our merchant vessels and their cargoes was a ready resource, and if to accomplish their purposes it became necessary to imprison the owners, captains, and crews, it was done. Rulers superseded rulers in Mexico in rapid succession, but still there was no change in this system of depredation. The Government of the United States made repeated reclamations on behalf of its citizens, but these were answered by the perpetration of new outrages.

Promises of redress made by Mexico in the most solemn forms were postponed or evaded. The files and records of the Department of State contain conclusive proofs of numerous lawless acts perpetrated upon the property and persons of our citizens by Mexico, and of wanton insults to our national flag. The interposition of our Government to obtain redress was again and again invoked under circumstances which no nation ought to disregard. It was hoped that these outrages would cease and that Mexico would be restrained by the laws which regulate the conduct of civilized nations in their intercourse with each other after the treaty of amity, commerce, and navigation of the 5th of April, 1831, was concluded between the two Republics; but this hope soon proved to be vain. The course of seizure and confiscation of the property of our citizens, the violation of their persons, and the insults to our flag pursued by Mexico previous to that time were scarcely suspended for even a brief period, although the treaty so clearly defines the rights and duties of the respective parties that it is impossible to misunderstand or mistake them. In less than seven years after the conclusion of that treaty our grievances had become so intolerable that in the opinion of President Jackson they should no longer be endured. In his message to Congress in February, 1837, he presented them to the consideration of that body, and declared that—

The length of time since some of the injuries have been committed, the repeated and unavailing applications for redress, the wanton character of some of the outrages upon the property and persons of our citizens, upon the officers and flag of the United States, independent of recent insults to this Government and people by the late extraordinary Mexican minister, would justify in the eyes of all nations immediate war.

In a spirit of kindness and forbearance, however, he recommended reprisals as a milder mode of redress. He declared that war should not be used as a remedy "by just and generous nations, confiding in their strength for injuries committed, if it can be honorably avoided," and added:

It has occurred to me that, considering the present embarrassed condition of that country, we should act with both wisdom and moderation by giving to Mexico one more opportunity to atone for the past before we take redress into our Own hands. To avoid all misconception on the part of Mexico, as well as to protect our own national character from reproach, this opportunity should be given with the avowed design and full preparation to take immediate satisfaction if it should not be obtained on a repetition of the demand for it. To this end I recommend that an act be passed authorizing reprisals, and the use of the naval force of the United States by the Executive against Mexico to enforce them, in the event of a refusal by the Mexican Government to come to an amicable adjustment of the matters in controversy between us upon another demand thereof made from on board out of our vessels of war on the coast of Mexico.

Committees of both Houses of Congress, to which this message of the President was referred, fully sustained his views of the character of the wrongs which we had suffered from Mexico, and recommended that another demand for redress should be made before authorizing war or reprisals. The Committee on Foreign Relations of the Senate, in their report, say:

After such a demand, should prompt justice be refused by the Mexican Government, we may appeal to all nations, not only for the equity and moderation with which we shall have acted toward a sister republic, but for the necessity which will then compel us to seek redress for our wrongs, either by actual war or by reprisals. The subject will then be presented before Congress, at the commencement of the next session, in a clear and distinct form, and the committee can not doubt but that such measures will be immediately adopted as may be necessary to vindicate the honor of the country and insure ample reparation to our injured fellow-citizens.

The Committee on Foreign Affairs of the House of Representatives made a similar recommendation. In their report they say that—

They fully concur with the President that ample cause exists for taking redress into our own hands, and believe that we should be justified in the opinion of other nations for taking such a step. But they are willing to try the experiment of another demand, made in the most solemn form, upon the justice of the Mexican Government before any further proceedings are adopted.

No difference of opinion upon the subject is believed to have existed in Congress at that time; the executive and legislative departments concurred; and yet such has been our forbearance and desire to preserve peace with Mexico that the wrongs of which we then complained, and which gave rise to these solemn proceedings, not only remain unredressed to this day, but additional causes of complaint of an aggravated character have ever since been accumulating. Shortly after these proceedings a special messenger was dispatched to Mexico to make a final demand for redress, and on the 20th of July, 1837, the demand was made. The reply of the Mexican Government bears date on the 29th of the same month, and contains assurances of the "anxious wish" of the Mexican Government "not to delay the moment of that final and equitable adjustment which is to terminate the existing difficulties between the two Governments;" that "nothing should be left undone which may contribute to the most speedy and equitable determination of the subjects which have so seriously engaged the attention of the American Government;" that the "Mexican Government would adopt as the only guides for its conduct the plainest principles of public right, the sacred obligations imposed by international law, and the religious faith of treaties," and that "whatever reason and justice may dictate respecting each case will be done." The assurance was further given that the decision of the Mexican Government upon each cause of complaint for which redress had been demanded should be communicated to the Government of the United States by the Mexican minister at Washington.

These solemn assurances in answer to our demand for redress were disregarded. By making them, however, Mexico obtained further delay. President Van Buren, in his annual message to Congress of the 5th of December, 1837, states that "although the larger number" of our demands for redress, "and many of them aggravated cases of personal wrongs, have been now for years before the Mexican Government, and some of the causes of national complaint, and those of the most offensive character, admitted of immediate, simple, and satisfactory replies, it is only within a few days past that any specific communication in answer to our last demand, made five months ago, has been received from the Mexican minister;" and that "for not one of our public complaints has satisfaction been given or offered, that but one of the cases of personal wrong has been favorably considered, and that but four cases of both descriptions out of all those formally presented and earnestly pressed have as yet been decided upon by the Mexican Government." President Van Buren, believing that it would be vain to make any further attempt to obtain redress by the ordinary means within the power of the Executive, communicated this opinion to Congress in the message referred to, in which he said:

On a careful and deliberate examination of their contents of the correspondence with the Mexican Government], and considering the spirit manifested by the Mexican Government, it has become my painful duty to return the subject as it now stands to Congress, to whom it belongs to decide upon the time, the mode, and the measure of redress.

Had the United States at that time adopted compulsory measures and taken redress into their own hands, all our difficulties with Mexico would probably have been long since adjusted and the existing war have been averted. Magnanimity and moderation on our part only had the effect to complicate these difficulties and render an amicable settlement of them the more embarrassing. That such measures of redress under similar provocations committed by any of the powerful nations of Europe would have been promptly resorted to by the United States can not be doubted. The national honor and the preservation of the national character throughout the world, as well as our own self-respect and the protection due to our own citizens, would have rendered such a resort indispensable. The history of no civilized nation in modern times has presented within so brief a period so many wanton attacks upon the honor of its flag and upon the property and persons of its citizens as had at that time been borne by the United States from the Mexican authorities and people. But Mexico was a sister republic on the North American continent, occupying a territory contiguous to our own, and was in a feeble and distracted condition, and these considerations, it is presumed, induced Congress to forbear still longer.

Instead of taking redress into our own hands, a new negotiation was entered upon with fair promises on the part of Mexico, but with the real purpose, as the event has proved, of indefinitely postponing the reparation which we demanded, and which was so justly due. This negotiation, after more than a year's delay, resulted in the convention of the 11th of April, 1839, "for the adjustment of claims of citizens of the United States of America upon the Government of the Mexican Republic." The joint board of commissioners created by this convention to examine and decide upon these claims was not organized until the month of August, 1840, and under the terms of the convention they were to terminate their duties within eighteen months from that time. Four of the eighteen months were consumed in preliminary discussions on frivolous and dilatory points raised by the Mexican commissioners, and it was not until the month of December, 1840, that they commenced the examination of the claims of our citizens upon Mexico. Fourteen months only remained to examine and decide upon these numerous and complicated cases. In the month of February, 1842, the term of the commission expired, leaving many claims undisposed of for want of time. The claims which were allowed by the board and by the umpire authorized by the convention to decide in case of disagreement between the Mexican and American commissioners amounted to $2,026,139.68. There were pending before the umpire when the commission expired additional claims, which had been examined and awarded by the American commissioners and had not been allowed by the Mexican commissioners, amounting to $928,627.88, upon which he did not decide, alleging that his authority had ceased with the termination of the joint commission. Besides these claims, there were others of American citizens amounting to $3,336,837.05, which had been submitted to the board, and upon which they had not time to decide before their final adjournment.

The sum of $2,026,139.68, which had been awarded to the claimants, was a liquidated and ascertained debt due by Mexico, about which there could be no dispute, and which she was bound to pay according to the terms of the convention. Soon after the final awards for this amount had been made the Mexican Government asked for a postponement of the time of making payment, alleging that it would be inconvenient to make the payment at the time stipulated. In the spirit of forbearing kindness toward a sister republic, which Mexico has so long abused, the United States promptly complied with her request. A second convention was accordingly concluded between the two Governments on the 30th of January, 1843, which upon its face declares that "this new arrangement is entered into for the accommodation of Mexico." By the terms of this convention all the interest due on the awards which had been made in favor of the claimants under the convention of the 11th of April, 1839, was to be paid to them on the 30th of April, 1843, and "the principal of the said awards and the interest accruing thereon" was stipulated to "be paid in five years, in equal installments every three months." Notwithstanding this new convention was entered into at the request of Mexico and for the purpose of relieving her from embarrassment, the claimants have only received the interest due on the 30th of April, 1843, and three of the twenty installments. Although the payment of the sum thus liquidated and confessedly due by Mexico to our citizens as indemnity for acknowledged acts of outrage and wrong was secured by treaty, the obligations of which are ever held sacred by all just nations, yet Mexico has violated this solemn engagement by failing and refusing to make the payment. The two installments due in April and July, 1844, under the peculiar circumstances connected with them, have been assumed by the United States and discharged to the claimants, but they are still due by Mexico. But this is not all of which we have just cause of complaint. To provide a remedy for the claimants whose cases were not decided by the joint commission under the convention of April 11, 1839, it was expressly stipulated by the sixth article of the convention of the 30th of January, 1843, that—

A new convention shall be entered into for the settlement of all claims of the Government and citizens of the United States against the Republic of Mexico which were not finally decided by the late commission which met in the city of Washington, and of all claims of the Government and citizens of Mexico against the United States.

In conformity with this stipulation, a third convention was concluded and signed at the city of Mexico on the 20th of November, 1843, by the plenipotentiaries of the two Governments, by which provision was made for ascertaining and paying these claims. In January, 1844, this convention was ratified by the Senate of the United States with two amendments, which were manifestly reasonable in their character. Upon a reference of the amendments proposed to the Government of Mexico, the same evasions, difficulties, and delays were interposed which have so long marked the policy of that Government toward the United States. It has not even yet decided whether it would or would not accede to them, although the subject has been repeatedly pressed upon its consideration. Mexico has thus violated a second time the faith of treaties by failing or refusing to carry into effect the sixth article of the convention of January, 1843.

Such is the history of the wrongs which we have suffered and patiently endured from Mexico through a long series of years. So far from affording reasonable satisfaction for the injuries and insults we had borne, a great aggravation of them consists in the fact that while the United States, anxious to preserve a good understanding with Mexico, have been constantly but vainly employed in seeking redress for past wrongs, new outrages were constantly occurring, which have continued to increase our causes of complaint and to swell the amount of our demands. While the citizens of the United States were conducting a lawful commerce with Mexico under the guaranty of a treaty of "amity, commerce, and navigation," many of them have suffered all the injuries which would have resulted from open war. This treaty, instead of affording protection to our citizens, has been the means of inviting them into the ports of Mexico that they might be, as they have been in numerous instances, plundered of their property and deprived of their personal liberty if they dared insist on their rights. Had the unlawful seizures of American property and the violation of the personal liberty of our citizens, to say nothing of the insults to our flag, which have occurred in the ports of Mexico taken place on the high seas, they would themselves long since have constituted a state of actual war between the two countries. In so long suffering Mexico to violate her most solemn treaty obligations, plunder our citizens of their property, and imprison their persons without affording them any redress we have failed to perform one of the first and highest duties which every government owes to its citizens, and the consequence has been that many of them have been reduced from a state of affluence to bankruptcy. The proud name of American citizen, which ought to protect all who bear it from insult and injury throughout the world, has afforded no such protection to our citizens in Mexico. We had ample cause of war against Mexico long before the breaking out of hostilities; but even then we forbore to take redress into our own hands until Mexico herself became the aggressor by invading our soil in hostile array and shedding the blood of our citizens.

Such are the grave causes of complaint on the part of the United States against Mexico—causes which existed long before the annexation of Texas to the American Union; and yet, animated by the love of peace and a magnanimous moderation, we did not adopt those measures of redress which under such circumstances are the justified resort of injured nations.

The annexation of Texas to the United States constituted no just cause of offense to Mexico. The pretext that it did so is wholly inconsistent and irreconcilable with well-authenticated facts connected with the revolution by which Texas became independent of Mexico. That this may be the more manifest, it may be proper to advert to the causes and to the history of the principal events of that revolution.

Texas constituted a portion of the ancient Province of Louisiana, ceded to the United States by France in the year 1803. In the year 1819 the United States, by the Florida treaty, ceded to Spain all that part of Louisiana within the present limits of Texas, and Mexico, by the revolution which separated her from Spain and rendered her an independent nation, succeeded to the rights of the mother country over this territory. In the year 1824 Mexico established a federal constitution, under which the Mexican Republic was composed of a number of sovereign States confederated together in a federal union similar to our own. Each of these States had its own executive, legislature, and judiciary, and for all except federal purposes was as independent of the General Government and that of the other States as is Pennsylvania or Virginia under our Constitution. Texas and Coahuila united and formed one of these Mexican States. The State constitution which they adopted, and which was approved by the Mexican Confederacy, asserted that they were "free and independent of the other Mexican United States and of every other power and dominion whatsoever," and proclaimed the great principle of human liberty that "the sovereignty of the state resides originally and essentially in the general mass of the individuals who compose it." To the Government under this constitution, as well as to that under the federal constitution, the people of Texas owed allegiance.

Emigrants from foreign countries, including the United States, were invited by the colonization laws of the State and of the Federal Government to settle in Texas. Advantageous terms were offered to induce them to leave their own country and become Mexican citizens. This invitation was accepted by many of our citizens in the full faith that in their new home they would be governed by laws enacted by representatives elected by themselves, and that their lives, liberty, and property would be protected by constitutional guaranties similar to those which existed in the Republic they had left. Under a Government thus organized they continued until the year 1835, when a military revolution broke out in the City of Mexico which entirely subverted the federal and State constitutions and placed a military dictator at the head of the Government. By a sweeping decree of a Congress subservient to the will of the Dictator the several State constitutions were abolished and the States themselves converted into mere departments of the central Government. The people of Texas were unwilling to submit to this usurpation. Resistance to such tyranny became a high duty. Texas was fully absolved from all allegiance to the central Government of Mexico from the moment that Government had abolished her State constitution and in its place substituted an arbitrary and despotic central government. Such were the principal causes of the Texan revolution. The people of Texas at once determined upon resistance and flew to arms. In the midst of these important and exciting events, however, they did not omit to place their liberties upon a secure and permanent foundation. They elected members to a convention, who in the month of March, 1836, issued a formal declaration that their "political connection with the Mexican nation has forever ended, and that the people of Texas do now constitute a free, sovereign, and independent Republic, and are fully invested with all the rights and attributes which properly belong to independent nations." They also adopted for their government a liberal republican constitution. About the same time Santa Anna, then the Dictator of Mexico, invaded Texas with a numerous army for the purpose of subduing her people and enforcing obedience to his arbitrary and despotic Government. On the 21st of April, 1836, he was met by the Texan citizen soldiers, and on that day was achieved by them the memorable victory of San Jacinto, by which they conquered their independence. Considering the numbers engaged on the respective sides, history does not record a more brilliant achievement. Santa Anna himself was among the captives.

In the month of May, 1836, Santa Anna acknowledged by a treaty with the Texan authorities in the most solumn form "the full, entire, and perfect independence of the Republic of Texas." It is true he was then a prisoner of war, but it is equally true that he had failed to reconquer Texas, and had met with signal defeat; that his authority had not been revoked, and that by virtue of this treaty he obtained his personal release. By it hostilities were suspended, and the army which had invaded Texas under his command returned in pursuance of this arrangement unmolested to Mexico.

From the day that the battle of San Jacinto was fought until the present hour Mexico has never possessed the power to reconquer Texas. In the language of the Secretary of State of the United States in a dispatch to our minister in Mexico under date of the 8th of July, 1842–

Mexico may have chosen to consider, and may still choose to consider, Texas as having been at all times since 1835, and as still continuing, a rebellious province; but the world has been obliged to take a very different view of the matter. From the time of the battle of San Jacinto, in April, 1836, to the present moment, Texas has exhibited the same external signs of national independence as Mexico herself, and with quite as much stability of government. Practically free and independent, acknowledged as a political sovereignty by the principal powers of the world, no hostile foot finding rest within her territory for six or seven years, and Mexico herself refraining for all that period from any further attempt to reestablish her own authority over that territory, it can not but be surprising to find Mr. De Bocanegra the secretary of foreign affairs of Mexico] complaining that for that whole period citizens of the United States or its Government have been favoring the rebels of Texas and supplying them with vessels, ammunition, and money, as if the war for the reduction of the Province of Texas had been constantly prosecuted by Mexico, and her success prevented by these influences from abroad.

In the same dispatch the Secretary of State affirms that—Since 1837 the United States have regarded Texas as an independent sovereignty as much as Mexico, and that trade and commerce with citizens of a government at war with Mexico can not on that account be regarded as an intercourse by which assistance and succor are given to Mexican rebels. The whole current of Mr. De Bocanegra's remarks runs in the same direction, as if the independence of Texas had not been acknowledged. It has been acknowledged; it was acknowledged in 1837 against the remonstrance and protest of Mexico, and most of the acts of any importance of which Mr. De Bocanegra complains flow necessarily from that recognition. He speaks of Texas as still being "an integral part of the territory of the Mexican Republic," but he can not but understand that the United States do not so regard it. The real complaint of Mexico, therefore, is in substance neither more nor less than a complaint against the recognition of Texan independence. It may be thought rather late to repeat that complaint, and not quite just to confine it to the United States to the exemption of England, France, and Belgium, unless the United States, having been the first to acknowledge the independence of Mexico herself, are to be blamed for setting an example for the recognition of that of Texas.

And he added that—

The Constitution, public treaties, and the laws oblige the President to regard Texas as an independent state, and its territory as no part of the territory of Mexico.

Texas had been an independent state, with an organized government, defying the power of Mexico to overthrow or reconquer her, for more than ten years before Mexico commenced the present war against the United States. Texas had given such evidence to the world of her ability to maintain her separate existence as an independent nation that she had been formally recognized as such not only by the United States, but by several of the principal powers of Europe. These powers had entered into treaties of amity, commerce, and navigation with her. They had received and accredited her ministers and other diplomatic agents at their respective courts, and they had commissioned ministers and diplomatic agents on their part to the Government of Texas. If Mexico, notwithstanding all this and her utter inability to subdue or reconquer Texas, still stubbornly refused to recognize her as an independent nation, she was none the less so on that account. Mexico herself had been recognized as an independent nation by the United States and by other powers many years before Spain, of which before her revolution she had been a colony, would agree to recognize her as such; and yet Mexico was at that time in the estimation of the civilized world, and in fact, none the less an independent power because Spain still claimed her as a colony. If Spain had continued until the present period to assert that Mexico was one of her colonies in rebellion against her, this would not have made her so or changed the fact of her independent existence. Texas at the period of her annexation to the United States bore the same relation to Mexico that Mexico had borne to Spain for many years before Spain acknowledged her independence, with this important difference, that before the annexation of Texas to the United States was consummated Mexico herself, by a formal act of her Government, had acknowledged the independence of Texas as a nation. It is true that in the act of recognition she prescribed a condition which she had no power or authority to impose—that Texas should not annex herself to any other power—but this could not detract in any degree from the recognition which Mexico then made of her actual independence. Upon this plain statement of facts, it is absurd for Mexico to allege as a pretext for commencing hostilities against the United States that Texas is still a part of her territory.

But there are those who, conceding all this to be true, assume the ground that the true western boundary of Texas is the Nueces instead of the Rio Grande, and that therefore in marching our

Army to the east bank of the latter river we passed the Texan line
and invaded the territory of Mexico. A simple statement of facts
known to exist will conclusively refute such an assumption. Texas,
as ceded to the United States by France in 1803, has been always
claimed as extending west to the Rio Grande or Rio Bravo. This
fact is established by the authority of our most eminent statesmen
at a period when the question was as well, if not better, understood
than it is at present. During Mr. Jefferson's Administration Messrs.
Monroe and Pinckney, who had been sent on a special mission
to Madrid, charged among other things with the adjustment of
boundary between the two countries, in a note addressed to the
Spanish minister of foreign affairs under date of the 28th of January, 1805, assert that the boundaries of Louisiana, as ceded to the
United States by France, "are the river Perdido on the east and the
river Bravo on the west," and they add that "the facts and principles
which justify this conclusion are so satisfactory to our Government
as to convince it that the United States have not a better right to
the island of New Orleans under the cession referred to than they
have to the whole district of territory which is above described."
Down to the conclusion of the Florida treaty, in February, 1819, by
which this territory was ceded to Spain, the United States asserted
and maintained their territorial rights to this extent. In the month
of June, 1818, during Mr. Monroe's Administration, information
having been received that a number of foreign adventurers had
landed at Galveston with the avowed purpose of forming a settlement in that vicinity, a special messenger was dispatched by the
Government of the United States with instructions from the Secretary of State to warn them to desist, should they be found there,
"or any other place north of the Rio Bravo, and within the territory
claimed by the United States." He was instructed, should they be
found in the country north of that river, to make known to them
"the surprise with which the President has seen possession thus
taken, without authority from the United States, of a place within
their territorial limits, and upon which no lawful settlement can be
made without their sanction." He was instructed to call upon them
to "avow under what national authority they profess to act," and to
give them due warning "that the place is within the United States,

who will suffer no permanent settlement to be made there under any authority other than their own." As late as the 8th of July, 1842, the Secretary of State of the United States, in a note addressed to our minister in Mexico, maintains that by the Florida treaty of 1819 the territory as far west as the Rio Grande was confirmed to Spain. In that note he states that—

By the treaty of the 22d of February, 1819, between the United States and Spain, the Sabine was adopted as the line of boundary between the two powers. Up to that period no considerable colonization had been effected in Texas; but the territory between the Sabine and the Rio Grande being confirmed to Spain by the treaty, applications were made to that power for grants of land, and such grants or permissions of settlement were in fact made by the Spanish authorities in favor of citizens of the United States proposing to emigrate to Texas in numerous families before the declaration of independence by Mexico.

The Texas which was ceded to Spain by the Florida treaty of 1819 embraced all the country now claimed by the State of Texas between the Nueces and the Rio Grande. The Republic of Texas always claimed this river as her western boundary, and in her treaty made with Santa Anna in May, 1836, he recognized it as such. By the constitution which Texas adopted in March, 1836, senatorial and representative districts were organized extending west of the Nueces. The Congress of Texas on the 19th of December, 1836, passed "An act to define the boundaries of the Republic of Texas," in which they declared the Rio Grande from its mouth to its source to be their boundary, and by the said act they extended their "civil and political jurisdiction" over the country up to that boundary. During a period of more than nine years which intervened between the adoption of her constitution and her annexation as one of the States of our Union Texas asserted and exercised many acts of sovereignty and jurisdiction over the territory and inhabitants west of the Nueces. She organized and defined the limits of counties extending to the Rio Grande; she established courts of justice and extended her judicial system over the territory; she established a custom-house and collected duties, and also post-offices and post-roads, in it; she established a land office and issued numerous grants for land within its limits; a senator and a representative residing in it were elected to the Congress of the Republic and served as such before the act of annexation took place. In both the Congress and convention of Texas which gave their assent to the terms of annexation to the United States proposed by our Congress were representatives residing west of the Nueces, who took part in the act of annexation itself. This was the Texas which by the act of our Congress of the 29th of December, 1845, was admitted as one of the States of our Union. That the Congress of the United States understood the State of Texas which they admitted into the Union to extend beyond the Nueces is apparent from the fact that on the 31st of December, 1845, only two days after the act of admission, they passed a law "to establish a collection district in the State of Texas," by which they created a port of delivery at Corpus Christi, situated west of the Nueces, and being the same point at which the Texas custom-house under the laws of that Republic had been located, and directed that a surveyor to collect the revenue should be appointed for that port by the President, by and with the advice and consent of the Senate. A surveyor was accordingly nominated, and confirmed by the Senate, and has been ever since in the performance of his duties. All these acts of the Republic of Texas and of our Congress preceded the orders for the advance of our Army to the east bank of the Rio Grande. Subsequently Congress passed an act "establishing certain post routes" extending west of the Nueces. The country west of that river now constitutes a part of one of the Congressional districts of Texas and is represented in the House of Representatives. The Senators from that State were chosen by a legislature in which the country west of that river was represented. In view of all these facts it is difficult to conceive upon what ground it can be maintained that in occupying the country west of the Nueces with our Army, with a view solely to its security and defense, we invaded the territory of Mexico. But it would have been still more difficult to justify the Executive, whose duty it is to see that the laws be faithfully executed, if in the face of all these proceedings, both of the Congress of Texas and of the United States, he had assumed the responsibility of yielding up the territory west of the Nueces to Mexico or of refusing to protect and defend this territory and its inhabitants, including Corpus Christi as well as the remainder of Texas, against the threatened Mexican invasion.

But Mexico herself has never placed the war which she has waged upon the ground that our Army occupied the intermediate territory between the Nueces and the Rio Grande. Her refuted pretension that Texas was not in fact an independent state, but a rebellious province, was obstinately persevered in, and her avowed purpose in commencing a war with the United States was to reconquer Texas and to restore Mexican authority over the whole territory—not to the Nueces only, but to the Sabine. In view of the proclaimed menaces of Mexico to this effect, I deemed it my duty, as a measure of precaution and defense, to order our Army to occupy a position on our frontier as a military post, from which our troops could best resist and repel any attempted invasion which Mexico might make. Our Army had occupied a position at Corpus Christi, west of the Nueces, as early as August, 1845, without complaint from any quarter. Had the Nueces been regarded as the true western boundary of Texas, that boundary had been passed by our Army many months before it advanced to the eastern bank of the Rio Grande. In my annual message of December last I informed Congress that upon the invitation of both the Congress and convention of Texas I had deemed it proper to order a strong squadron to the coasts of Mexico and to concentrate an efficient military force on the western frontier of Texas to protect and defend the inhabitants against the menaced invasion of Mexico. In that message I informed Congress that the moment the terms of annexation offered by the United States were accepted by Texas the latter became so far a part of our own country as to make it our duty to afford such protection and defense, and that for that purpose our squadron had been ordered to the Gulf and our Army to take a "position between the Nueces and the Del Norte" or Rio Grande and to "repel any invasion of the Texan territory which might be attempted by the Mexican forces."

It was deemed proper to issue this order, because soon after the President of Texas, in April, 1845, had issued his proclamation convening the Congress of that Republic for the purpose of submitting to that body the terms of annexation proposed by the United States the Government of Mexico made serious threats of invading the Texan territory. These threats became more imposing as it became more apparent in the progress of the question that the people of Texas would decide in favor of accepting the terms of annexation, and finally they had assumed such a formidable character as induced both the Congress and convention of Texas to request that a military force should be sent by the United States into her territory for the purpose of protecting and defending her against the threatened invasion. It would have been a violation of good faith toward the people of Texas to have refused to afford the aid which they desired against a threatened invasion to which they had been exposed by their free determination to annex themselves to our Union in compliance with the overture made to them by the joint resolution of our Congress. Accordingly, a portion of the Army was ordered to advance into Texas. Corpus Christi was the position selected by General Taylor. He encamped at that place in August, 1845, and the Army remained in that position until the 11th of March, 1846, when it moved westward, and on the 28th of that month reached the east bank of the Rio Grande opposite to Matamoras. This movement was made in pursuance of orders from the War Department, issued on the 13th of January, 1846. Before these orders were issued the dispatch of our minister in Mexico transmitting the decision of the council of government of Mexico advising that he should not be received, and also the dispatch of our consul residing in the City of Mexico, the former bearing date on the 17th and the latter on the 18th of December, 1845, copies of both of which accompanied my message to Congress of the 11th of May last, were received at the Department of State. These communications rendered it highly probable, if not absolutely certain, that our minister would not be received by the Government of General Herrera. It was also well known that but little hope could be entertained of a different result from General Paredes in case the revolutionary movement which he was prosecuting should prove successful, as was highly probable. The partisans of Paredes, as our minister in the dispatch referred to states, breathed the fiercest hostility against the United States, denounced the proposed negotiation as treason, and openly called upon the troops and the people to put down the Government of Herrera by force. The reconquest of Texas and war with the United States were openly threatened. These were the circumstances existing when it was deemed proper to order the Army under the command of General Taylor to advance to the western frontier of Texas and occupy a position on or near the Rio Grande.

The apprehensions of a contemplated Mexican invasion have been since fully justified by the event. The determination of Mexico to rush into hostilities with the United States was afterwards manifested from the whole tenor of the note of the Mexican minister of foreign affairs to our minister bearing date on the 12th of March, 1846. Paredes had then revolutionized the Government, and his minister, after referring to the resolution for the annexation of Texas which had been adopted by our Congress in March, 1845, proceeds to declare that–

A fact such as this, or, to speak with greater exactness, so notable an act of usurpation, created an imperious necessity that Mexico, for her own honor, should repel it with proper firmness and dignity. The supreme Government had beforehand declared that it would look upon such an act as a casus belli, and as a consequence of this declaration negotiation was by its very nature at an end, and war was the only recourse of the Mexican Government.

It appears also that on the 4th of April following General Paredes, through his minister of war, issued orders to the Mexican general in command on the Texan frontier to "attack" our Army "by every means which war permits." To this General Paredes had been pledged to the army and people of Mexico during the military revolution which had brought him into power. On the 18th of April, 1846, General Paredes addressed a letter to the commander on that frontier in which he stated to him: "At the present date I suppose you, at the head of that valiant army, either fighting already or preparing for the operations of a campaign;" and, "Supposing you already on the theater of operations and with all the forces assembled, it is indispensable that hostilities be commenced, yourself taking the initiative against the enemy."

The movement of our Army to the Rio Grande was made by the commanding general under positive orders to abstain from all aggressive acts toward Mexico or Mexican citizens, and to regard the relations between the two countries as peaceful unless Mexico should declare war or commit acts of hostility indicative of a state of war, and these orders he faithfully executed. Whilst occupying his position on the east bank of the Rio Grande, within the limits of Texas, then recently admitted as one of the States of our Union, the commanding general of the Mexican forces, who, in pursuance of the orders of his Government, had collected a large army on the opposite shore of the Rio Grande, crossed the river, invaded our territory, and commenced hostilities by attacking our forces. Thus, after all the injuries which we had received and borne from Mexico, and after she had insultingly rejected a minister sent to her on a mission of peace, and whom she had solemnly agreed to receive, she consummated her long course of outrage against our country by commencing an offensive war and shedding the blood of our citizens on our own soil.

The United States never attempted to acquire Texas by conquest. On the contrary, at an early period after the people of Texas had achieved their independence they sought to be annexed to the United States. At a general election in September, 1836, they decided with great unanimity in favor of "annexation," and in November following the Congress of the Republic authorized the appointment of a minister to bear their request to this Government. This Government, however, having remained neutral between Texas and Mexico during the war between them, and considering it due to the honor of our country and our fair fame among the nations of the earth that we should not at this early period consent to annexation, nor until it should be manifest to the whole world that the reconquest of Texas by Mexico was impossible, refused to accede to the overtures made by Texas. On the 12th of April, 1844, after more than seven years had elapsed since Texas had established her independence, a treaty was concluded for the annexation of that Republic to the United States, which was rejected by the Senate. Finally, on the 1st of March, 1845, Congress passed a joint resolution for annexing her to the United States upon certain preliminary conditions to which her assent was required. The solemnities which characterized the deliberations and conduct of the Government and people of Texas on the deeply interesting questions presented by these resolutions are known to the world. The Congress, the Executive, and the people of Texas, in a convention elected for that purpose, accepted with great unanimity the proposed terms of annexation, and thus consummated on her part the great act of restoring to our Federal Union a vast territory which had been ceded to Spain by the Florida treaty more than a quarter of a century before.

After the joint resolution for the annexation of Texas to the United States had been passed by our Congress the Mexican minister at Washington addressed a note to the Secretary of State, bearing date on the 6th of March, 1845, protesting against it as "an act of aggression the most unjust which can be found recorded in the annals of modern history, namely, that of despoiling a friendly nation like Mexico of a considerable portion of her territory," and protesting against the resolution of annexation as being an act "whereby the Province of Texas, an integral portion of the Mexican territory, is agreed and admitted into the American Union;" and he announced that as a consequence his mission to the United States had terminated, and demanded his passports, which were granted. It was upon the absurd pretext, made by Mexico (herself indebted for her independence to a successful revolution), that the Republic of Texas still continued to be, notwithstanding all that had passed, a Province of Mexico that this step was taken by the Mexican minister.

Every honorable effort has been used by me to avoid the war which followed, but all have proved vain. All our attempts to preserve peace have been met by insult and resistance on the part of Mexico. My efforts to this end commenced in the note of the Secretary of State of the 10th of March, 1845, in answer to that of the Mexican minister. Whilst declining to reopen a discussion which had already been exhausted, and proving again what was known to the whole world, that Texas had long since achieved her independence, the Secretary of State expressed the regret of this Government that Mexico should have taken offense at the resolution of annexation passed by Congress, and gave assurance that our "most strenuous efforts shall be devoted to the amicable adjustment of every cause of complaint between the two Governments and to the cultivation of the kindest and most friendly relations between the sister Republics." That I have acted in the spirit of this assurance will appear from the events which have since occurred. Notwithstanding Mexico had abruptly terminated all diplomatic intercourse with the United States, and ought, therefore, to have been the first to ask for its resumption, yet, waiving all ceremony, I embraced the earliest favorable opportunity "to ascertain from the Mexican Government whether they would receive an envoy from the United States intrusted with full power to adjust all the questions in dispute between the two Governments." In September, 1845, I believed the propitious moment for such an overture had arrived. Texas, by the enthusiastic and almost unanimous will of her people, had pronounced in favor of annexation. Mexico herself had agreed to acknowledge the independence of Texas, subject to a condition, it is true, which she had no right to impose and no power to enforce. The last lingering hope of Mexico, if she still could have retained any, that Texas would ever again become one of her Provinces, must have been abandoned.

The consul of the United States at the City of Mexico was therefore instructed by the Secretary of State on the 15th of September, 1845, to make the inquiry of the Mexican Government. The inquiry was made, and on the 15th of October, 1845, the minister of foreign affairs of the Mexican Government, in a note addressed to our consul, gave a favorable response, requesting at the same time that our naval force might be withdrawn from Vera Cruz while negotiations should be pending. Upon the receipt of this note our naval force was promptly withdrawn from Vera Cruz. A minister was immediately appointed, and departed to Mexico. Everything bore a promising aspect for a speedy and peaceful adjustment of all our difficulties. At the date of my annual message to Congress in December last no doubt was entertained but that he would be received by the Mexican Government, and the hope was cherished that all cause of misunderstanding between the two countries would be speedily removed. In the confident hope that such would be the result of his mission, I informed Congress that I forbore at that time to "recommend such ulterior measures of redress for the wrongs and injuries we had so long borne as it would have been proper to make had no such negotiation been instituted." To my surprise and regret the Mexican Government, though solemnly pledged to do so, upon the arrival of our minister in Mexico refused to receive and accredit him. When he reached Vera Cruz, on the 30th of November, 1845, he found that the aspect of affairs had undergone an unhappy change. The Government of General Herrera, who was at that time President of the Republic, was tottering to its fall. General Paredes, a military leader, had manifested his determination to overthrow the Government of Herrera by a military revolution, and one of the principal means which he employed to effect his purpose and render the Government of Herrera odious to the army and people of Mexico was by loudly condemning its determination to receive a minister of peace from the United States, alleging that it was the intention of Herrera, by a treaty with the United States, to dismember the territory of Mexico by ceding away the department of Texas. The Government of Herrera is believed to have been well disposed to a pacific adjustment of existing difficulties, but probably alarmed for its own security, and in order to ward off the danger of the revolution led by Paredes, violated its solemn agreement and refused to receive or accredit our minister; and this although informed that he had been invested with full power to adjust all questions in dispute between the two Governments. Among the frivolous pretexts for this refusal, the principal one was that our minister had not gone upon a special mission confined to the question of Texas alone, leaving all the outrages upon our flag and our citizens unredressed. The Mexican Government well knew that both our national honor and the protection due to our citizens imperatively required that the two questions of boundary and indemnity should be treated of together, as naturally and inseparably blended, and they ought to have seen that this course was best calculated to enable the United States to extend to them the most liberal justice. On the 30th of December, 1845, General Herrera resigned the Presidency and yielded up the Government to General Paredes without a struggle.

Thus a revolution was accomplished solely by the army commanded by Paredes, and the supreme power in Mexico passed into the hands of a military usurper who was known to be bitterly hostile to the United States.

Although the prospect of a pacific adjustment with the new Government was unpromising from the known hostility of its head to the United States, yet, determined that nothing should be left undone on our part to restore friendly relations between the two countries, our minister was instructed to present his credentials to the new Government and ask to be accredited by it in the diplomatic character in which he had been commissioned. These instructions he executed by his note of the 1st of March, 1846, addressed to the Mexican minister of foreign affairs, but his request was insultingly refused by that minister in his answer of the 12th of the same month. No alternative remained for our minister but to demand his passports and return to the United States.

Thus was the extraordinary spectacle presented to the civilized world of a Government, in violation of its own express agreement, having twice rejected a minister of peace invested with full powers to adjust all the existing differences between the two countries in a manner just and honorable to both. I am not aware that modern history presents a parallel case in which in time of peace one nation has refused even to hear propositions from another for terminating existing difficulties between them. Scarcely a hope of adjusting our difficulties, even at a remote day, or of preserving peace with Mexico, could be cherished while Paredes remained at the head of the Government. He had acquired the supreme power by a military revolution and upon the most solemn pledges to wage war against the United States and to reconquer Texas, which he claimed as a revolted province of Mexico. He had denounced as guilty of treason all those Mexicans who considered Texas as no longer constituting a part of the territory of Mexico and who were friendly to the cause of peace. The duration of the war which he waged against the United States was indefinite, because the end which he proposed of the reconquest of Texas was hopeless. Besides, there was good reason to believe from all his conduct that it was his intention to convert the Republic of Mexico into a monarchy and to call a foreign European prince to the throne. Preparatory to this end, he had during his short rule destroyed the liberty of the press, tolerating that portion of it only which openly advocated the establishment of a monarchy. The better to secure the success of his ultimate designs, he had by an arbitrary decree convoked a Congress, not to be elected by the free voice of the people, but to be chosen in a manner to make them subservient to his will and to give him absolute control over their deliberations.

Under all these circumstances it was believed that any revolution in Mexico founded upon opposition to the ambitious projects of Paredes would tend to promote the cause of peace as well as prevent any attempted European interference in the affairs of the North American continent, both objects of deep interest to the United States. Any such foreign interference, if attempted, must have been resisted by the United States. My views upon that subject were fully communicated to Congress in my last annual message. In any event, it was certain that no change whatever in the Government of Mexico which would deprive Paredes of power could be for the worse so far as the United States were concerned, while it was highly probable that any change must be for the better. This was the state of affairs existing when Congress, on the 13th of May last, recognized the existence of the war which had been commenced by the Government of Paredes; and it became an object of much importance, with a view to a speedy settlement of our difficulties and the restoration of an honorable peace, that Paredes should not retain power in Mexico.

Before that time there were symptoms of a revolution in Mexico, favored, as it was understood to be, by the more liberal party, and especially by those who were opposed to foreign interference and to the monarchical form of government. Santa Anna was then in exile in Havana, having been expelled from power and banished from his country by a revolution which occurred in December, 1844; but it was known that he had still a considerable party in his favor in Mexico. It was also equally well known that no vigilance which could be exerted by our squadron would in all probability have prevented him from effecting a landing somewhere on the extensive Gulf coast of Mexico if he desired to return to his country. He had openly professed an entire change of policy, had expressed his regret that he had subverted the federal constitution of 1824, and avowed that he was now in favor of its restoration. He had publicly declared his hostility, in strongest terms, to the establishment of a monarchy and to European interference in the affairs of his country. Information to this effect had been received, from sources believed to be reliable, at the date of the recognition of the existence of the war by Congress, and was afterwards fully confirmed by the receipt of the dispatch of our consul in the City of Mexico, with the accompanying documents, which are herewith transmitted. Besides, it was reasonable to suppose that he must see the ruinous consequences to Mexico of a war with the United States, and that it would be his interest to favor peace.

It was under these circumstances and upon these considerations that it was deemed expedient not to obstruct his return to Mexico should he attempt to do so. Our object was the restoration of peace, and, with that view, no reason was perceived why we should take part with Paredes and aid him by means of our blockade in preventing the return of his rival to Mexico. On the contrary, it was believed that the intestine divisions which ordinary sagacity could not but anticipate as the fruit of Santa Anna's return to Mexico, and his contest with Paredes, might strongly tend to produce a disposition with both parties to restore and preserve peace with the United States. Paredes was a soldier by profession and a monarchist in principle. He had but recently before been successful in a military revolution, by which he had obtained power. He was the sworn enemy of the United States, with which he had involved his country in the existing war. Santa Anna had been expelled from power by the army, was known to be in open hostility to Paredes, and publicly pledged against foreign intervention and the restoration of monarchy in Mexico. In view of these facts and circumstances it was that when orders were issued to the commander of our naval forces in the Gulf, on the 13th day of May last, the same day on which the existence of the war was recognized by Congress, to place the coasts of Mexico under blockade, he was directed not to obstruct the passage of Santa Anna to Mexico should he attempt to return.

A revolution took place in Mexico in the early part of August following, by which the power of Paredes was overthrown, and he has since been banished from the country, and is now in exile. Shortly afterwards Santa Anna returned. It remains to be seen whether his return may not yet prove to be favorable to a pacific adjustment of the existing difficulties, it being manifestly his interest not to persevere in the prosecution of a war commenced by Paredes to accomplish a purpose so absurd as the reconquest of Texas to the Sabine. Had Paredes remained in power, it is morally certain that any pacific adjustment would have been hopeless.

Upon the commencement of hostilities by Mexico against the United States the indignant spirit of the nation was at once aroused. Congress promptly responded to the expectations of the country, and by the act of the 13th of May last recognized the fact that war existed, by the act of Mexico, between the United States and that Republic, and granted the means necessary for its vigorous prosecution. Being involved in a war thus commenced by Mexico, and for the justice of which on our part we may confidently appeal to the whole world, I resolved to prosecute it with the utmost vigor. Accordingly the ports of Mexico on the Gulf and on the Pacific have been placed under blockade and her territory invaded at several important points. The reports from the Departments of War and of the Navy will inform you more in detail of the measures adopted in the emergency in which our country was placed and of the gratifying results which have been accomplished.

The various columns of the Army have performed their duty under great disadvantages with the most distinguished skill and courage. The victories of Palo Alto and Resaca de la Palma and of Monterey, won against greatly superior numbers and against most decided advantages in other respects on the part of the enemy, were brilliant in their execution, and entitle our brave officers and soldiers to the grateful thanks of their country. The nation deplores the loss of the brave officers and men who have gallantly fallen while vindicating and defending their country's rights and honor.

It is a subject of pride and satisfaction that our volunteer citizen soldiers, who so promptly responded to their country's call, with an experience of the discipline of a camp of only a few weeks, have borne their part in the hard-fought battle of Monterey with a constancy and courage equal to that of veteran troops and worthy of the highest admiration. The privations of long marches through the enemy's country and through a wilderness have been borne without a murmur. By rapid movements the Province of New Mexico, with Santa Fe, its capital, has been captured without bloodshed. The Navy has cooperated with the Army and rendered important services; if not so brilliant, it is because the enemy had no force to meet them on their own element and because of the defenses which nature has interposed in the difficulties of the navigation on the Mexican coast. Our squadron in the Pacific, with the cooperation of a gallant officer of the Army and a small force hastily collected in that distant country, has acquired bloodless possession of the Californias, and the American flag has been raised at every important point in that Province.

I congratulate you on the success which has thus attended our military and naval operations. In less than seven months after Mexico commenced hostilities, at a time selected by herself, we have taken possession of many of her principal ports, driven back and pursued her invading army, and acquired military possession of the Mexican Provinces of New Mexico, New Leon, Coahuila, Tamaulipas, and the Californias, a territory larger in extent than that embraced in the original thirteen States of the Union, inhabited by a considerable population, and much of it more than 1,000 miles from the points at which we had to collect our forces and commence our movements. By the blockade the import and export trade of the enemy has been cut off. Well may the American people be proud of the energy and gallantry of our regular and volunteer officers and soldiers. The events of these few months afford a gratifying proof that our country can under any emergency confidently rely for the maintenance of her honor and the defense of her rights on an effective force, ready at all times voluntarily to relinquish the comforts of home for the perils and privations of the camp. And though such a force may be for the time expensive, it is in the end economical, as the ability to command it removes the necessity of employing a large standing army in time of peace, and proves that our people love their institutions and are ever ready to defend and protect them.

While the war was in a course of vigorous and successful prosecution, being still anxious to arrest its evils, and considering that after the brilliant victories of our arms on the 8th and 9th of May last the national honor could not be compromitted by it, another overture was made to Mexico, by my direction, on the 27th of July last to terminate hostilities by a peace just and honorable to both countries. On the 31st of August following the Mexican Government declined to accept this friendly overture, but referred it to the decision of a Mexican Congress to be assembled in the early part of the present month. I communicate to you herewith a copy of the letter of the Secretary of State proposing to reopen negotiations, of the answer of the Mexican Government, and of the reply thereto of the Secretary of State,

The war will continue to be prosecuted with vigor as the best means of securing peace. It is hoped that the decision of the Mexican Congress, to which our last overture has been referred, may result in a speedy and honorable peace. With our experience, however, of the unreasonable course of the Mexican authorities, it is the part of wisdom not to relax in the energy of our military operations until the result is made known. In this view it is deemed important to hold military possession of all the Provinces which have been taken until a definitive treaty of peace shall have been concluded and ratified by the two countries.

The war has not been waged with a view to conquest, but, having been commenced by Mexico, it has been carried into the enemy's country and will be vigorously prosecuted there with a view to obtain an honorable peace, and thereby secure ample indemnity for the expenses of the war, as well as to our much-injured citizens, who hold large pecuniary demands against Mexico.

By the laws of nations a conquered country is subject to be governed by the conqueror during his military possession and until there is either a treaty of peace or he shall voluntarily withdraw from it. The old civil government being necessarily superseded, it is the right and duty of the conqueror to secure his conquest and to provide for the maintenance of civil order and the rights of the inhabitants. This right has been exercised and this duty performed by our military and naval commanders by the establishment of temporary governments in some of the conquered Provinces of Mexico, assimilating them as far as practicable to the free institutions of our own country. In the Provinces of New Mexico and of the Californias little, if any, further resistance is apprehended from the inhabitants to the temporary governments which have thus, from the necessity of the case and according to the laws of war, been established. It may be proper to provide for the security of these important conquests by making an adequate appropriation for the purpose of erecting fortifications and defraying the expenses necessarily incident to the maintenance of our possession and authority over them. [Here follow requests for appropriation, Treasury reports and other matters.]

With full reliance upon the wisdom and patriotism of your deliberations, it will be my duty, as it will be my anxious desire, to cooperate with you in every constitutional effort to promote the welfare and maintain the honor of our common country.

JAMES K. POLK

Citation: James K. Polk: "Second Annual Message," December 8, 1846. Online by Gerhard Peters and John T. Woolley, *The American Presidency Project*. http://www.presidency.ucsb.edu/ws/?pid=29487.

DOCUMENT 5
JAMES K. POLK. THIRD ANNUAL MESSAGE TO CONGRESS. DECEMBER 7, 1847

Fellow-Citizens of the Senate and of the House of Representatives:

The annual meeting of Congress is always an interesting event. The representatives of the States and of the people come fresh from their constituents to take counsel together for the common good.

After an existence of near three-fourths of a century as a free and independent Republic, the problem no longer remains to be solved whether man is capable of self-government. The success of our admirable system is a conclusive refutation of the theories of those in other countries who maintain that a "favored few" are born to rule and that the mass of mankind must be governed by force. Subject to no arbitrary or hereditary authority, the people are the only sovereigns recognized by our Constitution.

Numerous emigrants, of every lineage and language, attracted by the civil and religious freedom we enjoy and by our happy condition, annually crowd to our shores, and transfer their heart, not less than their allegiance, to the country whose dominion belongs alone to the people. No country has been so much favored, or should acknowledge with deeper reverence the manifestations of the divine protection. An all wise Creator directed and guarded us in our infant struggle for freedom and has constantly watched over our surprising progress until we have become one of the great nations of the earth.

It is in a country thus favored, and under a Government in which the executive and legislative branches hold their authority for limited periods alike from the people, and where all are responsible to their respective constituencies, that it is again my duty to communicate with Congress upon the state of the Union and the present condition of public affairs.

During the past year the most gratifying proofs are presented that our country has been blessed with a widespread and universal prosperity. There has been no period since the Government was founded when all the industrial pursuits of our people have been more successful or when labor in all branches of business has received a fairer or better reward. From our abundance we have been enabled to perform the pleasing duty of furnishing food for the starving millions of less favored countries.

In the enjoyment of the bounties of Providence at home such as have rarely fallen to the lot of any people, it is cause of congratulation that our intercourse with all the powers of the earth except Mexico continues to be of an amicable character.

It has ever been our cherished policy to cultivate peace and good will with all nations, and this policy has been steadily pursued by me. No change has taken place in our relations with Mexico since the adjournment of the last Congress. The war in which the United States were forced to engage with the Government of that country still continues.

I deem it unnecessary, after the full exposition of them contained in my message of the 11th of May, 1846, and in my annual message at the commencement of the session of Congress in December last, to reiterate the serious causes of complaint which we had against Mexico before she commenced hostilities.

It is sufficient on the present occasion to say that the wanton violation of the rights of person and property of our citizens committed by Mexico, her repeated acts of bad faith through a long series of years, and her disregard of solemn treaties stipulating for indemnity to our injured citizens not only constituted ample cause of war on our part, but were of such an aggravated character as would have justified us before the whole world in resorting to this extreme remedy. With an anxious desire to avoid a rupture between the two countries, we forbore for years to assert our clear rights by force, and continued to seek redress for the wrongs we had suffered by amicable negotiation in the hope that Mexico might yield to pacific counsels and the demands of justice. In this hope we were disappointed. Our minister of peace sent to Mexico was insultingly rejected. The Mexican Government refused even to hear the terms of adjustment which he was authorized to propose, and finally, under wholly unjustifiable pretexts, involved the two countries in war by invading the territory of the State of Texas, striking the first blow, and shedding the blood of our citizens on our own soil.

Though the United States were the aggrieved nation, Mexico commenced the war, and we were compelled in self-defense to repel the invader and to vindicate the national honor and interests by prosecuting it with vigor until we could obtain a just and honorable peace. On learning that hostilities had been commenced by Mexico I promptly communicated that fact, accompanied with a succinct statement of our other causes of complaint against Mexico, to Congress, and that body, by the act of the 13th of May, 1846, declared that "by the act of the Republic of Mexico a state of war exists between that Government and the United States." This act declaring "the war to exist by the act of the Republic of Mexico," and making provision for its prosecution "to a speedy and successful termination," was passed with great unanimity by Congress, there being but two negative votes in the Senate and but fourteen in the House of Representatives.

The existence of the war having thus been declared by Congress, it became my duty under the Constitution and the laws to conduct and prosecute it. This duty has been performed, and though at every stage of its progress I have manifested a willingness to terminate it by a just peace, Mexico has refused to accede to any terms which could be accepted by the United States consistently with the national honor and interest.

The rapid and brilliant successes of our arms and the vast extent of the enemy's territory which had been overrun and conquered before the close of the last session of Congress were fully known to that body. Since that time the war has been prosecuted with increased energy, and, I am gratified to state, with a success which commands universal admiration.. History presents no parallel of so many glorious victories achieved by any nation within so short a period. Our Army, regulars and volunteers, have covered themselves with imperishable honors. Whenever and wherever our forces have encountered the enemy, though he was in vastly superior numbers and often intrenched in fortified positions of his own selection and of great strength, he has been defeated. Too much praise can not be bestowed upon our officers and men, regulars and volunteers, for their gallantry, discipline, indomitable courage, and perseverance, all seeking the post of danger and vying with each other in deeds of noble daring.

While every patriot's heart must exult and a just national pride animate every bosom in beholding the high proofs of courage, consummate military skill, steady discipline, and humanity to the vanquished enemy exhibited by our gallant Army, the nation is called to mourn over the loss of many brave officers and soldiers, who have fallen in defense of their country's honor and interests. The brave dead met their melancholy fate in a foreign land, nobly discharging their duty, and with their country's flag waving triumphantly in the face of the foe. Their patriotic deeds are justly appreciated, and will long be remembered by their grateful countrymen. The parental care of the Government they loved and served should be extended to their surviving families.

Shortly after the adjournment of the last session of Congress the gratifying intelligence was received of the signal victory of Buena Vista, and of the fall of the city of Vera Cruz, and with it the strong castle of San Juan de Ulloa, by which it was defended. Believing that after these and other successes so honorable to our arms and so disastrous to Mexico the period was propitious to afford her another opportunity, if she thought proper to embrace it, to enter into negotiations for peace, a commissioner was appointed to proceed to the headquarters of our Army with full powers to enter upon negotiations and to conclude a just and honorable treaty of peace. He was not directed to make any new overtures of peace, but was the bearer of a dispatch from the Secretary of State of the

United States to the minister of foreign affairs of Mexico, in reply to one received from the latter of the 22d of February, 1847, in which the Mexican Government was informed of his appointment and of his presence at the headquarters of our Army, and that he was invested with full powers to conclude a definitive treaty of peace whenever the Mexican Government might signify a desire to do so. While I was unwilling to subject the United States to another indignant refusal, I was yet resolved that the evils of the war should not be protracted a day longer than might be rendered absolutely necessary by the Mexican Government.

Care was taken to give no instructions to the commissioner which could in any way interfere with our military operations or relax our energies in the prosecution of the war. He possessed no authority in any manner to control these operations. He was authorized to exhibit his instructions to the general in command of the Army, and in the event of a treaty being concluded and ratified on the part of Mexico he was directed to give him notice of that fact. On the happening of such contingency, and on receiving notice thereof, the general in command was instructed by the Secretary of War to suspend further active military operations until further orders. These instructions were given with a view to intermit hostilities until the treaty thus ratified by Mexico could be transmitted to Washington and receive the action of the Government of the United States. The commissioner was also directed on reaching the Army to deliver to the general in command the dispatch which he bore from the Secretary of State to the minister of foreign affairs of Mexico, and on receiving it the general was instructed by the Secretary of War to cause it to be transmitted to the commander of the Mexican forces, with a quest that it might be communicated to his Government. The commissioner did not reach the headquarters of the Army until after another brilliant victory had crowned our arms at Cerro Gordo. The dispatch which he bore from the Secretary of War to the general in command of the Army was received by that officer, then at Jalapa, on the 7th of May, 1847, together with the dispatch from the Secretary of State to the minister of foreign affairs of Mexico, having been transmitted to him from Vera Cruz. The commissioner arrived at the headquarters of the Army a few days afterwards. His presence with the Army and his diplomatic character were made known to the Mexican Government from Puebla on the 12th of June, 1847, by the transmission of the dispatch from the Secretary of State to the minister of foreign affairs of Mexico.

Many weeks elapsed after its receipt, and no overtures were made nor was any desire expressed by the Mexican Government to enter into negotiations for peace.

Our Army pursued its march upon the capital, and as it approached it was met by formidable resistance. Our forces first encountered the enemy, and achieved signal victories in the severely contested battles of Contreras and Churubusco. It was not until after these actions had resulted in decisive victories and the capital of the enemy was within our power that the Mexican Government manifested any disposition to enter into negotiations for peace, and even then, as events have proved, there is too much reason to believe they were insincere, and that in agreeing to go through the forms of negotiation the object was to gain time to strengthen the defenses of their capital and to prepare for fresh resistance.

The general in command of the Army deemed it expedient to suspend hostilities temporarily by entering into an armistice with a view to the opening of negotiations. Commissioners were appointed on the part of Mexico to meet the commissioner on the part of the United States. The result of the conferences which took place between these functionaries of the two Governments was a failure to conclude a treaty of peace. The commissioner of the United States took with him the project of a treaty already prepared, by the terms of which the indemnity required by the United States was a cession of territory.

It is well known that the only indemnity which it is in the power of Mexico to make in satisfaction of the just and long-deferred claims of our citizens against her and the only means by which she can reimburse the United States for the expenses of the war is a cession to the United States of a portion of her territory. Mexico has no money to pay, and no other means of making the required indemnity. If we refuse this, we can obtain nothing else. To reject indemnity by refusing to accept a cession of territory would be to abandon all our just demands, and to wage the war, bearing all its expenses, without a purpose or definite object.

A state of war abrogates treaties previously existing between the belligerents and a treaty of peace puts an end to all claims for indemnity for tortious acts committed under the authority of one government against the citizens or subjects of another unless they are provided for in its stipulations. A treaty of peace which would terminate the existing war without providing for indemnity would enable Mexico, the acknowledged debtor and herself the aggressor in the war, to relieve herself from her just liabilities. By such a treaty our citizens who hold just demands against her would have no remedy either against Mexico or their own Government. Our duty to these citizens must forever prevent such a peace, and no treaty which does not provide ample means of discharging these demands can receive my sanction.

A treaty of peace should settle all existing differences between the two countries. If an adequate cession of territory should be made by such a treaty, the United States should release Mexico from all her liabilities and assume their payment to our own citizens. If instead of this the United States were to consent to a treaty by which Mexico should again engage to pay the heavy amount of indebtedness which a just indemnity to our Government and our citizens would impose on her, it is notorious that she does not possess the means to meet such an undertaking. From such a treaty no result could be anticipated but the same irritating disappointments which have heretofore attended the violations of similar treaty stipulations on the part of Mexico. Such a treaty would be but a temporary cessation of hostilities, without the restoration of the friendship and good understanding which should characterize the future intercourse between the two countries.

That Congress contemplated the acquisition of territorial indemnity when that body made provision for the prosecution of the war is obvious. Congress could not have meant when, in May, 1846, they appropriated $10,000,000 and authorized the President to employ the militia and naval and military forces of the United States and to accept the services of 50,000 volunteers to enable him to prosecute the war, and when, at their last session, and after

our Army had invaded Mexico, they made additional appropriations and authorized the raising of additional troops for the same
purpose, that no indemnity was to be obtained from Mexico at
the conclusion of the war; and yet it was certain that if no Mexican territory was acquired no indemnity could be obtained. It is
further manifest that Congress contemplated territorial indemnity
from the fact that at their last session an act was passed, upon the
Executive recommendation, appropriating $3,000,000 with that ex-
press object. This appropriation was made "to enable the President
to conclude a treaty of peace, limits, and boundaries with the Republic of Mexico, to be used by him in the event that said treaty,
when signed by the authorized agents of the two Governments
and duly ratified by Mexico, shall call for the expenditure of the
same or any part thereof." The object of asking this appropriation
was distinctly stated in the several messages on the subject which
I communicated to Congress. Similar appropriations made in 1803
and 1806, which were referred to, were intended to be applied in
part consideration for the cession of Louisiana and the Floridas. In
like manner it was anticipated that in settling the terms of a treaty
of "limits and boundaries" with Mexico a cession of territory estimated to be of greater value than the amount of our demands
against her might be obtained, and that the prompt payment of this
sum in part consideration for the territory ceded, on the conclusion
of a treaty and its ratification on her part, might be an inducement
with her to make such a cession of territory as would be satisfactory to the United States; and although the failure to conclude such a
treaty has rendered it unnecessary to use any part of the $3,000,000
appropriated by that act, and the entire sum remains in the Treasury, it is still applicable to that object should the contingency occur
making such application proper.

The doctrine of no territory is the doctrine of no indemnity, and if sanctioned would be a public acknowledgment that our
country was wrong and that the war declared by Congress with extraordinary unanimity was unjust and should be abandoned—an admission unfounded in fact and degrading to the national character.

The terms of the treaty proposed by the United States were
not only just to Mexico, but, considering the character and amount

of our claims, the unjustifiable and unprovoked commencement of hostilities by her, the expenses of the war to which we have been subjected, and the success which had attended our arms, were deemed to be of a most liberal character.

The commissioner of the United States was authorized to agree to the establishment of the Rio Grande as the boundary from its entrance into the Gulf to its intersection with the southern boundary of New Mexico, in north latitude about 32 degree, and to obtain a cession to the United States of the Provinces of New Mexico and the Californias and the privilege of the right of way across the Isthmus of Tehuantepec. The boundary of the Rio Grande and the cession to the United States of New Mexico and Upper California constituted an ultimatum which our commissioner was under no circumstances to yield.

That it might be manifest, not only to Mexico, but to all other nations, that the United States were not disposed to take advantage of a feeble power by insisting upon wrestling from her all the other Provinces, including many of her principal towns and cities, which we had conquered and held in our military occupation but were willing to conclude a treaty in a spirit of liberality, our commissioner was authorized to stipulate for the restoration to Mexico of all our other conquests.

As the territory to be acquired by the boundary proposed might be estimated to be of greater value than a fair equivalent for our just demands, our commissioner was authorized to stipulate for the payment of such additional pecuniary consideration as was deemed reasonable.

The terms of a treaty proposed by the Mexican commissioners were wholly inadmissible. They negotiated as if Mexico were the victorious, and not the vanquished, party. They must have known that their ultimatum could never be accepted. It required the United States to dismember Texas by surrendering to Mexico that part of the territory of that State lying between the Nueces and the Rio Grande, included within her limits by her laws when she was an independent republic, and when she was annexed to the United States and admitted by Congress as one of the States of our Union. It contained no provision for the payment by Mexico of the just claims of our citizens. It required indemnity to Mexican citizens for injuries they may have sustained by our troops in the prosecution of the war. It demanded the right for Mexico to levy and collect the Mexican tariff of duties on goods imported into her ports while in our military occupation during the war, and the owners of which had paid to officers of the United States the military contributions which had been levied upon them; and it offered to cede to the United States, for a pecuniary consideration, that part of Upper California lying north of latitude 37°. Such were the unreasonable terms proposed by the Mexican commissioners.

The cession to the United States by Mexico of the Provinces of New Mexico and the Californias, as proposed by the commissioner of the United States, it was believed would be more in accordance with the convenience and interests of both nations than any other cession of territory which it was probable Mexico could be induced to make.

It is manifest to all who have observed the actual condition of the Mexican Government for some years past and at present that if these Provinces should be retained by her she could not long continue to hold and govern them. Mexico is too feeble a power to govern these Provinces, lying as they do at a distance of more than 1,000 miles from her capital, and if attempted to be retained by her they would constitute but for a short time even nominally a part of her dominions. This would be especially the case with Upper California.

The sagacity of powerful European nations has long since directed their attention to the commercial importance of that Province, and there can be little doubt that the moment the United States shall relinquish their present occupation of it and their claim to it as indemnity an effort would be made by some foreign power to possess it, either by conquest or by purchase. If no foreign government should acquire it in either of these modes, an independent revolutionary government would probably be established by the inhabitants and such foreigners as may remain in or remove to the country as soon as it shall be known that the United States have abandoned it. Such a government would be too feeble long to maintain its separate independent existence, and would finally become annexed to or be a dependent colony of some more powerful state. Should any foreign government attempt to possess it as a colony, or otherwise to incorporate it with itself, the principle avowed by President Monroe in 1824, and reaffirmed in my first annual message, that no foreign power shall with our consent be permitted to plant or establish any new colony or dominion on any part of the North American continent must be maintained. In maintaining this principle and in resisting its invasion by any foreign power we might be involved in other wars more expensive and more difficult than that in which we are now engaged. The Provinces of New Mexico and the Californias are contiguous to the territories of the United States, and if brought under the government of our laws their resources–mineral, agricultural, manufacturing, and commercial–would soon be developed.

Upper California is bounded on the north by our Oregon possessions, and if held by the United States would soon be settled by a hardy, enterprising, and intelligent portion of our population. The Bay of San Francisco and other harbors along the Californian coast would afford shelter for our Navy, for our numerous whale ships, and other merchant vessels employed in the Pacific Ocean, and would in a short period become the marts of an extensive and profitable commerce with China and other countries of the East.

These advantages, in which the whole commercial world would participate, would at once be secured to the United States by the cession of this territory; while it is certain that as long as it remains a part of the Mexican dominions they can be enjoyed neither by Mexico herself nor by any other nation.

New Mexico is a frontier Province, and has never been of any considerable value to Mexico. From its locality it is naturally connected with our Western settlements. The territorial limits of the State of Texas, too, as defined by her laws before her admission into our Union, embrace all that portion of New Mexico lying east of the Rio Grande, while Mexico still claims to hold this territory as a part of her dominions. The adjustment of this question of boundary is important.

There is another consideration which induced the belief that the Mexican Government might even desire to place this Province under the protection of the Government of the United States. Numerous bands of fierce and warlike savages wander over it and upon its borders. Mexico has been and must continue to be too feeble to restrain them from committing depredations, robberies, and murders, not only upon the inhabitants of New Mexico itself, but upon those of the other northern States of Mexico. It would be a blessing to all these northern States to have their citizens protected against them by the power of the United States. At this moment many Mexicans, principally females and children, are in captivity among them. If New Mexico were held and governed by the United States, we could effectually prevent these tribes from committing such outrages, and compel them to release these captives and restore them to their families and friends.

In proposing to acquire New Mexico and the Californias, it was known that but an inconsiderable portion of the Mexican people would be transferred with them, the country embraced within these Provinces being chiefly an uninhabited region.

These were the leading considerations which induced me to authorize the terms of peace which were proposed to Mexico. They were rejected, and, negotiations being at an end, hostilities were renewed. An assault was made by our gallant Army upon the strongly fortified places near the gates of the City of Mexico and upon the city itself, and after several days of severe conflict the Mexican forces, vastly superior in number to our own, were driven from the city, and it was occupied by our troops.

Immediately after information was received of the unfavorable result of the negotiations, believing that his continued presence with the Army could be productive of no good, I determined to recall our commissioner. A dispatch to this effect was transmitted to him on the 6th of October last. The Mexican Government will be informed of his recall, and that in the existing state of things I shall not deem it proper to make any further overtures of peace, but shall be at all times ready to receive and consider any proposals which may be made by Mexico.

Since the liberal proposition of the United States was authorized to be made, in April last, large expenditures have been incurred and the precious blood of many of our patriotic fellow-citizens has been shed in the prosecution of the war. This consideration and the obstinate perseverance of Mexico in protracting the war must influence the terms of peace which it may be deemed proper hereafter to accept. Our arms having been everywhere victorious, having subjected to our military occupation a large portion of the enemy's country, including his capital, and negotiations for peace having failed, the important questions arise, in what manner the war ought to be prosecuted and what should be our future policy. I can not doubt that we should secure and render available the conquests which we have already made, and that with this view we should hold and occupy by our naval and military forces all the ports, towns, cities, and Provinces now in our occupation or which may hereafter fall into our possession; that we should press forward our military operations and levy such military contributions on the enemy as may, as far as practicable, defray the future expenses of the war.

Had the Government of Mexico acceded to the equitable and liberal terms proposed, that mode of adjustment would have been preferred, Mexico having declined to do this and failed to offer any other terms which could be accepted by the United States, the national honor, no less than the public interests, requires that the war should be prosecuted with increased energy and power until a just and satisfactory peace can be obtained. In the meantime, as Mexico refuses all indemnity, we should adopt measures to indemnify ourselves by appropriating permanently a portion of her territory. Early after the commencement of the war New Mexico and the Californias were taken possession of by our forces. Our military and naval commanders were ordered to conquer and hold them, subject to be disposed of by a treaty of peace.

These Provinces are now in our undisputed occupation, and have been so for many months, all resistance on the part of Mexico having ceased within their limits. I am satisfied that they should never be surrendered to Mexico. Should Congress concur with me in this opinion, and that they should be retained by the United States as indemnity, I can perceive no good reason why the civil jurisdiction and laws of the United States should not at once be extended over them. To wait for a treaty of peace such as we are willing to make, by which our relations toward them would not be changed, can not be good policy; whilst our own interest and that of the people inhabiting them require that a stable, responsible, and free government under our authority should as soon as possible be established over them. Should Congress, therefore, determine to hold these Provinces permanently, and that they shall hereafter be considered as constituent parts of our country, the early establishment of Territorial governments over them will be important for the more perfect protection of persons and property; and I recommend that such Territorial governments be established. It will promote peace and tranquillity among the inhabitants, by allaying all apprehension that they may still entertain of being again subjected to the jurisdiction of Mexico. I invite the early and favorable consideration of Congress to this important subject.

Besides New Mexico and the Californias, there are other Mexican Provinces which have been reduced to our possession by conquest. These other Mexican Provinces are now governed by our military and naval commanders under the general authority which is conferred upon a conqueror by the laws of war. They should continue to be held, as a means of coercing Mexico to accede to just terms of peace. Civil as well as military officers are required to conduct such a government. Adequate compensation, to be drawn from contributions levied on the enemy, should be fixed by law for such officers as may be thus employed. What further provision may become necessary and what final disposition it may be proper to make of them must depend on the future progress of the war and the course which Mexico may think proper hereafter to pursue.

With the views I entertain I can not favor the policy which has been suggested, either to withdraw our Army altogether or to retire to a designated line and simply hold and defend it. To withdraw our Army altogether from the conquests they have made by deeds of unparalleled bravery, and at the expense of so much blood and treasure, in a just war on our part, and one which, by the act of the enemy, we could not honorably have avoided, would be to degrade the nation in its own estimation and in that of the world. To retire to a line and simply hold and defend it would not terminate the war. On the contrary, it would encourage Mexico to persevere and tend to protract it indefinitely. It is not to be expected that Mexico, after refusing to establish such a line as a permanent boundary when our victorious Army are in possession of her capital and in the heart of her country, would permit us to hold it without resistance. That she would continue the war, and in the most harassing and annoying forms, there can be no doubt. A border warfare of the most savage character, extending over a long line, would be unceasingly waged. It would require a large army to be kept constantly in the field, stationed at posts and garrisons along such a line, to protect and defend it. The enemy, relieved from the pressure of our arms on his coasts and in the populous parts of the interior, would direct his attention to this line, and, selecting an isolated post for attack, would concentrate his forces upon it. This would be a condition of affairs which the Mexicans, pursuing their favorite system of guerrilla warfare, would probably prefer to any other. Were we to assume a defensive attitude on such a line, all the advantages of such a state of war would be on the side of the enemy. We could levy no contributions upon him, or in any other way make him feel the pressure of the war, but must remain inactive and await his approach, being in constant uncertainty at what point on the line or at what time he might make an assault. He may assemble and organize an overwhelming force in the interior on his own side of the line, and, concealing his purpose, make a sudden assault upon some one of our posts so distant from any other as to prevent the possibility of timely succor or reenforcements, and in this way our gallant Army would be exposed to the danger of being cut off in detail; or if by their unequaled bravery and prowess everywhere exhibited during this war they should repulse the enemy, their numbers stationed at any one post may be too small to pursue him. If the enemy be repulsed in one attack, he would have nothing to do but to retreat to his own side of the line, and, being in no fear of a pursuing army, may reenforce himself at leisure for another attack on the same or some other post. He may, too, cross the line between our posts, make rapid incursions into the country which we hold, murder the inhabitants, commit depredations on them, and then retreat to the interior before a sufficient force can be concentrated to pursue him. Such would probably be the harassing character of

a mere defensive war on our part. If our forces when attacked, or
threatened with attack, be permitted to cross the line, drive back
the enemy, and conquer him, this would be again to invade the enemy's country after having lost all the advantages of the conquests
we have already made by having voluntarily abandoned them. To
hold such a line successfully and in security it is far from being certain that it would not require as large an army as would be necessary
to hold all the conquests we have already made and to continue the
prosecution of the war in the heart of the enemy's country. It is
also far from being certain that the expenses of the war would be
diminished by such a policy. I am persuaded that the best means of
vindicating the national honor and interest and of bringing the war
to an honorable close will be to prosecute it with increased energy
and power in the vital parts of the enemy's country.

In my annual message to Congress of December last I declared that– The war has not been waged with a view to conquest,
but, having been commenced by Mexico, it has been carried into
the enemy's country and will be vigorously prosecuted there with
a view to obtain an honorable peace, and thereby secure ample indemnity for the expenses of the war, as well as to our much-injured
citizens, who hold large pecuniary demands against Mexico.

Such, in my judgment, continues to be our true policy; indeed,
the only policy which will probably secure a permanent peace.

It has never been contemplated by me, as an object of the war,
to make a permanent conquest of the Republic of Mexico or to
annihilate her separate existence as an independent nation. On the
contrary, it has ever been my desire that she should maintain her
nationality, and under a good government adapted to her condition be a free, independent, and prosperous Republic. The United
States were the first among the nations to recognize her independence, and have always desired to be on terms of amity and good
neighborhood with her. This she would not suffer. By her own
conduct we have been compelled to engage in the present war. In
its prosecution we seek not her overthrow as a nation, but in vindicating our national honor we seek to obtain redress for the wrongs
she has done us and indemnity for our just demands against her.
We demand an honorable peace, and that peace must bring with it

indemnity for the past and security for the future. Hitherto Mexico has refused all accommodation by which such a peace could be obtained.

Whilst our armies have advanced from victory to victory from the commencement of the war, it has always been with the olive branch of peace in their hands, and it has been in the power of Mexico at every step to arrest hostilities by accepting it.

One great obstacle to the attainment of peace has undoubtedly arisen from the fact that Mexico has been so long held in subjection by one faction or military usurper after another, and such has been the condition of insecurity in which their successive governments have been placed that each has been deterred from making peace lest for this very cause a rival faction might expel it from power. Such was the fate of President Herrera's administration in 1845 for being disposed even to listen to the overtures of the United States to prevent the war, as is fully confirmed by an official correspondence which took place in the month of August last between him and his Government, a copy of which is herewith communicated. "For this cause alone the revolution which displaced him from power was set on foot" by General Paredes. Such may be the condition of insecurity of the present Government.

There can be no doubt that the peaceable and well-disposed inhabitants of Mexico are convinced that it is the true interest of their country to conclude an honorable peace with the United States, but the apprehension of becoming the victims of some military faction or usurper may have prevented them from manifesting their feelings by any public act. The removal of any such apprehension would probably cause them to speak their sentiments freely and to adopt the measures necessary for the restoration of peace. With a people distracted and divided by contending factions and a Government subject to constant changes by successive revolutions, the continued successes of our arms may fail to secure a satisfactory peace. In such event it may become proper for our commanding generals in the field to give encouragement and assurances of protection to the friends of peace in Mexico in the establishment and maintenance of a free republican government of their own choice, able and willing to conclude a peace which would be just to them and secure to us the indemnity we demand. This may become the only mode of obtaining such a peace. Should such be the result, the war which Mexico has forced upon us would thus be converted into an enduring blessing to herself. After finding her torn and distracted by factions, and ruled by military usurpers, we should then leave her with a republican government in the enjoyment of real independence and domestic peace and prosperity, performing all her relative duties in the great family of nations and promoting her own happiness by wise laws and their faithful execution.

If, after affording this encouragement and protection, and after all the persevering and sincere efforts we have made from the moment Mexico commenced the war, and prior to that time, to adjust our differences with her, we shall ultimately fail, then we shall have exhausted all honorable means in pursuit of peace, and must continue to occupy her country with our troops, taking the full measure of indemnity into our own hands, and must enforce the terms which our honor demands.

To act otherwise in the existing state of things in Mexico, and to withdraw our Army without a peace, would not only leave all the wrongs of which we complain unredressed, but would be the signal for new and fierce civil dissensions and new revolutions–all alike hostile to peaceful relations with the United States. Besides, there is danger, if our troops were withdrawn before a peace was conducted, that the Mexican people, wearied with successive revolutions and deprived of protection for their persons and property, might at length be inclined to yield to foreign influences and to cast themselves into the arms of some European monarch for protection from the anarchy and suffering which would ensue. This, for our own safety and in pursuance of our established policy, we should be compelled to resist. We could never consent that Mexico should be thus converted into a monarchy governed by a foreign prince.

Mexico is our near neighbor, and her boundaries are coterminous with our own through the whole extent across the North American continent, from ocean to ocean. Both politically and commercially we have the deepest interest in her regeneration and prosperity. Indeed, it is impossible that, with any just regard to our own safety, we can ever become indifferent to her fate.

It may be that the Mexican Government and people have misconstrued or misunderstood our forbearance and our objects in desiring to conclude an amicable adjustment of the existing differences between the two countries. They may have supposed that we would submit to terms degrading to the nation, or they may have drawn false inferences from the supposed division of opinion in the United States on the subject of the war, and may have calculated to gain much by protracting it, and, indeed, that we might ultimately abandon it altogether without insisting on any indemnity, territorial or otherwise. Whatever may be the false impressions under which they have acted, the adoption and prosecution of the energetic policy proposed must soon undeceive them.

In the future prosecution of the war the enemy must be made to feel its pressure more than they have heretofore done. At its commencement it was deemed proper to conduct it in a spirit of forbearance and liberality. With this end in view, early measures were adopted to conciliate, as far as a state of war would permit, the mass of the Mexican population; to convince them that the war was waged, not against the peaceful inhabitants of Mexico, but against their faithless Government, which had commenced hostilities; to remove from their minds the false impressions which their designing and interested rulers had artfully attempted to make, that the war on our part was one of conquest, that it was a war against their religion and their churches, which were to be desecrated and overthrown, and that their rights of person and private property would be violated. To remove these false impressions, our commanders in the field were directed scrupulously to respect their religion, their churches, and their church property, which were in no manner to be violated; they were directed also to respect the rights of persons and property of all who should not take up arms against us.

Assurances to this effect were given to the Mexican people by Major General Taylor in a proclamation issued in pursuance of instructions from the Secretary of War in the month of June, 1846, and again by Major-General Scott, who acted upon his own convictions of the propriety of issuing it, in a proclamation of the 11th of May, 1847. In this spirit of liberality and conciliation, and with a view to prevent the body of the Mexican population from taking up arms against us, was the war conducted on our part. Provisions and other supplies furnished to our Army by Mexican citizens were paid for at fair and liberal prices, agreed upon by the parties. After the lapse of a few months it became apparent that these assurances and this mild treatment had failed to produce the desired effect upon the Mexican population. While the war had been conducted on our part according to the most humane and liberal principles observed by civilized nations, it was waged in a far different spirit on the part of Mexico. Not appreciating our forbearance, the Mexican people generally became hostile to the United States, and availed themselves of every opportunity to commit the most savage excesses upon our troops. Large numbers of the population took up arms, and, engaging in guerrilla warfare, robbed and murdered in the most cruel manner individual soldiers or small parties whom accident or other causes had separated from the main body of our Army; bands of guerrilleros and robbers infested the roads, harassed our trains, and whenever it was in their power cut off our supplies.

The Mexicans having thus shown themselves to be wholly incapable of appreciating our forbearance and liberality, it was deemed proper to change the manner of conducting the war, by making them feel its pressure according to the usages observed under similar circumstances by all other civilized nations.

Accordingly, as early as the 22d of September, 1846, instructions were given by the Secretary of War to Major-General Taylor to "draw supplies" for our Army "from the enemy without paying for them, and to require contributions for its support, if in that way he was satisfied he could get abundant supplies for his forces." In directing the execution of these instructions much was necessarily left to the discretion of the commanding officer, who was best acquainted with the circumstances by which he was surrounded, the wants of the Army, and the practicability of enforcing the measure. General Taylor, on the 26th of October, 1846, replied from Monterey that "it would have been impossible hitherto, and is so now, to sustain the Army to any extent by forced contributions of money or supplies." For the reasons assigned by him, he did not adopt the policy of his instructions, but declared his readiness to do so "should the Army in its future operations reach a portion of the country which may be made to supply the troops with advantage." He continued to pay for the articles of supply which were drawn from the enemy's country.

Similar instructions were issued to Major-General Scott on the 3d of April, 1847, who replied from Jalapa on the 20th of May, 1847, that if it be expected "that the Army is to support itself by forced contributions levied upon the country we may ruin and exasperate the inhabitants and starve ourselves." The same discretion was given to him that had been to General Taylor in this respect. General Scott, for the reasons assigned by him, also continued to pay for the articles of supply for the Army which were drawn from the enemy.

After the Army had reached the heart of the most wealthy portion of Mexico it was supposed that the obstacles which had before that time prevented it would not be such as to render impracticable the levy of forced contributions for its support, and on the 1st of September and again on the 6th of October, 1847, the order was repeated in dispatches addressed by the Secretary of War to General Scott, and his attention was again called to the importance of making the enemy bear the burdens of the war by requiring them to furnish the means of supporting our Army, and he was directed to adopt this policy unless by doing so there was danger of depriving the Army of the necessary supplies. Copies of these dispatches were forwarded to General Taylor for his government.

On the 31st of March last I caused an order to be issued to our military and naval commanders to levy and collect a military contribution upon all vessels and merchandise which might enter any of the ports of Mexico in our military occupation, and to apply such contributions toward defraying the expenses of the war. By virtue of the right of conquest and the laws of war, the conqueror, consulting his own safety or convenience, may either exclude foreign commerce altogether from all such ports or permit it upon such terms and conditions as he may prescribe. Before the principal ports of Mexico were blockaded by our Navy the revenue derived from import duties under the laws of Mexico was paid into the Mexican treasury. After these ports had fallen into our military possession the blockade was raised and commerce with them permitted upon prescribed terms and conditions. They were opened to the trade of all nations upon the payment of duties more moderate in their amount than those which had been previously levied by Mexico, and the revenue, which was formerly paid into the Mexican treasury, was directed to be collected by our military and naval officers and applied to the use of our Army and Navy. Care was taken that the officers, soldiers, and sailors of our Army and Navy should be exempted from the operations of the order, and, as the merchandise imported upon which the order operated must be consumed by Mexican citizens, the contributions exacted were in effect the seizure of the public revenues of Mexico and the application of them to our own use. In directing this measure the object was to compel the enemy to contribute as far as practicable toward the expenses of the war.

For the amount of contributions which have been levied in this form I refer you to the accompanying reports of the Secretary of War and of the Secretary of the Navy, by which it appears that a sum exceeding half a million of dollars has been collected. This amount would undoubtedly have been much larger but for the difficulty of keeping open communications between the coast and the interior, so as to enable the owners of the merchandise imported to transport and vend it to the inhabitants of the country. It is confidently expected that this difficulty will to a great extent be soon removed by our increased forces which have been sent to the field.

Measures have recently been adopted by which the internal as well as the external revenues of Mexico in all places in our military occupation will be seized and appropriated to the use of our Army and Navy.

The policy of levying upon the enemy contributions in every form consistently with the laws of nations, which it may be practicable for our military commanders to adopt, should, in my judgment, be rigidly enforced, and orders to this effect have accordingly been given. By such a policy, at the same time that our own Treasury will be relieved from a heavy drain, the Mexican people will be made to feel the burdens of the war, and, consulting their own interests, may be induced the more readily to require their rulers to accede to a just peace.

After the adjournment of the last session of Congress events transpired in the prosecution of the war which in my judgment required a greater number of troops in the field than had been anticipated. The strength of the Army was accordingly increased by "accepting" the services of all the volunteer forces authorized by the act of the 13th of May, 1846, without putting a construction on that act the correctness of which was seriously questioned. The volunteer forces now in the field, with those which had been "accepted" to "serve for twelve months" and were discharged at the end of their term of service, exhaust the 50,000 men authorized by that act. Had it been clear that a proper construction of the act warranted it, the services of an additional number would have been called for and accepted; but doubts existing upon this point, the power was not exercised. It is deemed important that Congress should at an early period of their session confer the authority to raise an additional regular force to serve during the war with Mexico and to be discharged upon the conclusion and ratification of a treaty of peace. I invite the attention of Congress to the views presented by the Secretary of War in his report upon this subject.

I recommend also that authority be given by law to call for and accept the services of an additional number of volunteers, to be exercised at such time and to such extent as the emergencies of the service may require. [Here follows commentaries on neutral nations, budget reports, and other matters on federal revenues and expenditures.]

Invoking the blessing of the Almighty Ruler of the Universe upon your deliberations, it will be my highest duty, no less than my sincere pleasure, to cooperate with you in all measures which may tend to promote the honor and enduring welfare of our common country.

JAMES K. POLK

Citation: James K. Polk: "Third Annual Message," December 7, 1847. Online by Gerhard Peters and John T. Woolley, *The American Presidency Project*. http://www.presidency.ucsb.edu/ws/?pid=29488.

DOCUMENT 6
RESOLUTIONS IN THE UNITED STATES
HOUSE OF REPRESENTATIVES

Introduced by Abraham Lincoln, Representative from Illinois.

DECEMBER 22, 1847

1. Whereas, The President of the United States, in his message of May 11, 1846, has declared that "the Mexican Government not only refused to receive him [the envoy of the United States], or to listen to his propositions, but, after a long-continued series of menaces, has at last invaded our territory and shed the blood of our fellow-citizens on our own soil";
2. And again, in his message of December 8, 1846, that "we had ample cause of war against Mexico long before the breaking out of hostilities; but even then we forbore to take redress into our own hands until Mexico herself became the aggressor, by invading our soil in hostile array, and shedding the blood of our citizens";
3. And yet again, in his message of December 7, 1847, that "the Mexican Government refused even to hear the terms of adjustment which he [our minister of peace] was authorized to propose, and finally, under wholly unjustifiable pretexts, involved the two countries in war, by invading the territory of the State of Texas, striking the first blow, and shedding the blood of our citizens on our own soil";

4. And whereas, This House is desirous to obtain a full knowl-
    edge of all the facts which go to establish whether the particu-
    lar spot on which the blood of our citizens was so shed was or
    was not at that time our own soil: therefore,

5. Resolved, By the House of Representatives, that the President
    of the United States be respectfully requested to inform this
    House:

6. First. Whether the spot on which the blood of our citizens
    was shed, as in his message declared, was or was not within
    the territory of Spain, at least after the treaty of 1819, until the
    Mexican revolution.

7. Second. Whether that spot is or is not within the territory
    which was wrested from Spain by the revolutionary govern-
    ment of Mexico.

8. Third. Whether that spot is or is not within a settlement of
    people, which settlement has existed ever since long before the
    Texas revolution, and until its inhabitants fled before the ap-
    proach of the United States army.

9. Fourth. Whether that settlement is or is not isolated from any
    and all other settlements by the Gulf and the Rio Grande on
    the south and west, and by wide uninhabited regions on the
    north and east.

10. Fifth. Whether the people of that settlement, or a majority of
    them, or any of them, have ever submitted themselves to the
    government or laws of Texas or of the United States, by con-
    sent or by compulsion, either by accepting office, or voting at
    elections, or paying tax, or serving on juries, or having process
    served upon them, or in any other way.

11. Sixth. Whether the people of that settlement did or did not flee
    from the approach of the United States army, leaving unpro-
    tected their homes and their growing crops, before the blood
    was shed, as in the message stated; and whether the first blood,
    so shed, was or was not shed within the enclosure of one of
    the people who had thus fled from it.

12. Seventh. Whether our citizens, whose blood was shed, as in his
    message declared, were or were not, at that time, armed offi-

cers and soldiers, sent into that settlement by the military order of the President, through the Secretary of War.

13. Eighth. Whether the military force of the United States was or was not so sent into that settlement after General Taylor had more than once intimated to the War Department that, in his opinion, no such movement was necessary to the defense or protection of Texas.

Congressional Globe, 30th Cong. 1st Sess. 64 (1847).
https://www.loc.gov/law/help/usconlaw/pdf/Mexican.war.pdf

NOTE: *On January 3, 1848, in the course of a debate on a bill to honor Gen. Zachary Taylor and thank him for his services during the Mexican War, Rep. George Ashmun (Whig, Mass.) proposed an amendment stating that the war had been "unnecessarily and unconstitutionally begin by the president of the United States." It was approved 85-81 with Lincoln voting in favor. It was subsequently known as the "Ashmun Amendment" and is referred to as such by Lincoln in documents which follow.*

DOCUMENT 7
THE WAR WITH MEXICO: SPEECH IN THE UNITED STATES HOUSE OF REPRESENTATIVES

Abraham Lincoln January 12, 1848

Mr. Chairman:

Some, if not all the gentlemen on, the other side of the House, who have addressed the committee within the last two days, have spoken rather complainingly, if I have rightly understood them, of the vote given a week or ten days ago, declaring that the war with Mexico was unnecessarily and unconstitutionally commenced by the President [James K Polk]. I admit that such a vote should not be given, in mere party wantonness, and that the one given, is justly censurable, if it have no other, or better foundation. I am one of those who joined in that vote; and I did so under my best impression of the truth of the case. How I got this impression, and how it may possibly be removed, I will now try to show. When the war began, it was my opinion that all those who, because of knowing too little, or because of knowing too much, could not conscientiously approve the conduct of the President, in the beginning of it, should, nevertheless, as good citizens and patriots, remain silent on that point, at least till the war should be ended. Some leading democrats, including Ex President Van Buren, have taken this same view, as I understand them; and I adhered to it, and acted upon it, until since I took my seat here; and I think I should still adhere to it, were it not that the President and his friends will not allow it to be so. Besides the continual effort of the President to argue every silent vote given for supplies, into an endorsement of the justice and wisdom of his conduct–besides that singularly candid paragraph, in his late message in which he tells us that Congress, with great unanimity, only two in the Senate and fourteen in the House dissenting, had declared that, "by the act of the Republic of Mexico, a state of war exists between that Government and the United States," when the same journals that informed him of this, also informed him, that when that declaration stood disconnected from the question of supplies, sixty-seven in the House, and not fourteen merely, voted against it–besides this open attempt to prove, by telling the truth, what he could not prove by telling the whole truth–demanding of all who will not submit to be misrepresented, in justice to themselves, to speak out–besides all this, one of my colleagues (Mr. Richardson) at a very early day in the session brought in a set of resolutions, expressly endorsing the original justice of the war on the part of the President. Upon these resolutions, when they shall be put on their passage I shall be compelled to vote; so that I can not be silent, if I would. Seeing this, I went about preparing myself to give the vote understandingly when it should come. I carefully examined the President's messages, to ascertain what he himself had said and proved upon the point. The result of this examination was to make the impression, that taking for true, all the President states as facts, he falls far short of proving his justification; and that the President would have gone farther with his proof, if it had not been for the small matter, that the truth would not permit him. Under the impression thus made, I gave the vote before mentioned. I propose now to give, concisely, the process of the examination I made, and how I reached the conclusion I did. The President, in his first war message of May 1846, declares that the soil was ours on which hostilities were commenced by Mexico; and he repeats that declaration, almost in the same language, in each successive annual message, thus showing that he esteems that point, a highly essential one. In the importance of that point, I entirely agree with the President. To my judgment, it is the very point, upon which he should be justified, or condemned. In his message of Dec. 1846, it seems to have occurred to him, as is certainly true, that title–ownership–to

soil, or anything else, is not a simple fact; but is a conclusion following one or more simple facts; and that it was incumbent upon him,
to present the facts, from which he concluded, the soil was ours, on
which the first blood of the war was shed.

Accordingly a little below the middle of page twelve in the
message last referred to, he enters upon that task; forming an issue,
and introducing testimony, extending the whole, to a little below
the middle of page fourteen. Now I propose to try to show, that
the whole of this,–issue and evidence–is, from beginning to end,
the sheerest deception. The issue, as he presents it, is in these words
"But there are those who, conceding all this. to be true, assume the
ground that the true western boundary of Texas is the Nueces,
instead of the Rio Grande; and that, therefore, in marching our
army to the east bank of the latter river, we passed the Texan line,
and invaded the territory of Mexico." Now this issue is made up
of two affirmatives and no negative. The main deception of it is,
that it assumes as true, that one river or the other is necessarily
the boundary; and cheats the superficial thinker entirely out of the
idea, that possibly the boundary is somewhere between the two,
and not actually at either. A further deception is that it will let in evidence, which a true issue would exclude. A true issue, made by the
President, would be about as follows "I say, the soil was ours, on
which the first blood was shed; there are those who say it was not."

I now proceed to examine the Presidents evidence, as applicable to such an issue. When that evidence is analyzed, it is all included in the following propositions:

1. That the Rio Grande was the Western boundary of Louisiana
    as we purchased it of France in 1803.
2. That the Republic of Texas always claimed the Rio Grande, as
    her Western boundary.
3. That by various acts, she had claimed it on paper.
4. That Santa Anna, in his treaty with Texas, recognized the Rio
    Grande, as her boundary.
5. That Texas before, and the U. S. after, annexation had exercised
    jurisdiction beyond the Nueces–between the two rivers.

6.   That our Congress, understood the boundary of Texas to extend beyond the Nueces.

Now for each of these in its turn.

His first item is, that the Rio Grande was the Western boundary
of Louisiana, as we purchased it of France in 1803; and seeming to
expect this to be disputed, he argues over the amount of nearly a
page, to prove it true; at the end of which he lets us know, that by
the treaty of 1819, we sold to Spain the whole country from the Rio
Grande eastward, to the Sabine. Now, admitting for the present,
that the Rio Grande, was the boundary of Louisiana, what, under
heaven, had that to do with the present boundary between us and
Mexico? How, Mr. Chairman, the line, that once divided your land
from mine, can still be the boundary between us, after I have sold
my land to you, is, to me, beyond all comprehension. And how any
man, with an honest purpose only, of proving the truth, could ever
have thought of introducing such a fact to prove such an issue, is
equally incomprehensible. His next piece of evidence is that "The
Republic of Texas always claimed this river (Rio Grande) as her
western boundary[.]" That is not true, in fact. Texas has claimed
it, but she has not always claimed it. There is, at least, one distinguished exception. Her state constitution,–the republic's most solemn, and well considered act–that which may, without impropriety,
be called her last will and testament revoking all others–makes no
such claim. But suppose she had always claimed it. Has not Mexico always claimed the contrary? so that there is but claim against
claim, leaving nothing proved, until we get back of the claims, and
find which has the better foundation. Though not in the order in
which the President presents his evidence, I now consider that class
of his statements, which are, in substance, nothing more than that
Texas has, by various acts of her convention and congress, claimed
the Rio Grande, as her boundary, on paper. I mean here what he
says about the fixing of the Rio Grande as her boundary in her old
constitution (not her state constitution) about forming congressional districts, counties &c &c. Now all of this is but naked claim;
and what I have already said about claims is strictly applicable to
this. If I should claim your land, by word of mouth, that certainly

would not make it mine; and if I were to claim it by a deed which I had made myself, and with which, you had had nothing to do, the claim would be quite the same, in substance–or rather, in utter nothingness. I next consider the President's statement that Santa Anna in his treaty with Texas, recognized the Rio Grande, as the western boundary of Texas. Besides the position, so often taken that Santa Anna, while a prisoner of war–a captive–could not bind Mexico by a treaty, which I deem conclusive–besides this, I wish to say something in relation to this treaty, so called by the President, with Santa Anna. If any man would like to be amused by a sight of that little thing, which the President calls by that big name, he can have it, by turning to Niles' Register volume 50, page 336. And if anyone should suppose that Niles' Register is a curious repository of so mighty a document, as a solemn treaty between nations, I can only say that I learned, to a tolerable degree [of] certainty, by enquiry at the State Department, that the President himself, never saw it anywhere else. By the way, I believe I should not err, if I were to declare, that during the first ten years of the existence of that document, it was never, by any body, called a treaty–that it was never so called, till the President, in his extremity, attempted, by so calling it, to wring something from it in justification of himself in connection with the Mexican war. It has none of the distinguishing features of a treaty. It does not call itself a treaty. Santa Anna does not therein, assume to bind Mexico; he assumes only to act as the President-Commander-in-chief of the Mexican Army and Navy; stipulates that the then present hostilities should cease, and that he would not himself take up arms, nor influence the Mexican people to take up arms, against Texas during the existence of the war of independence [.] He did not recognize the independence of Texas; he did not assume to put an end to the war; but clearly indicated his expectation of its continuance; he did not say one word about boundary, and, most probably, never thought of it. It is stipulated therein that the Mexican forces should evacuate the territory of Texas, passing to the other side of the Rio Grande; and in another article, it is stipulated that, to prevent collisions between the armies, the Texan army should not approach nearer than within five leagues–of what is not said–but clearly, from the object stated it is—of the Rio Grande. Now, if this is a treaty, recognizing the Rio Grande, as the boundary of Texas, it contains the singular feature, of stipulating, that Texas shall not go within five leagues of her own boundary.

Next comes the evidence of Texas before annexation, and the United States, afterwards, exercising jurisdiction beyond the Nueces, and between the two rivers. This actual exercise of jurisdiction, is the very class or quality of evidence we want. It is excellent so far as it goes; but does it go far enough? He tells us it went beyond the Nueces; but he does not tell us it went to the Rio Grande. He tells us, jurisdiction was exercised between the two rivers, but he does not tell us it was exercised over all the territory between them. Some simple minded people, think it is possible, to cross one river and go beyond it without going all the way to the next—that jurisdiction may be exercised between two rivers without covering all the country between them. I know a man, not very unlike myself, who exercises jurisdiction over a piece of land between the Wabash and the Mississippi; and yet so far is this from being all there is between those rivers, that it is just one hundred and fifty two feet long by fifty wide, and no part of it much within a hundred miles of either. He has a neighbor between him and the Mississippi,—that is, just across the street, in that direction—whom, I am sure, he could neither persuade nor force to give up his habitation; but which nevertheless, he could certainly annex, if it were to be done, by merely standing on his own side of the street and claiming it, or even, sitting down, and writing a deed for it.

But next the President tells us, the Congress of the United States understood the state of Texas they admitted into the union, to extend beyond the Nueces. Well, I suppose they did. I certainly so understood it. But how far beyond? That Congress did not understand it to extend clear to the Rio Grande, is quite certain by the fact of their joint resolutions, for admission, expressly leaving all questions of boundary to future adjustment. And it may be added, that Texas herself, is proved to have had the same understanding of it, that our Congress had, by the fact of the exact conformity of her new constitution, to those resolutions.

I am now through the whole of the President's evidence; and it is a singular fact, that if anyone should declare the President sent the army into the midst of a settlement of Mexican people, who had never submitted, by consent or by force, to the authority of Texas or of the United States, and that there, and thereby, the first blood of the war was shed, there is not one word in all the President has said, which would either admit or deny the declaration. This strange omission, it does seem to me, could not have occurred but by design. My way of living leads me to be about the courts of justice; and there, I have sometimes seen a good lawyer, struggling for his client's neck, in a desperate case, employing every artifice to work round, befog, and cover up, with many words, some point arising in the case, which he dared not admit, and yet could not deny. Party bias may help to make it appear so; but with all the allowance I can make for such bias, it still does appear to me, that just such, and from just such necessity, is the President's struggle in this case.

Some time after my colleague (Mr. Richardson) introduced the resolutions I have mentioned, I introduced a preamble, resolution, and interrogatories intended to draw the President out, if possible, on this hitherto untrodden ground. To show their relevancy, I propose to state my understanding of the true rule for ascertaining the boundary between Texas and Mexico. It is, that wherever Texas was exercising jurisdiction, was hers; and wherever Mexico was exercising jurisdiction, was hers; and that whatever separated the actual exercise of jurisdiction of the one, from that of the other, was the true boundary between them. If, as is probably true, Texas was exercising jurisdiction along the western bank of the Nueces, and Mexico was exercising it along the eastern bank of the Rio Grande, then neither river was the boundary; but the uninhabited country between the two, was. The extent of our territory in that region depended, not on any treaty-fixed boundary (for no treaty had attempted it) but on revolution Any people anywhere, being inclined and having the power, have the right to rise up, and shake off the existing government, and form a new one that suits them better. This is a most valuable,– most sacred right–a right, which we hope and believe, is to liberate the world. Nor is this right confined to cases in which the whole people of an existing government, may choose to exercise it. Any portion of such people that can, may revolutionize, and make their own, of so much of the territory as they inhabit. More than this, a majority of any portion of such people may revolutionize, putting down a minority, intermingled with, or near about them, who may oppose their movement. Such minority, was precisely the case, of the Tories of our own revolution. It is a quality of revolutions not to go by old lines, or old laws; but to break up both, and make new ones. As to the country now in question, we bought it of France in 1803, and sold it to Spain in 1819, according to the President's statements. After this, all Mexico, including Texas, revolutionized against Spain; and still later, Texas revolutionized against Mexico. In my view, just so far as she carried her revolution, by obtaining the actual, willing or unwilling, submission of the people, so far, the country was hers, and no farther. Now sir, for the purpose of obtaining the very best evidence, as to whether Texas had actually carried her revolution, to the place where the hostilities of the present war commenced, let the President answer the interrogatories, I proposed, as before mentioned, or some other similar ones. Let him answer, fully, fairly, and candidly. Let him answer with facts, and not with arguments. Let him remember he sits where Washington sat, and so remembering, let him answer, as Washington would answer. As a nation should not, and the Almighty will not, be evaded, so let him attempt no envasion—no equivocation. And if, so answering, he can show that the soil was ours, where the first blood of the war was shed—that it was not within an inhabited country, or, if within such, that the inhabitants had submitted themselves to the civil authority of Texas, or of the United States, and that the same is true of the site of Fort Brown, then I am with him for his justification. In that case I, shall be most happy to reverse the vote I gave the other day. I have a selfish motive for desiring that the President may do this. I expect to give some votes, in connection with the war, which, without his so doing, will be of doubtful propriety in my own judgment, but which will be free from the doubt if he does so. But if he cannot, or will not do this—if on any pretence, or no pretence, he shall refuse or omit it, then I shall be fully convinced, of what I more than

suspect already, that he is deeply conscious of being in the wrong
that he feels the blood of this war, like the blood of Abel, is crying
to Heaven against him. That originally having some strong motive—
what, I will not stop now to give my opinion concerning—to involve
the two countries in a war, and trusting to escape scrutiny, by fixing
the public gaze upon the exceeding brightness of military glory—
that attractive rainbow, that rises in showers of blood—that ser-
pent's eye, that charms to destroy he plunged into it, and has swept,
on and on, till, disappointed in his calculation of the ease with
which Mexico might be subdued, he now finds himself, he knows
not where. How like the half insane mumbling of a fever-dream, is
the whole war part of his late message! At one time telling us that
Mexico has nothing whatever, that we can get, but territory; at another, showing us how we can support the war, by levying contributions on Mexico. At one time, urging the national honor, the security of the future, the prevention of foreign interference, and
even, the good of Mexico herself, as among the objects of the war;
at another, telling us, that "to reject indemnity, by refusing to accept
a cession of territory, would be to abandon all our just demands,
and to wage the war, bearing all it's expenses, without a purpose or
definite object[.]" So then, the national honor, security of the future, and everything but territorial indemnity, may be considered
the no-purposes, and indefinite, objects of the war! But, having it
now settled that territorial indemnity is the only object, we are
urged to seize, by legislation here, all that he was content to take, a
few months ago, and the whole province of lower California to
boot, and to still carry on the war—to take all we are fighting for,
and still fight on. Again, the President is resolved, under all circumstances, to have full territorial indemnity for the expenses of the
war; but he forgets to tell us how we are to get the excess, after
those expenses shall have surpassed the value of the whole of the
Mexican territory. So again, he insists that the separate national
existence of Mexico, shall be maintained; but he does not tell us
how this can be done, after we shall have taken all her territory. Lest
the questions, I here suggest, be considered speculative merely, let
me be indulged a moment in trying [to] show they are not. The war
has gone on some twenty months; for the expenses of which, to-

gether with an inconsiderable old score, the President now claims about one half of the Mexican territory; and that, by far the better half, so far as concerns our ability to make anything out of it. It is comparatively uninhabited; so that we could establish land offices in it, and raise some money in that way. But the other half is already inhabited, as I understand it, tolerably densely for the nature of the country; and all its lands, or all that are valuable, already appropriated as private property. How then are we to make anything out of these lands with this encumbrance on them? or how, remove the encumbrance? I suppose no one will say we should kill the people, or drive them out, or make slaves of them, or even confiscate their property. How then can we make much out of this part of the territory? If the prosecution of the war has, in expenses, already equaled the better half of the country, how long it's future prosecution, will be in equaling, the less valuable half, is not a speculative, but a practical question, pressing closely upon us. And yet it is a question which the President seems to never have thought of. As to the mode of terminating the war, and securing peace, the President is equally wandering and indefinite. First, it is to be done by a more vigorous prosecution of the war in the vital parts of the enemies country; and, after apparently, talking himself tired, on this point, the President drops down into a half despairing tone, and tells us that "with a people distracted and divided by contending factions, and a government subject to constant changes, by successive revolutions, the continued success of our arms may fail to secure a satisfactory peace[.]" Then he suggests the propriety of wheedling the Mexican people to desert the counsels of their own leaders, and trusting in our protection, to set up a government from which we can secure a satisfactory peace; telling us, that "this may become the only mode of obtaining such a peace." But soon he falls into doubt of this too; and then drops back on to the already half abandoned ground of "more vigorous prosecution.["] All this shows that the President is, in no wise, satisfied with his own positions. First he takes up one, and in attempting to argue us into it, he argues himself out of it; then seizes another, and goes through the same process; and then, confused at being able to think of nothing new, he snatches up the old one again, which he has some time before cast off. His mind, tasked beyond its power, is running hither and thither, like some tortured creature, on a burning surface, finding no position, on which it can settle down, and be at ease.

Again, it is a singular omission in this message, that it, nowhere intimates when the President expects the war to terminate. At its beginning, Genl. Scott was, by this same President, driven into disfavor, if not disgrace, for intimating that peace could not be conquered in less than three or four months. But now, at the end of about twenty months, during which time our arms have given us the most splendid successes—every department, and every part, land and water, officers and privates, regulars and volunteers, doing all that men could do, and hundreds of things which it had ever before been thought men could not do,—after all this, this same President gives us a long message, without showing us, that, as to the end, he himself, has, even an imaginary conception. As I have before said, he knows not where he is. He is a bewildered, confounded, and miserably perplexed man. God grant he may be able to show, there is not something about his conscious, more painful than all his mental perplexity!

Roy P. Basler, Ed. *The Collected Works of Abraham Lincoln,* vol 1. (New Brunswick: Rutgers University Press, 1953), 431-42.

DOCUMENT 8
LINCOLN'S LETTERS TO WILLIAM HERNDON ON THE MEXICAN WAR

REGARDING SPEECH ON MEXICAN WAR

TO WILLIAM H. HERNDON.

WASHINGTON, February 1, 1848.

DEAR WILLIAM:–Your letter of the 19th ultimo was received last night, and for which I am much obliged.

The only thing in it that I wish to talk to you at once about is that because of my vote for Ashmun's amendment you fear that you and I disagree about the war. I regret this, not because of any fear we shall remain disagreed after you have read this letter, but because if you misunderstand I fear other good friends may also. That vote affirms that the war was unnecessarily and unconstitutionally commenced by the President; and I will stake my life that if you had been in my place you would have voted just as I did. Would you have voted what you felt and knew to be a lie? I know you would not. Would you have gone out of the House–skulked the vote? I expect not. If you had skulked one vote, you would have had to skulk many more before the end of the session. Richardson's resolutions, introduced before I made any move or gave any vote upon the subject, make the direct question of the justice of the war; so that no man can be silent if he would. You are compelled to speak; and your only alternative is to tell the truth or a lie. I cannot doubt which you would do.

This vote has nothing to do in determining my votes on the questions of supplies. I have always intended, and still intend, to vote supplies; perhaps not in the precise form recommended by the President, but in a better form for all purposes, except Loco-foco party purposes. It is in this particular you seem mistaken. The Locos are untiring in their efforts to make the impression that all who vote supplies or take part in the war do of necessity approve the President's conduct in the beginning of it; but the Whigs have from the beginning made and kept the distinction between the two. In the very first act nearly all the Whigs voted against the preamble declaring that war existed by the act of Mexico; and yet nearly all of them voted for the supplies. As to the Whig men who have participated in the war, so far as they have spoken in my hearing they do not hesitate to denounce as unjust the President's conduct in the beginning of the war. They do not suppose that such denunciation is directed by undying hatred to him, as The Register would have it believed. There are two such Whigs on this floor (Colonel Haskell and Major James) The former fought as a colonel by the side of Colonel Baker at Cerro Gordo, and stands side by side with me in the vote that you seem dissatisfied with. The latter, the history of whose capture with Cassius Clay you well know, had not arrived here when that vote was given; but, as I understand, he stands ready to give just such a vote whenever an occasion shall present. Baker, too, who is now here, says the truth is undoubtedly that way; and whenever he shall speak out, he will say so. Colonel Doniphan, too, the favorite Whig of Missouri, and who overran all Northern Mexico, on his return home in a public speech at St. Louis condemned the administration in relation to the war. If I remember, G. T. M. Davis, who has been through almost the whole war, declares in favor of Mr. Clay; from which I infer that he adopts the sentiments of Mr. Clay, generally at least. On the other hand, I have heard of but one Whig who has been to the war attempting to justify the President's conduct. That one was Captain Bishop, editor of the

Charleston Courier, and a very clever fellow. I do not mean this letter for the public, but for you. Before it reaches you, you will have seen and read my pamphlet speech, and perhaps been scared anew by it. After you get over your scare, read it over again, sentence by sentence, and tell me honestly what you think of it. I condensed all I could for fear of being cut off by the hour rule, and when I got through I had spoken but forty-five minutes.

Yours forever,

A. LINCOLN.

ON THE MEXICAN WAR

TO WILLIAM H. HERNDON.

WASHINGTON, February 15, 1848.

DEAR WILLIAM:–Your letter of the 29th January was received last night. Being exclusively a constitutional argument, I wish to submit some reflections upon it in the same spirit of kindness that I know actuates you. Let me first state what I understand to be your position. It is that if it shall become necessary to repel invasion, the President may, without violation of the Constitution, cross the line and invade the territory of another country, and that whether such necessity exists in any given case the President is the sole judge.

Before going further consider well whether this is or is not your position. If it is, it is a position that neither the President himself, nor any friend of his, so far as I know, has ever taken. Their only positions are–first, that the soil was ours when the hostilities commenced; and second, that whether it was rightfully ours or not, Congress had annexed it, and the President for that reason was bound to defend it; both of which are as clearly proved to be false in fact as you can prove that your house is mine. The soil was not ours, and Congress did not annex or attempt to annex it. But to return to your position. Allow the President to invade a neighboring nation whenever he shall deem it necessary to repel an invasion, and you allow him to do so whenever he may choose to say he deems it necessary for such purpose, and you allow him to make war at pleasure. Study to see if you can fix any limit to his power in this respect, after having given him so much as you propose. If today he should choose to say he thinks it necessary to invade Canada to prevent the British from invading us, how could you stop him? You may say to him,—"I see no probability of the British invading us"; but he will say to you, "Be silent: I see it, if you don't."

The provision of the Constitution giving the war making power to Congress was dictated, as I understand it, by the following reasons: kings had always been involving and impoverishing their people in wars, pretending generally, if not always, that the good of the people was the object. This our convention understood to be the most oppressive of all kingly oppressions, and they resolved to so frame the Constitution that no one man should hold the power of bringing this oppression upon us. But your view destroys the whole matter, and places our President where kings have always stood. Write soon again.

Yours truly,

A. LINCOLN.

DOCUMENT 9
TREATY OF GUADALUPE HIDALGO;
FEBRUARY 2, 1848

*TREATY OF PEACE, FRIENDSHIP, LIMITS, AND SETTLEMENT
BETWEEN THE UNITED STATES OF AMERICA AND THE
UNITED MEXICAN STATES CONCLUDED AT GUADALUPE
HIDALGO, FEBRUARY 2, 1848; RATIFICATION ADVISED BY
SENATE, WITH AMENDMENTS, MARCH 10, 1848; RATIFIED BY
PRESIDENT, MARCH 16, 1848; RATIFICATIONS EXCHANGED
AT QUERETARO, MAY 30, 1848; PROCLAIMED, JULY 4, 1848.*

IN THE NAME OF ALMIGHTY GOD

The United States of America and the United Mexican States animated by a sincere desire to put an end to the calamities of the war
which unhappily exists between the two Republics and to establish
Upon a solid basis relations of peace and friendship, which shall
confer reciprocal benefits upon the citizens of both, and assure the
concord, harmony, and mutual confidence wherein the two people should live, as good neighbors have for that purpose appointed their respective plenipotentiaries, that is to say: The President
of the United States has appointed Nicholas P. Trist, a citizen of
the United States, and the President of the Mexican Republic has
appointed Don Luis Gonzaga Cuevas, Don Bernardo Couto, and
Don Miguel Atristain, citizens of the said Republic; Who, after a
reciprocal communication of their respective full powers, have,

under the protection of Almighty God, the author of peace, arranged, agreed upon, and signed the following: Treaty of Peace, Friendship, Limits, and Settlement between the United States of America and the Mexican Republic.

ARTICLE I
There shall be firm and universal peace between the United States of America and the Mexican Republic, and between their respective countries, territories, cities, towns, and people, without exception of places or persons.

ARTICLE II
Immediately upon the signature of this treaty, a convention shall be entered into between a commissioner or commissioners appointed by the General-in-chief of the forces of the United States, and such as may be appointed by the Mexican Government, to the end that a provisional suspension of hostilities shall take place, and that, in the places occupied by the said forces, constitutional order may be reestablished, as regards the political, administrative, and judicial branches, so far as this shall be permitted by the circumstances of military occupation.

ARTICLE III
Immediately upon the ratification of the present treaty by the Government of the United States, orders shall be transmitted to the commanders of their land and naval forces, requiring the latter (provided this treaty shall then have been ratified by the Government of the Mexican Republic, and the ratifications exchanged) immediately to desist from blockading any Mexican ports and requiring the former (under the same condition) to commence, at the earliest moment practicable, withdrawing all troops of the United States then in the interior of the Mexican Republic, to points that shall be selected by common agreement, at a distance from the seaports not exceeding thirty leagues; and such evacuation of the interior of the Republic shall be completed with the least possible delay; the Mexican Government hereby binding itself to afford every facility in its power for rendering the same convenient to the

troops, on their march and in their new positions, and for promoting a good understanding between them and the inhabitants. In like manner orders shall be despatched to the persons in charge of the custom houses at all ports occupied by the forces of the United States, requiring them (under the same condition) immediately to deliver possession of the same to the persons authorized by the Mexican Government to receive it, together with all bonds and evidences of debt for duties on importations and on exportations, not yet fallen due. Moreover, a faithful and exact account shall be made out, showing the entire amount of all duties on imports and on exports, collected at such custom-houses, or elsewhere in Mexico, by authority of the United States, from and after the day of ratification of this treaty by the Government of the Mexican Republic; and also an account of the cost of collection; and such entire amount, deducting only the cost of collection, shall be delivered to the Mexican Government, at the city of Mexico, within three months after the exchange of ratifications.

The evacuation of the capital of the Mexican Republic by the troops of the United States, in virtue of the above stipulation, shall be completed in one month after the orders there stipulated for shall have been received by the commander of said troops, or sooner if possible.

ARTICLE IV
Immediately after the exchange of ratifications of the present treaty all castles, forts, territories, places, and possessions, which have been taken or occupied by the forces of the United States during the present war, within the limits of the Mexican Republic, as about to be established by the following article, shall be definitely restored to the said Republic, together with all the artillery, arms, apparatus of war, munitions, and other public property, which were in the said castles and forts when captured, and which shall remain there at the time when this treaty shall be duly ratified by the Government of the Mexican Republic. To this end, immediately upon the signature of this treaty, orders shall be despatched to the American officers commanding such castles and forts, securing against the removal or destruction of any such artillery, arms, apparatus

of war, munitions, or other public property. The city of Mexico, within the inner line of intrenchments surrounding the said city, is comprehended in the above stipulation, as regards the restoration of artillery, apparatus of war, & c.

The final evacuation of the territory of the Mexican Republic, by the forces of the United States, shall be completed in three months from the said exchange of ratifications, or sooner if possible; the Mexican Government hereby engaging, as in the foregoing article to use all means in its power for facilitating such evacuation, and rendering it convenient to the troops, and for promoting a good understanding between them and the inhabitants.

If, however, the ratification of this treaty by both parties should not take place in time to allow the embarcation of the troops of the United States to be completed before the commencement of the sickly season, at the Mexican ports on the Gulf of Mexico, in such case a friendly arrangement shall be entered into between the General-in-Chief of the said troops and the Mexican Government, whereby healthy and otherwise suitable places, at a distance from the ports not exceeding thirty leagues, shall be designated for the residence of such troops as may not yet have embarked, until the return of the healthy season. And the space of time here referred to as, comprehending the sickly season shall be understood to extend from the first day of May to the first day of November.

All prisoners of war taken on either side, on land or on sea, shall be restored as soon as practicable after the exchange of ratifications of this treaty. It is also agreed that if any Mexicans should now be held as captives by any savage tribe within the limits of the United States, as about to be established by the following article, the Government of the said United States will exact the release of such captives and cause them to be restored to their country.

ARTICLE V

The boundary line between the two Republics shall commence in the Gulf of Mexico, three leagues from land, opposite the mouth of the Rio Grande, otherwise called Rio Bravo del Norte, or Opposite the mouth of its deepest branch, if it should have more than one branch emptying directly into the sea; from thence up the middle of that river, following the deepest channel, where it has more than one, to the point where it strikes the southern boundary of New Mexico; thence, westwardly, along the whole southern boundary of New Mexico (which runs north of the town called Paso) to its western termination; thence, northward, along the western line of New Mexico, until it intersects the first branch of the river Gila; (or if it should not intersect any branch of that river, then to the point on the said line nearest to such branch, and thence in a direct line to the same); thence down the middle of the said branch and of the said river, until it empties into the Rio Colorado; thence across the Rio Colorado, following the division line between Upper and Lower California, to the Pacific Ocean.

The southern and western limits of New Mexico, mentioned in the article, are those laid down in the map entitled "Map of the United Mexican States, as organized and defined by various acts of the Congress of said republic, and constructed according to the best authorities. Revised edition. Published at New York, in 1847, by J. Disturnell," of which map a copy is added to this treaty, bearing the signatures and seals of the undersigned Plenipotentiaries. And, in order to preclude all difficulty in tracing upon the ground the limit separating Upper from Lower California, it is agreed that the said limit shall consist of a straight line drawn from the middle of the Rio Gila, where it unites with the Colorado, to a point on the coast of the Pacific Ocean, distant one marine league due south of the southernmost point of the port of San Diego, according to the plan of said port made in the year 1782 by Don Juan Pantoja, second sailing-master of the Spanish fleet, and published at Madrid in the year 1802, in the atlas to the voyage of the schooners Sutil and Mexicana; of which plan a copy is hereunto added, signed and sealed by the respective Plenipotentiaries.

In order to designate the boundary line with due precision, upon authoritative maps, and to establish upon the ground landmarks which shall show the limits of both republics, as described in the present article, the two Governments shall each appoint a commissioner and a surveyor, who, before the expiration of one year from the date of the exchange of ratifications of this treaty, shall meet at the port of San Diego, and proceed to run and mark the said boundary in its whole course to the mouth of the Rio Bravo del Norte. They shall keep journals and make out plans of their operations; and the result agreed upon by them shall be deemed a part of this treaty, and shall have the same force as if it were inserted therein. The two Governments will amicably agree regarding what may be necessary to these persons, and also as to their respective escorts, should such be necessary.

The boundary line established by this article shall be religiously respected by each of the two republics, and no change shall ever be made therein, except by the express and free consent of both nations, lawfully given by the General Government of each, in conformity with its own constitution.

ARTICLE VI

The vessels and citizens of the United States shall, in all time, have a free and uninterrupted passage by the Gulf of California, and by the river Colorado below its confluence with the Gila, to and from their possessions situated north of the boundary line defined in the preceding article; it being understood that this passage is to be by navigating the Gulf of California and the river Colorado, and not by land, without the express consent of the Mexican Government.

If, by the examinations which may be made, it should be ascertained to be practicable and advantageous to construct a road, canal, or railway, which should in whole or in part run upon the river Gila, or upon its right or its left bank, within the space of one marine league from either margin of the river, the Governments of both republics will form an agreement regarding its construction, in order that it may serve equally for the use and advantage of both countries.

ARTICLE VII

The river Gila, and the part of the Rio Bravo del Norte lying below the southern boundary of New Mexico, being, agreeably to the fifth article, divided in the middle between the two republics, the navigation of the Gila and of the Bravo below said boundary shall be free and common to the vessels and citizens of both countries; and neither shall, without the consent of the other, construct any work that may impede or interrupt, in whole or in part, the exercise of this right; not even for the purpose of favoring new methods of navigation. Nor shall any tax or contribution, under any denomination or title, be levied upon vessels or persons navigating the same or upon merchandise or effects transported thereon, except in the case of landing upon one of their shores. If, for the purpose of making the said rivers navigable, or for maintaining them in such state, it should be necessary or advantageous to establish any tax or contribution, this shall not be done without the consent of both Governments.

The stipulations contained in the present article shall not impair the territorial rights of either republic within its established limits.

ARTICLE VIII

Mexicans now established in territories previously belonging to Mexico, and which remain for the future within the limits of the United States, as defined by the present treaty, shall be free to continue where they now reside, or to remove at any time to the Mexican Republic, retaining the property which they possess in the said territories, or disposing thereof, and removing the proceeds wherever they please, without their being subjected, on this account, to any contribution, tax, or charge whatever.

Those who shall prefer to remain in the said territories may either retain the title and rights of Mexican citizens, or acquire those of citizens of the United States. But they shall be under the obligation to make their election within one year from the date of the exchange of ratifications of this treaty; and those who shall remain in the said territories after the expiration of that year, without having declared their intention to retain the character of Mexicans, shall be considered to have elected to become citizens of the United States.

In the said territories, property of every kind, now belonging to Mexicans not established there, shall be inviolably respected. The present owners, the heirs of these, and all Mexicans who may hereafter acquire said property by contract, shall enjoy with respect to it guarantees equally ample as if the same belonged to citizens of the United States.

ARTICLE IX

The Mexicans who, in the territories aforesaid, shall not preserve the character of citizens of the Mexican Republic, conformably with what is stipulated in the preceding article, shall be incorporated into the Union of the United States. and be admitted at the proper time (to be judged of by the Congress of the United States) to the enjoyment of all the rights of citizens of the United States, according to the principles of the Constitution; and in the mean time, shall be maintained and protected in the free enjoyment of their liberty and property, and secured in the free exercise of their religion without; restriction.

ARTICLE X

[Stricken out]

ARTICLE XI

Considering that a great part of the territories, which, by the present treaty, are to be comprehended for the future within the limits of the United States, is now occupied by savage tribes, who will hereafter be under the exclusive control of the Government of the United States, and whose incursions within the territory of Mexico would be prejudicial in the extreme, it is solemnly agreed that all such incursions shall be forcibly restrained by the Government of the United States whensoever this may be necessary; and that when they cannot be prevented, they shall be punished by the said Government, and satisfaction for the same shall be exacted all in the same way, and with equal diligence and energy, as if the same incursions were meditated or committed within its own territory, against its own citizens.

It shall not be lawful, under any pretext whatever, for any inhabitant of the United States to purchase or acquire any Mexican, or any foreigner residing in Mexico, who may have been captured by Indians inhabiting the territory of either of the two republics; nor to purchase or acquire horses, mules, cattle, or property of any kind, stolen within Mexican territory by such Indians.

And in the event of any person or persons, captured within Mexican territory by Indians, being carried into the territory of the United States, the Government of the latter engages and binds itself, in the most solemn manner, so soon as it shall know of such captives being within its territory, and shall be able so to do, through the faithful exercise of its influence and power, to rescue them and return them to their country. or deliver them to the agent or representative of the Mexican Government. The Mexican authorities will, as far as practicable, give to the Government of the United States notice of such captures; and its agents shall pay the expenses incurred in the maintenance and transmission of the rescued captives; who, in the mean time, shall be treated with the utmost hospitality by the American authorities at the place where they may be. But if the Government of the United States, before receiving such notice from Mexico, should obtain intelligence, through any other channel, of the existence of Mexican captives within its territory, it will proceed forthwith to effect their release and delivery to the Mexican agent, as above stipulated.

For the purpose of giving to these stipulations the fullest possible efficacy, thereby affording the security and redress demanded by their true spirit and intent, the Government of the United States will now and hereafter pass, without unnecessary delay, and always vigilantly enforce, such laws as the nature of the subject may require. And, finally, the sacredness of this obligation shall never be lost sight of by the said Government, when providing for the removal of the Indians from any portion of the said territories, or for its being settled by citizens of the United States; but, on the contrary, special care shall then be taken not to place its Indian occupants under the necessity of seeking new homes, by committing those invasions which the United States have solemnly obliged themselves to restrain.

ARTICLE XII

In consideration of the extension acquired by the boundaries of the United States, as defined in the fifth article of the present treaty, the Government of the United States engages to pay to that of the Mexican Republic the sum of fifteen millions of dollars.

Immediately after the treaty shall have been duly ratified by the Government of the Mexican Republic, the sum of three millions of dollars shall be paid to the said Government by that of the United States, at the city of Mexico, in the gold or silver coin of Mexico The remaining twelve millions of dollars shall be paid at the same place, and in the same coin, in annual installments of three millions of dollars each, together with interest on the same at the rate of six per centum per annum. This interest shall begin to run upon the whole sum of twelve millions from the day of the ratification of the present treaty by–the Mexican Government, and the first of the installments shall be paid-at the expiration of one year from the same day. Together with each annual installment, as it falls due, the whole interest accruing on such installment from the beginning shall also be paid.

ARTICLE XIII
The United States engage, moreover, to assume and pay to the claimants all the amounts now due them, and those hereafter to become due, by reason of the claims already liquidated and decided against the Mexican Republic, under the conventions between the two republics severally concluded on the eleventh day of April, eighteen hundred and thirty-nine, and on the thirtieth day of January, eighteen hundred and forty-three; so that the Mexican Republic shall be absolutely exempt, for the future, from all expense whatever on account of the said claims.

ARTICLE XIV
The United States do furthermore discharge the Mexican Republic from all claims of citizens of the United States, not heretofore decided against the Mexican Government, which may have arisen previously to the date of the signature of this treaty; which discharge shall be final and perpetual, whether the said claims be rejected or be allowed by the board of commissioners provided for in the following article, and whatever shall be the total amount of those allowed.

ARTICLE XV
The United States, exonerating Mexico from all demands on account of the claims of their citizens mentioned in the preceding

article, and considering them entirely and forever canceled, whatever their amount may be, undertake to make satisfaction for the same, to an amount not exceeding three and one-quarter millions of dollars. To ascertain the validity and amount of those claims, a board of commissioners shall be established by the Government of the United States, whose awards shall be final and conclusive; provided that, in deciding upon the validity of each claim, the boa shall be guided and governed by the principles and rules of decision prescribed by the first and fifth articles of the unratified convention, concluded at the city of Mexico on the twentieth day of November, one thousand eight hundred and forty-three; and in no case shall an award be made in favour of any claim not embraced by these principles and rules.

If, in the opinion of the said board of commissioners or of the claimants, any books, records, or documents, in the possession or power of the Government of the Mexican Republic, shall be deemed necessary to the just decision of any claim, the commissioners, or the claimants through them, shall, within such period as Congress may designate, make an application in writing for the same, addressed to the Mexican Minister of Foreign Affairs, to be transmitted by the Secretary of State of the United States; and the Mexican Government engages, at the earliest possible moment after the receipt of such demand, to cause any of the books, records, or documents so specified, which shall be in their possession or power (or authenticated copies or extracts of the same), to be transmitted to the said Secretary of State, who shall immediately deliver them over to the said board of commissioners; provided that no such application shall be made by or at the instance of any claimant, until the facts which it is expected to prove by such books, records, or documents, shall have been stated under oath or affirmation.

ARTICLE XVI
Each of the contracting parties reserves to itself the entire right to fortify whatever point within its territory it may judge proper so to fortify for its security.

ARTICLE XVII

The treaty of amity, commerce, and navigation, concluded at the city of Mexico, on the fifth day of April, A. D. 1831, between the United States of America and the United Mexican States, except the additional article, and except so far as the stipulations of the said treaty may be incompatible with any stipulation contained in the present treaty, is hereby revived for the period of eight years from the day of the exchange of ratifications of this treaty, with the same force and virtue as if incorporated therein; it being understood that each of the contracting parties reserves to itself the right, at any time after the said period of eight years shall have expired, to terminate the same by giving one year's notice of such intention to the other party.

ARTICLE XVIII

All supplies whatever for troops of the United States in Mexico, arriving at ports in the occupation of such troops previous to the final evacuation thereof, although subsequently to the restoration of the custom-houses at such ports, shall be entirely exempt from duties and charges of any kind; the Government of the United States hereby engaging and pledging its faith to establish and vigilantly to enforce, all possible guards for securing the revenue of Mexico, by preventing the importation, under cover of this stipulation, of any articles other than such, both in kind and in quantity, as shall really be wanted for the use and consumption of the forces of the United States during the time they may remain in Mexico. To this end it shall be the duty of all officers and agents of the United States to denounce to the Mexican authorities at the respective ports any attempts at a fraudulent abuse of this stipulation, which they may know of, or may have reason to suspect, and to give to such authorities all the aid in their power with regard thereto; and every such attempt, when duly proved and established by sentence of a competent tribunal, They shall be punished by the confiscation of the property so attempted to be fraudulently introduced.

ARTICLE XIX

With respect to all merchandise, effects, and property whatsoever, imported into ports of Mexico, whilst in the occupation of the forces of the United States, whether by citizens of either republic, or by citizens or subjects of any neutral nation, the following rules shall be observed:

(1) All such merchandise, effects, and property, if imported previously to the restoration of the custom-houses to the Mexican authorities, as stipulated for in the third article of this treaty, shall be exempt from confiscation, although the importation of the same be prohibited by the Mexican tariff.

(2) The same perfect exemption shall be enjoyed by all such merchandise, effects, and property, imported subsequently to the restoration of the custom-houses, and previously to the sixty days fixed in the following article for the coming into force of the Mexican tariff at such ports respectively; the said merchandise, effects, and property being, however, at the time of their importation, subject to the payment of duties, as provided for in the said following article.

(3) All merchandise, effects, and property described in the two rules foregoing shall, during their continuance at the place of importation, and upon their leaving such place for the interior, be exempt from all duty, tax, or imposts of every kind, under whatsoever title or denomination. Nor shall they be there subject to any charge whatsoever upon the sale thereof.

(4) All merchandise, effects, and property, described in the first and second rules, which shall have been removed to any place in the interior, whilst such place was in the occupation of the forces of the United States, shall, during their continuance therein, be exempt from all tax upon the sale or consumption thereof, and from every kind of impost or contribution, under whatsoever title or denomination.

(5) But if any merchandise, effects, or property, described in the first and second rules, shall be removed to any place not occupied at the time by the forces of the United States, they shall, upon their introduction into such place, or upon their sale or consumption there, be subject to the same duties which, under the Mexican laws, they would be required to pay in such cases if they had been

imported in time of peace, through the maritime custom-houses, and had there paid the duties conformably with the Mexican tariff.

(6) The owners of all merchandise, effects, or property, described in the first and second rules, and existing in any port of Mexico, shall have the right to reship the same, exempt from all tax, impost, or contribution whatever.

With respect to the metals, or other property, exported from any Mexican port whilst in the occupation of the forces of the United States, and previously to the restoration of the custom-house at such port, no person shall be required by the Mexican authorities, whether general or state, to pay any tax, duty, or contribution upon any such exportation, or in any manner to account for the same to the said authorities.

ARTICLE XX

Through consideration for the interests of commerce generally, it is agreed, that if less than sixty days should elapse between the date of the signature of this treaty and the restoration of the custom houses, conformably with the stipulation in the third article, in such case all merchandise, effects and property whatsoever, arriving at the Mexican ports after the restoration of the said custom-houses, and previously to the expiration of sixty days after the day of signature of this treaty, shall be admitted to entry; and no other duties shall be levied thereon than the duties established by the tariff found in force at such custom-houses at the time of the restoration of the same. And to all such merchandise, effects, and property, the rules established by the preceding article shall apply.

ARTICLE XXI

If unhappily any disagreement should hereafter arise between the Governments of the two republics, whether with respect to the interpretation of any stipulation in this treaty, or with respect to any other particular concerning the political or commercial relations of the two nations, the said Governments, in the name of those nations, do promise to each other that they will endeavour, in the most sincere and earnest manner, to settle the differences so arising, and to preserve the state of peace and friendship in which the two countries are now placing themselves, using, for this end, mutual representations and pacific negotiations. And if, by these means, they should not be enabled to come to an agreement, a resort shall not, on this account, be had to reprisals, aggression, or hostility of any kind, by the one republic against the other, until the Government of that which deems itself aggrieved shall have maturely considered, in the spirit of peace and good neighbourship, whether it would not be better that such difference should be settled by the arbitration of commissioners appointed on each side, or by that of a friendly nation. And should such course be proposed by either party, it shall be acceded to by the other, unless deemed by it altogether incompatible with the nature of the difference, or the circumstances of the case.

ARTICLE XXII

If (which is not to be expected, and which God forbid) war should unhappily break out between the two republics, they do now, with a view to such calamity, solemnly pledge themselves to each other and to the world to observe the following rules; absolutely where the nature of the subject permits, and as closely as possible in all cases where such absolute observance shall be impossible:

(1). The merchants of either republic then residing in the other shall be allowed to remain twelve months (for those dwelling in the interior), and six months (for those dwelling at the seaports) to collect their debts and settle their affairs; during which periods they shall enjoy the same protection, and be on the same footing, in all respects, as the citizens or subjects of the most friendly nations; and, at the expiration thereof, or at any time before, they shall have full liberty to depart, carrying off all their effects without molestation or hindrance, conforming therein to the same laws which the citizens or subjects of the most friendly nations are required to conform to. Upon the entrance of the armies of either nation into the territories of the other, women and children, ecclesiastics, scholars of every faculty, cultivators of the earth, merchants, artisans, manufacturers, and fishermen, unarmed and inhabiting unfortified towns, villages, or places, and in general all persons whose occupations are for the common subsistence and benefit of mankind, shall be allowed to continue their respective employments, unmolested in their persons.

Nor shall their houses or goods be burnt or otherwise destroyed, nor their cattle taken, nor their fields wasted, by the armed force into whose power, by the events of war, they may happen to fall; but if the necessity arise to take anything from them for the use of such armed force, the same shall be paid for at an equitable price. All churches, hospitals, schools, colleges, libraries, and other establishments for charitable and beneficent purposes, shall be respected, and all persons connected with the same protected in the discharge of their duties, and the pursuit of their vocations.

(2). In order that the fate of prisoners of war may be alleviated all such practices as those of sending them into distant, inclement or unwholesome districts, or crowding them into close and noxious places, shall be studiously avoided. They shall not be confined in dungeons, prison ships, or prisons; nor be put in irons, or bound or otherwise restrained in the use of their limbs. The officers shall enjoy liberty on their paroles, within convenient districts, and have comfortable quarters; and the common soldiers shall be dispose(in cantonments, open and extensive enough for air and exercise and lodged in barracks as roomy and good as are provided by the party in whose power they are for its own troops. But if any office shall break his parole by leaving the district so assigned him, or any other prisoner shall escape from the limits of his cantonment after they shall have been designated to him, such individual, officer, or other prisoner, shall forfeit so much of the benefit of this article as provides for his liberty on parole or in cantonment. And if any officer so breaking his parole or any common soldier so escaping from the limits assigned him, shall afterwards be found in arms previously to his being regularly exchanged, the person so offending shall be dealt with according to the established laws of war. The officers shall be daily furnished, by the party in whose power they are, with as many rations, and of the same articles, as are allowed either in kind or by commutation, to officers of equal rank in its own army; and all others shall be daily furnished with such ration as is allowed to a common soldier in its own service; the value of all which supplies shall, at the close of the war, or at periods to be agreed upon between the respective commanders, be paid by the other party, on a mutual adjustment of accounts for the subsistence of prisoners; and such accounts shall not be mingled with or set off against any others, nor the balance due on them withheld, as a compensation or reprisal for any cause whatever, real or pretended Each party shall be allowed to keep a commissary of prisoners, appointed by itself, with every cantonment of prisoners, in possession of the other; which commissary shall see the prisoners as often as he pleases; shall be allowed to receive, exempt from all duties a taxes, and to distribute, whatever comforts may be sent to them by their friends; and shall be free to transmit his reports in open letters to the party by whom he is employed. And it is declared that neither the pretense that war dissolves all treaties, nor any other whatever, shall be considered as annulling or suspending the solemn covenant contained in this article. On the contrary, the state of war is precisely that for which it is provided; and, during which, its stipulations are to be as sacredly observed as the most acknowledged obligations under the law of nature or nations.

ARTICLE XXIII
This treaty shall be ratified by the President of the United States of America, by and with the advice and consent of the Senate thereof; and by the President of the Mexican Republic, with the previous approbation of its general Congress; and the ratifications shall be exchanged in the City of Washington, or at the seat of Government of Mexico, in four months from the date of the signature hereof, or sooner if practicable. In faith whereof we, the respective Plenipotentiaries, have signed this treaty of peace, friendship, limits, and settlement, and have hereunto affixed our seals respectively. Done in quintuplicate, at the city of Guadalupe Hidalgo, on the second day of February, in the year of our Lord one thousand eight hundred and forty-eight.

N. P. TRIST
LUIS P. CUEVAS
BERNARDO COUTO
MIGL. ATRISTAIN

Source: Treaties and Conventions between the United States of America and Other Powers Since July 4, 1776 Washington, DC : Government Printing Office, 1871

DOCUMENT 10
TO WILLIAM H. HERNDON

WASHINGTON, June 22, 1848.

DEAR WILLIAM:–Last night I was attending a sort of caucus of the Whig members, held in relation to the coming Presidential election. The whole field of the nation was scanned, and all is high hope and confidence. Illinois is expected to better her condition in this race.

Under these circumstances, judge how heartrending it was to come to my room and find and read your discouraging letter of the 15th. We have made no gains, but have lost "H. R. Robinson, Turner, Campbell, and four or five more." Tell Arney to reconsider, if he would be saved. Baker and I used to do something, but I think you attach more importance to our absence than is just. There is another cause. In 1840, for instance, we had two senators and five representatives in Sangamon; now we have part of one senator and two representatives. With quite one third more people than we had then, we have only half the sort of offices which are sought by men of the speaking sort of talent. This, I think, is the chief cause. Now, as to the young men. You must not wait to be brought forward by the older men. For instance, do you suppose that I should ever have got into notice if I had waited to be hunted up and pushed forward by older men? You young men get together and form a "Rough and Ready Club," and have regular meetings and speeches. Take in everybody you can get. Harrison Grimsley, L. A. Enos, Lee Kimball, and C. W. Matheny will do to begin the thing; but as you go along gather up all the shrewd, wild boys about town, whether just of age, or a little under age, Chris. Logan, Reddick Ridgely, Lewis Zwizler, and hundreds such. Let every one play the part he can play best,–some speak, some sing, and all "holler." Your meetings will be of evenings; the older men, and the women, will go to hear you; so that it will not only contribute to the election of "Old Zach," but will be an interesting pastime, and improving to the intellectual faculties of all engaged. Don't fail to do this.

You ask me to send you all the speeches made about "Old Zach," the war, etc. Now this makes me a little impatient. I have regularly sent you the Congressional Globe and Appendix, and you cannot have examined them, or you would have discovered that they contain every speech made by every man in both houses of Congress, on every subject, during the session. Can I send any more? Can I send speeches that nobody has made? Thinking it would be most natural that the newspapers would feel interested to give at least some of the speeches to their readers, I at the beginning of the session made arrangements to have one copy of the Globe and Appendix regularly sent to each Whig paper of the district. And yet, with the exception of my own little speech, which was published in two only of the then five, now four, Whig papers, I do not remember having seen a single speech, or even extract from one, in any single one of those papers. With equal and full means on both sides, I will venture that the State Register has thrown before its readers more of Locofoco speeches in a month than all the Whig papers of the district have done of Whig speeches during the session.

If you wish a full understanding of the war, I repeat what I believe I said to you in a letter once before, that the whole, or nearly so, is to be found in the speech of Dixon of Connecticut. This I sent you in pamphlet as well as in the Globe. Examine and study every sentence of that speech thoroughly, and you will understand the whole subject. You ask how Congress came to declare that war had existed by the act of Mexico. Is it possible you don't understand that yet? You have at least twenty speeches in your possession that fully explain it. I will, however, try it once more. The news reached Washington of the commencement of hostilities on the Rio Grande, and of the great peril of General Taylor's army. Everybody, Whigs and Democrats, was for sending them aid, in men and money. It was necessary to pass a bill for this. The Locos had a majority in both houses, and they brought in a bill with a preamble saying: Whereas, War exists by the act of Mexico, therefore we send General Taylor money. The Whigs moved to strike out the preamble, so that they could vote to send the men and money, without saying anything about how the war commenced; but being in the minority, they were voted down, and the preamble was retained.

Then, on the passage of the bill, the question came upon them, Shall we vote for preamble and bill together, or against both together? They did not want to vote against sending help to General Taylor, and therefore they voted for both together. Is there any difficulty in understanding this? Even my little speech shows how this was; and if you will go to the library, you may get the Journal of 1845-46, in which you will find the whole for yourself.

We have nothing published yet with special reference to the Taylor race; but we soon will have, and then I will send them to everybody. I made an internal-improvement speech day before yesterday, which I shall send home as soon as I can get it written out and printed,—and which I suppose nobody will read.

Your friend as ever,
A. LINCOLN.

TO: W. H. HERNDON.

WASHINGTON, July 10, 1848.

DEAR WILLIAM:

Your letter covering the newspaper slips was received last night. The subject of that letter is exceedingly painful to me, and I cannot but think there is some mistake in your impression of the motives of the old men. I suppose I am now one of the old men; and I declare on my veracity, which I think is good with you, that nothing could afford me more satisfaction than to learn that you and others of my young friends at home were doing battle in the contest and endearing themselves to the people and taking a stand far above any I have ever been able to reach in their admiration. I cannot conceive that other men feel differently. Of course I cannot demonstrate what I say; but I was young once, and I am sure I was never ungenerously thrust back. I hardly know what to say. The way for a young man to rise is to improve himself every way he can, never suspecting that anybody wishes to hinder him. Allow me to assure you that suspicion and jealousy never did help any man in any situation. There may sometimes be ungenerous attempts to keep a young man down; and they will succeed, too, if he allows his mind to be diverted from its true channel to brood over the attempted injury. Cast about and see if this feeling has not injured every person you have ever known to fall into it.

Now, in what I have said I am sure you will suspect nothing but sincere friendship.

I would save you from a fatal error. You have been a studious young man. You are far better informed on almost all subjects than I ever have been. You cannot fail in any laudable object unless you allow your mind to be improperly directed. I have some the advantage of you in the world's experience, merely by being older; and it is this that induces me to advise. You still seem to be a little mistaken about the Congressional Globe and Appendix. They contain all of the speeches that are published in any way. My speech and Dayton's speech which you say you got in pamphlet form are both word for word in the Appendix. I repeat again, all are there.

Your friend, as ever,
A. LINCOLN.

From Classic Literature in the Public Domain Library. Great Britain. Accessed Sept. 16, 2015. http://www.classic-literature.co.uk/american-authors/19th-century/abraham-lincoln/

DOCUMENT 11
LINCOLN TO ROMERO
(LETTER OF JANUARY 21, 1861)

Ocampo to Romero, December 22, 1860. Reservada, Numero 17, Archivo de Relaciones Exteriores, México, D.F.

Instructions: You are to proceed to the place of residence of President-elect Lincoln and in the name of the government make clear the desire which animates President Juárez of entering into the most cordial relations with the government of the United States.

Mr. Matias Romero
Springfield, Ills.
Jan 21, 1861

Mr. Dear Sir,
Allow me to thank you for your polite call as Charge d'Affaires of Mexico. While, as yet I can do no official act on behalf of the United States, as one of its citizens I tender the expression of my sincere wishes for the happiness, prosperity and liberty of yourself, your government, and its people.
Your Obt. Servant,
A. LINCOLN

DOCUMENT 12
MATÍAS ROMERO TO THE SECRETARY OF EXTERIOR RELATIONS

May 16, 1862

Wishing to inform the president of the United States of the condition of our affairs, while at the same time learning his ideas and views for the future regarding French intervention on this continent, I have resolved to call upon him with the required frequency. Although my character near this government is not the most appropriate for possessing the right to be received by the president, I have determined to commit this small irregularity for my country's sake.

This morning I had the first interview with Lincoln [since his arrival in Washington]. To see him I adopted the pretext of expressing my condolences at his loss of a son this past February. Short before taking leave of him, I congratulated him on the success of his recent trip to Fortress Monroe, expressing my wish to see peace established in the United State, because, in great part, the settlement of thing in Mexico depends on that. I expounded a little on the themes that the European expedition was undertaken in the belief that the United States was permanently divided, that the French policy in Mexico was hostile to this nation, and that an identity of interested exists between our two countries. He had always believed, he replied, that the settlement of Mexico's present difficulties depended upon the course events would take here.

Since Mexican affairs were a matter of such importance, I told him, I would take the liberty of coming occasionally in an unofficial capacity to speak with him on these matters. [2:184]

DOCUMENT 13
EXECUTIVE MANSION, WASHINGTON, AUGUST 22, 1862.

Hon. Horace Greeley:

Dear Sir.

I have just read yours of the 19th. addressed to myself through the New-York Tribune. If there be in it any statements, or assumptions of fact, which I may know to be erroneous, I do not, now and here, controvert them. If there be in it any inferences which I may believe to be falsely drawn, I do not now and here, argue against them. If there be perceptable in it an impatient and dictatorial tone, I waive it in deference to an old friend, whose heart I have always supposed to be right.

As to the policy I "seem to be pursuing" as you say, I have not meant to leave any one in doubt.

I would save the Union. I would save it the shortest way under the Constitution. The sooner the national authority can be restored; the nearer the Union will be "the Union as it was." If there be those who would not save the Union, unless they could at the same time *saves* slavery, I do not agree with them. If there be those who would not save the Union unless they could at the same time *destroy* slavery, I do not agree with them. My paramount object in this struggle *is* to save the Union, and is *not* either to save or to destroy slavery. If I could save the Union without freeing *any* slave

I would do it, and if I could save it by freeing *all* the slaves I would do it; and if I could save it by freeing some and leaving others alone I would also do that. What I do about slavery, and the colored race, I do because I believe it helps to save the Union; and what I forbear, I forbear because I do *not* believe it would help to save the Union. I shall do *less* whenever I shall believe what I am doing hurts the cause, and I shall do *more* whenever I shall believe doing more will help the cause. I shall try to correct errors when shown to be errors; and I shall adopt new views so fast as they shall appear to be true views.

I have here stated my purpose according to my view of *official* duty; and I intend no modification of my oft-expressed *personal* wish that all men every where could be free.

Yours,
A. Lincoln.

Abraham Lincoln. "Letter to Horace Greeley, August 22, 1862. http://www.abrahamlincolnonline.org/lincoln/speeches/greeley. htm

DOCUMENT 14
THE EMANCIPATION PROCLAMATION

January 1, 1863

A Transcription

By the President of the United States of America:

A Proclamation.

Whereas, on the twenty-second day of September, in the year of our Lord one thousand eight hundred and sixty-two, a proclamation was issued by the President of the United States, containing, among other things, the following, to wit:

"That on the first day of January, in the year of our Lord one thousand eight hundred and sixty-three, all persons held as slaves within any State or designated part of a State, the people whereof shall then be in rebellion against the United States, shall be then, thenceforward, and forever free; and the Executive Government of the United States, including the military and naval authority thereof, will recognize and maintain the freedom of such persons, and will do no act or acts to repress such persons, or any of them, in any efforts they may make for their actual freedom.

"That the Executive will, on the first day of January aforesaid, by proclamation, designate the States and parts of States, if any, in which the people thereof, respectively, shall then be in rebellion against the United States; and the fact that any State, or the people thereof, shall on that day be, in good faith, represented in the Congress of the United States by members chosen thereto at elections wherein a majority of the qualified voters of such State shall have participated, shall, in the absence of strong countervailing testimony, be deemed conclusive evidence that such State, and the people thereof, are not then in rebellion against the United States."

Now, therefore I, Abraham Lincoln, President of the United States, by virtue of the power in me vested as Commander-in-Chief, of the Army and Navy of the United States in time of actual armed rebellion against the authority and government of the United States, and as a fit and necessary war measure for suppressing said rebellion, do, on this first day of January, in the year of our Lord one thousand eight hundred and sixty-three, and in accordance with my purpose so to do publicly proclaimed for the full period of one hundred days, from the day first above mentioned, order and designate as the States and parts of States wherein the people thereof respectively, are this day in rebellion against the United States, the following, to wit:

Arkansas, Texas, Louisiana, (except the Parishes of St. Bernard, Plaquemines, Jefferson, St. John, St. Charles, St. James Ascension, Assumption, Terrebonne, Lafourche, St. Mary, St. Martin, and Orleans, including the City of New Orleans) Mississippi, Alabama, Florida, Georgia, South Carolina, North Carolina, and Virginia, (except the forty-eight counties designated as West Virginia, and also the counties of Berkley, Accomac, Northampton, Elizabeth City, York, Princess Ann, and Norfolk, including the cities of Norfolk and Portsmouth[)], and which excepted parts, are for the present, left precisely as if this proclamation were not issued.

And by virtue of the power, and for the purpose aforesaid, I do order and declare that all persons held as slaves within said designated States, and parts of States, are, and henceforward shall be free; and that the Executive government of the United States, including the military and naval authorities thereof, will recognize and maintain the freedom of said persons.

And I hereby enjoin upon the people so declared to be free to abstain from all violence, unless in necessary self-defence; and

I recommend to them that, in all cases when allowed, they labor faithfully for reasonable wages.

And I further declare and make known, that such persons of suitable condition, will be received into the armed service of the United States to garrison forts, positions, stations, and other places, and to man vessels of all sorts in said service.

And upon this act, sincerely believed to be an act of justice, warranted by the Constitution, upon military necessity, I invoke the considerate judgment of mankind, and the gracious favor of Almighty God.

In witness whereof, I have hereunto set my hand and caused the seal of the United States to be affixed.

Done at the City of Washington, this first day of January, in the year of our Lord one thousand eight hundred and sixty three, and of the Independence of the United States of America the eighty-seventh.

By the President:
ABRAHAM LINCOLN

WILLIAM H. SEWARD
Secretary of State.

(National Archives document. US Printing Service. Public Domain).

DOCUMENT 15
MATÍAS ROMERO TO THE SECRETARY
OF EXTERIOR RELATIONS

May 16, 1865.

On the 9th Grant came with six people from his staff to dine with me. During the meal he and his aides appeared to enjoy themselves and manifested considerable cordiality. It was not the proper occasion to continue the conversation commenced with the general on the 8th {where Grant indicated that he might be willing to resign his commission now that the South had surrendered, and lead an independent force into Mexico to drive the French out], so I limited myself to speaking of general news, which, in our interest, should have come to his attention.

Afterward I had no chance to see him alone. To achieve this purpose, I decided to go to Philadelphia, where he also had to go at the end of last week. Grant had invited my sister to visit Mrs. Grant in that city. Unfortunately, my sister could not go, but I offered to accompany him if he would advise me on which train he was leaving. He graciously sent me word that he would go on Saturday the 13th on the 11:15 a.m. train. I arranged my trip and met him on that train. He traveled quite indisposed. Because he rested most of the way, I could not speak to him during the trip.

Upon our arrival in Philadelphia, he invited me to stay at his house. Although the general was quite indisposed a large part of the time we were there, I had a more ample opportunity to tell him what I wished. His indisposition actually favored me, permitting me to spend all my time with him. Otherwise, receiving the people who wanted to see him, I would scarcely have seen him alone in his own house.

My principle objective was to learn if he had decided to go to Mexico. Since I last wrote you on this matter, the idea has occurred to me that it is perhaps more desirable for him to remain here because his elevated position will present him many opportunities to help us. With regard to whose goes to the Republic, especially in view of what will have to be done there, we can find others who would serve us with equal advantage. I did not find it desirable, then, to insist much on his decision to go to Mexico. At the same time I discovered that he did not believe that his going [to Mexico] was necessary to throw the French out of the Republic.

The danger that this note might fall into our enemies' hands, plus the little to be achieved by referring in minute detail to the tenor of my conversation with Grant, prompt me to deviate on this occasion form my custom of reporting to the supreme government every little step I take here to promote the interests of the Republic.

The success of the plan formed here will depend in large part on the secrecy maintained regarding its details. This consideration, no less than my desire not to compromised our best friends, forces me to limit myself to informing you that all goes well here according to our wishes. Soon we will be able to obtain all the assistance we need from this country.

The notes.106, 107, and 108 of this ministry contain all the authorizations and instructions from the supreme government which I could desire regarding this affair, including authorization to contract with the U.S. government for U.S. officers and a cadre to fight in Mexico to expel the French. [5:315-16]

Matías Romero to the Secretary of Exterior Relations

December 20, 1865.

Yesterday I went to Grant's office and found him preparing to leave. I inquired if he had sent instructions to Sheridan. He replied that he had sent a very succinct telegram. However, the very next day, he added, he would write Sheridan a private letter conveying all the necessary details. Even if the president has great interest for our cause, Grant noted, he cannot openly take sides in the question while the United States remains neutral. He was going to recommend the best course to Sheridan, he continued, which would be for Sheridan to proceed as he best saw fit without awaiting instructions, but rather considering consummated facts. [5:912-13]

DOCUMENT 16
INVITATION TO ROMERO
FROM MAJOR US POLITICAL, BUSINESS
AND CULTURAL LEADERS

New York, September 16, 1867,
His Excellency, Senor Matias Romero
Envoy Extraordinary and Minister Plenipotentiary, from Mexico
Washington, D.C.

Sir:
The undersigned citizens of New York, desirous to testify in some public manner their esteem for your character as the representative of the Mexican Government, their appreciation of the services you have rendered your country by steadily adhering to its cause under the greatest discouragements, and their interest in the welfare of Mexico invite you to a dinner at such time as may suit your convenience to appoint.
Respectfully, your obedient Servants,
PETER COOPER,
WM. H. ASPINWALL,
PAIL SPOFFORD,
M.H. GRINNELL,
H.H. VAN DYCK,
HENRY CLEWS,
SAM'L COURTNEY,
JAMES ROBB,

CHAS. W. SANDFORD,

FRANCIS SKIDDY,

SHEPARD GANDY,

PARK GODWIN,

WM. R GARRISON,

BENJ. HOLLIDAY

ELLIOTT C. COWDIN,

WM. C. BRYANT,

JAMES. W. BEEKMAN,

HIRAN BARNEY

WM E. DODGE, JR.,

JOHN JAY,

HENRY WARD BEECHER,

DAN'L BUTTERFIELD,

THEODORE ROOSEVELT

JOHN A STEWART

HENRY A. SMYTHE

DAVID HOADLEY

RUFUS INGALLS,

JAS. A WHITING

J. GRANT WILSON

WM.G. FARGO

DOCUMENT 17
ROMERO'S RESPONSE

Washington, September 18, 1867

Gentlemen:

I have been honored with the letter you had the kindness to address me on the 16th instant, inviting me to a Dinner at such time as may suit my convenience to appoint.

It is very gratifying to me, gentlemen, that such good friends of mine and prominent citizens of New York as you, who have encouraged me throughout the contest, would now tender me this significant demonstration, selecting a time when I am about returning home, after having obtained, thanks to a merciful Providence the patriotism of the Mexican people and the noble sympathy of the people of the United States, a crowning success in all the objects of my labors.

I take this flattering demonstration to be the renewed expression of your sympathy for the efforts of the Mexican people in defending the Independence of their Country and the institutions of their choice, and for the patriotic conduct of the Republican Government which did so much to achieve success.

It will afford me a great deal of pleasure to meet you in the proposed social celebration of our success which will, in my opinion, prove advantageous to this country as well as my own, and for which we are so much indebted to you.

Availing myself of the privilege you have been good enough to grant me, I will name Wednesday the 2nd of October, as convenient to me, and hope that this time may be acceptable to you.

I am, Gentlemen, with high respect, most truly

Your obedient servant, M. Romero

Source: https://archive.org/stream/banquettoseorm00newy/ban-quettoseorm00newy_djvu.txt

DOCUMENT 18
MATÍAS ROMERO TO THE SECRETARY
OF EXTERIOR RELATIONS

October 5, 1867

Today at midday I went to the White House to take leave formally of President Johnson. Shortly after I arrived at the White House, Johnson received me. I regretted having to leave this country, where I have so many friends and unforgettable memories, I told him, but I considered it my duty to return to my country. I carried with me, I added, the most agreeable memories of his fine treatment of me in our official relations, of the sympathy he expressed for our cause, and of his very distinguished service for us from his high position. I told him I would take the greatest pleasure in testifying about this to my government and to my fellow citizens.

Johnson thanked me with some emotion for these sentiments. He was not very demonstrative he told me, but his sincerest sympathies have always been with us. Although he did not speak as much as others, he added, he believed no one exceeded him in sympathy for Mexico. He was pleased and satisfied with the result [of the intervention] believing the developments were most favorable for Mexico. Very sincerely desiring us to consolidate peace in the Republic now, he judged, we need only peace to become a prosperous, happy nation. The Liberal party's preponderance, he though, now seemed sufficiently strong to maintain the factions in check and to consolidate the peace. In conclusion, he wished me a happy voyage and a quick return

I thanked Johnson for his kind remarks and took leave of him. His sincere manner and his cordial and frank words persuaded me that his sympathy for us had been and is more profound and sincere than generally believed. [10:428]

Sources of Romero correspondence. *Correspondencia de la legación mexicana en Washington durante la intervención extrajera, 1860-1868.* 10 vols. (México: Imprenta del Gobierno, 1870-92.) English translations by Thomas D. Schoonover and Ebba Wesner Schoonover, *Mexican Lobby. Matías Romero in Washington, 1861-1867.* Thomas D. Schoonover. Lexington: The University Press of Kentucky, 1986.

BIBLIOGRAPHY

I. Manuscripts, Papers, and Documents

A. *Archivo Nacional de México*
Archivo de Defensa, Expediente XI/481, Cosas sobre los soldados que se
llaman San Patricios.
———. Reglamento sobre el Curso de Particulares Contra los Enemigos
de la Nación.
Archivo General de la Secretaría de Relaciones Exteriores, H/252 Des-
posición para que los soldados irlandes...
Cartas y Misc. Papeles del Gral. Mariano Arista con Documentos sobre la
Guerra entre México y los Estados Unidos del Norte.
Matías Romero, "Communication to the Minister of Foreign Relations,"
Chicago, January 23, 1861. Reservada, Numero 17. Archivo de Rela-
ciones Exteriores, Mexico.
B. *Banco de México*
Correspondencia de la legación mexicana en Washington durante la inter-
vención extranjera 1860-1868.
Archivo histórico de Matías Romero: Catalogo descriptiva, corresponden-
cia recibida.
Diario personal de Matías Romero 1855-1865 editado por Emma Cosió
Villegas.
C. *Archivo de Benito Juárez*
Biblioteca Nacional de México. (San Agustín). Fondo Reservado, México.
D. *Library of Congress*
Zachary Taylor Papers.

E. *Brown University, John Hay Library*
The Paul R. Dupree Mexican History Collection
The George L. Church Collection
F. *University of Texas, Latin American Collection*
J.H. Smith Transcripts. Riva Palacio Papers. Valentín Gómez Farías Papers.
G. *Museo de las Intervenciones, Churubusco, México*
Intervención del Lic. Sergio Yáñez de la Barrera, Cordinador de Asesores
y Director Jurídico del Departamento de Distrito Federal en Alvaro-Obregón, Durante el CXXVII Aniversario Luctuoso del Batallón
de San Patricio.
"Intervención Norteamericana 1846-1848," MS (undated) elaborado por
Laura Herrera Serna.

II. Printed Documents

29th Congress, 1st Session. House Executive Document 196, Message
from the President ...Relative to an Invasion and Commencement
of Hostilities by Mexico.

29th Congress, 2nd Session. Senate Document 4. Report of the secretary
of War...Killed, Wounded, or Missing in the Battles of Palo Alto and
Resaca de Palma.

30th Congress, 1st Session, Senate Executive Document 1, Message from
the President...at the Commencement of the First Session of the
Thirtieth Congress.

30th Congress, 1st Session. House Executive Document 17. Correspondence with General Taylor.

30th Congress, 1st Session. House Executive Document 56. Correspondence Between the Secretary of War and Generals Scott and Taylor
and Between General Scott and Mr. Trist.

30th Congress, 1st Session. House Executive Document 59. Correspondence Between the Secretary of War and General Scott.

30th Congress, 1st Session. House Executive Document 60. Mexican War
Correspondence.

30th Congress, 1st Session. Senate Executive Document 14. Message
from the President...Relative To Forced Contributions.

30th Congress, 1st Session. Senate executive Document 20. Message from
the President... in Relation to the Negotiations...During the Suspension of Hostilities After the Battles of Contreras and Churubusco.

30th Congress, 1st Session. Senate Executive Document 36. Report of the Secretary of War Showing the Number of Troops in the Service...the Killed and Wounded &c.

30th Congress, 2nd Session. Executive Document 1. Message from the President...at the Commencement of the Second Session of the Thirtieth Congress.

Complete Treaty of Guadalupe-Hidalgo, February 2, 1848, as ratified. Treaties and Conventions between the United States of America and Other Powers Since July 4, 1776. (Washington, DC: Government Printing Office, 1871).

37th Congress, 1st Session, Senate Executive Document 1, House Executive Documents 1 and 54.

37th Congress, 2nd Session, House Executive Document 100.

39th Congress, 1st Session, House Executive Document 1

39th Congress, 2nd Session, House Executive Document 29.

40th Congress, 1st Session, Senate Executive Document 20. House Executive Document 1.

III. Newspapers

Baltimore *Niles National Register.*
Boston *Times.*
Brooklyn *Daily Eagle*
Chihuahua *The Anglo-Saxon.*
Daily Delta.
Diario del Gobierno de la República Mexicana.
Guadalajara *El Informador.*
Los Angeles Times.
La Opinión.
Mexico City *The American Star*
El Correo Nacional.
El Monitor Republicano
El Siglo Diez y Nueve.
El Sol de México.
New Orleans *Picayune.*
New York *Evening Post.*
New York *Morning News*
New York Herald
New York Tribune

The North American.
Novedades.
Periódico Oficial.
Richmond *Tribune*
Richmond *Jeffersonian*
Siglo Diezinueve
Siglo Veintiuno.
Washington *National Intelligencer.*

IV. Contemporaneous periodicals and journals

American Review.
Graham's Magazine.
Harper's Weekly.
Liberator.
The Pioneer.
The Spirit of the Times.
United States Magazine and Democratic Review.

V. Accounts by Contemporaries (1845-1850)

Alcaraz, Ramón et al, eds. *Apuntes para la historia de la guerra entre México y los Estados Unidos.* Mexico: M. Paynó, 1848.
——. *The Other Side; Or Notes for the History of the War Between Mexico and the United States.* Trans. By Albert C. Ramsey. New York: J. Wiley, 1850.
Ampudia, Pedro de. *Manifiesto del General Ampudia a Sus Conciudadanos.* México: Ignacio Cumplido, 1847.
Balbontín, Manuel. *La invasión americana, 1846 a 1847. Apuntes del Subteniente de Artillería Manuel Balbontín.* México: Gonzalo A. Esteva, 1883.
Ballentine, George. *Autobiography of an English Soldier in the United States Army, Comprising Observations in the States and Mexico.* New York: Stronger & Townsend, 1853.
Bosh García, Carlos. *Material para la Historia Diplomática de México (México y los Estados Unidos, 1820-1848).* México: Escuela Nacional de Ciencias Politicas Y Sociales, 1957.
Clark, Amasa G. *Reminiscences of a Centenarian, as Told by Amasa Gleason Clark, Veteran of the Mexican War, to Cora Tope Clark.* Ed. by J. Marvin Hunter, Sr. Bandera: n.p., 1930.

Calderon de la Barca, Fanny. *Life in Mexico. The Letters of Fanny Calderon de la Barca.* Garden City: Anchor Books, 1970.

Chamberlain, Samuel E. *My Confession.* Written and illustrated by Samuel Emery Chamberlain. New York: Harper & Bros., 1851, reprint, 1956.

Connelley, William Elsey, ed. *Doniphan's Expedition and the Conquest of New Mexico and California.* Topeka: n.p., 1907.

Davis, George T.M. *Autobiography of the Late Col. Geo. T. M. Davis, Captain and Aide-de-Camp Scott's Army of Invasion (Mexico),* New York: n.p., 1853.

DeHart, William C. Capt. (Former Judge-Advocate). *Observations On Military Law, and the Constitution and Practice of Courts-Martial with a Summary of the Law of Evidence as Applicable to Military Trials.* New York: Wiley and Putnam, 1846.

Edwards, Frank S. *A Campaign in New Mexico With Colonel Doniphan.* Philadelphia: Carey & Hart, 1847.

García, Genaro y Pereyra, Carlos, eds. *México durante su guerra con los Estados Unidos en Documentos inéditos o muy raros para la historia de México.* México: Editorial Bouret, 1906.

[Giddings, Luther]. *Sketches of the Campaign in Northern Mexico by an Officer of the First Regiment of Ohio Volunteers.* New York: George P. Putnam & Co., 1853.

Grant, Ulysses S. *Personal Memoirs of U.S. Grant.* 2 vols. New York: Charles A. Webster & Co., 1885-86.

Henry, William S. *Campaign Sketches of the War With Mexico.* New York: Harper & Bros., 1847.

Herndon, William H. *Recollections of Abraham Lincoln: The True Story of a Great Life.* Charleston: CreateSpace, 2014. Kindle edition.

Hitchcock, Ethan A. *Fifty Years in Camp and Field; Dairy of Major General Ethan Allen Hitchcock, U.S.A.* ed. W. A. Croffut. New York: G.P. Putnam's Sons, 1909.

Jay, William A. *A Review of the Causes and Consequences of the Mexican War.* Boston: Benjamin B. Mussey, 1849.

Lincoln, Abraham. *The Writings of Abraham Lincoln. All volumes.* New York: Waxkeep Publishing, 2013. Kindle Edition.

Livermore, Abiel Abbot. *The War With Mexico Reviewed.* Boston: American Peace Society, 1850.

Moore, H. Judge. *Scott's Campaign in Mexico from the Rendezvous on the Island of Lobos to the Taking of the City.* Charlestown: J.B. Nixon, 1849.

O'Sullivan, John L. "Annexation," *United States Magazine and Democratic Review,* vol. 27, no. LXXXV (July/August 1845): 5-10.

Oswendal, J. Jacob. *Notes of the Mexican War 1846-47-48.* Philadelphia: n.p., 1885.

Prieto, Guillermo. *Memorias de mis tiempos, 1828 a 1853.* 2 vols. México: Editorial Patria, 1948.

Quaife, Milo Milton, ed. *The Dairy of James K. Polk During His Presidency, 1845 to 1849.* 4 vols. Chicago: A.C. McClurg & Co., 1910.

Ramsey, Albert C., trans. *The Other Side: Or, Notes for the History of the War Between Mexico and the United States.* New York: John Wiley, 1850.

Reilly, James. "An Artilleryman's Story," *Journal of the Military Service Institution 33* (1903):438-46.

Ruxton, George Frederick Augustus. *Adventures in Mexico and the Rocky Mountains.* New York: Harper and Bros., 1848.

Samson, William H., ed. *Letters of Zachary Taylor from the Battle-Fields of the Mexican War.* Reprinted from the originals in the collection of Mr. William K. Bixby of St. Louis, Mo. Rochester: The Genesee Press, 1908.

Santa Anna, Antonio López de. *Detalle de las Operaciones Ocurridas en la Defensa de la Capital de la República, Atacada por el Ejército de los Estados-Unidos del Norte en el Año de 1847.* México: Ignacio Cumplido.

———. *The Eagle. The Autobiography of Santa Anna.* Ed. Ann Fears Crawford. Austin: The Pemberton Press, 1967.

———. *Las Guerras de México con Tejas y los EstadosUnidos.* México: Ch. Bouret, 1910.

———. *Mi Historia Militar y Política 1810-1874.* México: Ch. Bouret, 1905.

[Scott, John A.] *Encarnacion Prisoners, Comprising An Account of the March of the Kentucky Cavalry from Louisville to the Rio Grande.* Louisville: Prentice & Weissanger, 1848.

Scott, Winfield. *Memoirs of Lieut. General Scott, LL.D. Written by Himself.* New York: Shelton & Co. 1864.

Semmes, Raphael. *The Campaign of General Scott in the Valley of Mexico.* Cincinnati: More and Anderson, 1852.

———. *Service Afloat and Ashore During the Mexican War.* Cincinnati: William H. Moore, 1851.

Sherman, William. *The Memoirs of William T. Sherman.* New York: Harper Torch, 1885. Kindle Edition, 2014.

Sheridan, Philip H. *Personal Memoirs of P.H. Sheridan, General, United States Army.* New York: Charles Webster, 1888. Kindle Edition.

Smith, George Winston, and Charles Judah, eds. *Chronicles of the Gringos: The U.S. Army in the Mexican War, 1846-48, Accounts of Eyewitnesses and Combatants.* Albuquerque: University of New Mexico Press, 1968.

Stevenson, Sara York. *Maximilian in Mexico: A Woman's Reminiscences of the French Intervention.* New York: Century, 1899.

Thompson, Waddy. *Recollections of Mexico.* New York: Wiley and Putnam, 1846.

Valencia, Gabriel. *Detalladlas Acciones de los Días 19 y 20 en los Campos de Padierna, y Otros Pormenores Recientemente Comunicados por Personas Fidedignas.* Morelia: Ignacio Arango, 1847.

Wise, Henry A., Lt., U.S.N. *Los Gringos, or, an Inside View of Mexico and California, with Wanderings in Peru, Chile, and Polynesia.* New York: Baker and Scribner, 1849.

VI. Other, non-contemporary, secondary sources, and monographs

Adams, William Lawrence. *Pennsylvania's Amazon Princess Railroad,* Bloomington: AuthorHouse, 2012.

Allen, Debra J. *Historical Dictionary of U.S. Diplomacy from the Revolution to Secession.* Lanham: Scarecrow Press, 2012.

Arteta, Begoña. *Destino Manifiesto: Viajeros anglosajones en México, 1830-1840.* México: Ediciones Gernika, 1989.

Baker, Kimball. *"The Saint Patrick's Fought For Their Skins and Mexico."* Smithsonian 8 (1978): 94-101.

Basler, Roy P. ed. The Collected Works of Abraham Lincoln, Vol 1, New Brunswick: Rutgers University Press, 1953.

——. *The Collected Works of Abraham Lincoln,* Vol. II, Rockville: Wildside Press, 2008.

Bauer, K. Jack. *The Mexican War: 1846-48.* New York: Macmillan Co., 1974.

Berthoff, Roland. *An Unsettled People.* New York: Harper and Row, 1971.

Bill, Alfred Hoyt. *Rehearsal for Conflict: The War With Mexico 1845-1848.* New York: Alfred A. Knopf, 1947.

Billington, Ray Allan. *The Protestant Crusade: 1800-1860.* New York: Rinehart and Company, 1938.

Blaisdell, Bob. *The Wit and Wisdom of Abraham Lincoln.* New York: Dive Publications, Inc, 2005.

Blumenthal, Shirley, and Ozer, Jerome S. *Coming to America.* New York: Delacourt Press, 1980.

Brockway, Thomas P. *Documentos Básicos de la Política Exterior Estadounidense.* Traducción: Mario A. Marino. Argentina: Editorial Agora, 1958.

Brueck, Gene M. *Mexico Views Manifest Destiny 1821-1846.* Albuquerque: University of New Mexico Press, 1975.

Bustamante, Carlos María de. *El nuevo Bernal Díaz del Castillo o sea Historia de la invasión de los angloamericanos en México.* México: Secretaría Educación Pública, 1949.

Callcott, Wilfred Hardy. *Church and State in Mexico.* Durham: Duke University Press, 1926.

———. *Santa Anna. The Story of An Enigma Which Once Was Mexico.* Norman: University of Oklahoma Press, 1936.

Cantú, Gastón García. *Las invasiones norteamericanas en México.* México: Ediciones Era, 1971.

Carney, Stephen A. C *The Occupation of Mexico May 1846-July 1848.* West Point. US Army Center of Military History, 2015.

Castillo Fernández, Francisco del. *Apuntes para la historia de San Ángel.* México: Museo Nacional de Arqueología, Historia y Etnología, 1913.

Castillo Negrete, Emilio del. *Invasión de los Norteamericanos en México.* 4 vols. México: n.p., 1890-91.

Chartrand, René. *The Mexican Adventure 1861-67* (Men-At-War Series). Oxford: Osprey Publishing Company. 1994.

Clary, David A. *Eagles and Empire.* New York: Bantam Books, 2009.

Connor, Seymour V, and Odie B. Faulk. *North America Divided. The Mexican War, 1846-1848.* New York: Oxford University Press, 1971.

Cox, Patricia. *Batallón de San Patricio.* México: Editorial Stylo, 1954.

Curtis, Edmund. *History of Ireland.* London: Oxford University Press, 1937.

Day, Mark R. "The Passion of the San Patricios," *Irish American Magazine,* May-June (1993): 44-48.

DeVoto, Benard. *The Year of Decison: 1846.* Boston: Little, Brown and Company, 1943.

DiLorenzo, Thomas. *Lincoln Unmasked: What You're Not Supposed to Know About Dishonest Abe.* New York: Three Rivers Press, 2006.

———. *The Real Lincoln: A New Look At Abraham Lincoln, His Agenda and An Unnecessary War.* New York: Three Rivers Press, 2003.

Donald, David Herbert. *Lincoln.* New York: Touchstone, 1995.

Downey, Fairfax. "The Tragic Story of the San Patricio Battalion," *The American Heritage Reader.* New York: Dell Publishing Company, 1956.

Eisenhower, John. S.D. *So Far From God. The U.S. War With Mexico 1846-1848.* New York: Doubleday, 1989.

Elson, John. "The Destruction of Old Mexico," *Time,* April 11, 1994.

Erlich, Paul, et al., eds. *The Golden Door.* New York: Ballantine Books, 1979.

Fanfani, Amintore. *Catholicism, Protestantism and Capitalism.* New York: Sheed & Ward, 1955.

Findley, Paul. *A. Lincoln, The Crucible of Congress: The Years Which Forged His Greatness.* Fairfield, CA: James Stevenson Publisher, 2004.

Finnerty, John F. *John F. Finnerty Reports Porfirian Mexico,* 1879. Ed. by. Wilbert H. Timmons. El Paso: Texas Western Press, 1974.

Finke, Detmar H. "The Organization and Uniforms of the San Patricios Units of the Mexican Army, 1846-1848." *Military Collector and Historian* 9 (1957): 36-38.

Fisher, Louis. *The Mexican War and Lincoln's "Spot Resolutions."* Damascus: Pennyhill Press, 2009.

Fogarty, Jim. "The Irish Who Died For Mexico," *Ireland's Own,* December (1990): 20-21.

Foster, R.F., ed. *The Oxford History of Ireland.* New York/Oxford: Oxford University Press, 1989.

Frías, Heriberto. *La guerra contra los Gringos.* México: Ediciones Leega/Jucar, 1984.

Fuentes, Carlos. *The Buried Mirror: Reflections on Spain and the New World,* 1862-1867. Boston: Houghton Mifflin, 1992.

Gallagher, Gary W., Ed. *The Spotsylvania Campaign.* Chapel Hill: University of North Carolina Press, 1998.

Gallagher, Thomas. *Paddy's Lament: Ireland 1846-1847, Prelude To Hatred.* New York: Harcourt, Brace & Company, 1982.

Greeley, Andrew M. *That Most Distressful Nation.* Chicago: Quadrangle Books, 1972.

Greenberg, Amy S. *A Wicked War. Polk Clay, Lincoln and the 1846 U.S. Invasion of Mexico.* New York: Alfred A. Knopf, 2012.

Grabman, Richard. *Gods, Gachupines and Gringos: A People's History of Mexico.* Mazatlán: Editorial Mazatlán, 2008.

[Harney, William S.] "General Harney," *Journal of the United States Cavalry Association* 3 (1890): 1-8.

Haley, Alex. *Roots.* New York: Doubleday, 1976.

Hammond, Scott J. et al., ed. *Classics of American Political Thought.* Vol. 1. Indianapolis: Hackett Publishing Company, 2007.

Hanke, Lewis. "A Note on the Life and Publications of Colonel George Earl Church." Providence: Transportation Engineers, 1965.

Hart, John Mason. *Empire and Revolution: The Americans in Mexico Since the Civil War.* Berkeley: University of California Press, 2002.

Henry, Robert Selph. *The Story of the Mexican War.* Indianapolis/New York: The Bobbs-Merrill Company, 1950.

Heitman, Francis, comp. *Historical Register and Dictionary of the United States Army from Its Organization, Sept. 29, 1789 to March 2, 1903.* 2 vols. Washington: Government Printing Office, 1903.

Hogan, Michael. *The Irish Soldiers of Mexico.* Guadalajara: Fondo Editorial Universitario, 1997.

Holt, Thaddeus. "Checkmate At Mexico City," *The Quarterly Journal of Military History.* (Spring 1990): 82-93.

Hopkins, G.T. "The San Patricio Battalion In The Mexican War," *The U.S. Cavalry Journal* 24 (1913): 279-84.

Johannsen, Robert W. *To The Halls of the Montezumas: The Mexican War In The American Imagination.* New York/Oxford: Oxford University Press, 1985.

Jones, Oakah C., Jr. *Santa Anna.* New York: Twayne Publishing, 1968.

Kane, John J. *Catholic-Protestant Conflicts in America.* Chicago: Regnery, 1955.

Knobel, Dale T. *Paddy and the Republic. Ethnicity and Nationality in Antebellum America.* Middletown: Wesleyan University Press, 1986.

Krueger, Carl. *Saint Patrick's Battalion.* New York: Dutton & Co., 1960.

Lavender, David. *Climax at Buena Vista.* Philadelphia: J.P. Lippincott, 1966.

Lowell, James Russell. *The Biglow Papers, A Critical Edition.* DeKalb: Northern Illinois University, 1917.

Mahoney, Tom. "50 Hanged and 11 Branded, The Story of the San Patricio Battalion," *Southwest Review* 32 (1947): 373-77.

Martínez, Leopoldo C. *La Intervención Norteamericana en México 1846-1848.* México: Panorama Editorial, 1991.

Matthews, Chris. *A Flag To Fly.* San Francisco: Spectrum Theater Company, 1987.

May, Robert E. "Invisible Men: Blacks and the U.S. Army In the Mexican War," *The Historian,* vol. XLIX, No. 4 (August, 1987): 463-477.

———. *Slavery, Race, and Conquest in the Tropics: Lincoln, Douglas, and the Future of Latin America,* New York: Cambridge University Press, 2013

Mayo, C.M. *The Last Prince of the Mexican Empire.* Denver: Unbridled Books, 2009.

McClure, Alexander K. *Lincoln's Yarns and Stories.* Chicago: John C. Winston Company, n/d. Public domain. Kindle Edition, 2012.McHugh, Michael J. *George B. McClellan: The Disposable Patriot.* Arlington Heights: Christian Liberty Press, 1998.

Merklin, Lewis, Jr. *They Chose Honor.* Philadelphia: University of Pennsylvania, 1974.

McEniry, Sister Blanche M. *American Catholics in the War With Mexico.* Washington: Catholic University of America, 1937.

McCornack, Richard B. "The San Patricio Deserters in the Mexican War," *The Americas* 8 (1951): 131-42.

McGee, Thomas D'Arcy. *History of the Irish Settlers in North America.* Baltimore: Genealogical Publishing, 1952.

McHenry, J. Patrick. *A Short History of Mexico.* Garden City: Dolphin Books, 1952.

McPherson, Edward. *The Political History of the United States During the Great Rebellion: From November 6, 1860 to July 4, 1864. Including a Classified Summary of the Legislation of the Second Session of the Thirty-sixth Congress, the Three Sessions of the Thirty-seventh Congress. And the Votes Thereon, and the Important Executive, Judicial and Politico-military facts of the Eventful Period; Together with the Organization Legislation and General Procedure of the Rebel Legislature.* London: Forgotten Books, 2015.

Meltzer, Milton. *Bound For the Rio Grande: The Mexican Struggle 1845-1850.* New York: Alfred A. Knopf, 1974.

Merk, Frederick. *Manifest Destiny and Mission in American History.* New York: Random House, 1966.

Meyer, Michael C. and Sherman, William L. *The Course of Mexican History.* New York/Oxford: Oxford University Press, 1979.

Mills, Bronwyn, Mills, ed. *The Mexican War (America At War).* New York: Facts On File, 1992.

Military Laws of the United States. Washington: Government Printing Office, 1915.

Miller, Robert Ryal. *Mexico: A History.* Norman: University of Oklahoma, 1985.

———. *Shamrock and Sword: The Saint Patrick's Battalion in the U.S.-Mexican War.* Norman: University of Oklahoma, 1989.

Morrison, Samuel Elliot. *The Oxford History of the American People. Vol. II.* New York: Mentor Books, 1965.

Muñoz, Rafael F. *Santa Anna: El dictador resplandeciente.* México: Fondo de Cultura Económica, 1983.

Neve, Carlos D. *Historia gráfica del ejército mexicano.* Cuernavaca: Quesada Brandi, 1967.

Nicols, Edward J. *Zach Taylor's Little Army.* Garden City: Doubleday & Co., 1963.

O'Flaherty, Daniel. *General Jo Shelby, Undefeated Rebel.* Chapel Hill: University of North Carolina Press, 1954.

Paz, Octavio. *The Labyrinth of Solitude: Life and Thought in Mexico.* Trans. by Lysander Kemp. New York: Grove Press, 1961.

Potter, George F. *To The Golden Door: The Story of the Irish In Ireland and America.* Boston: Little Brown & Co., 1960.

Peraino, Kevin. *Lincoln in the World: The Making of a Statesman and the Dawn of American Power.* New York: Crown Publishers, 2013.

Ramírez, José Fernando. *Mexico During the War With the United States.* Ed. Walter V. Scholes. Trans. Elliot B. Scheer. Columbia: University of Missouri, 1950.

Rea, Vargas, ed. *Apuntes Históricos Sobre los Acontecimientos Notables de la Guerra Entre México y los Estados Unidos del Norte.* México: Biblioteca Aportación Histórica, 1945.

Reavis, L.U. *The Life and Military Service of Gen. William Selby Harney.* St.Louis: Bryan, Brand and Co., 1878.

Riva Palacio, Vicente, ed. *México através de los siglos.* 5 vols. México: Ballesca y Cía, 1887-89.

Roa Bárcena, José M. *Recuerdos de la invasión nortemericana.* (1846-1848). 3 vols. México: Editorial Porrúa, 1947.

Robinson, Cecil, ed. *The View From Chapultepec: Mexican Writers on the Mexican-American War.* Tucson: University of Arizona Press, 1979.

Ruiz, Ramón Eduardo. *The Mexican War: Was It Manifest Destiny?* New York: Holt, Rinehart and Winston, 1963.

Schiller, A. Arthur. *Military Law: Statutes, Regulations, Orders, Judicial Decisions, and Opinions of the Judge Advocates-General.* St. Paul: West Publishing Company, 1952.

Schoonover, Thomas D., ed. *Mexican Lobby: Matías Romero in Washington 1861-1867.* Lexington: The University of Kentucky Press, 1986.

Schroeder, John H. *Mr. Polk's War: American Opposition and Dissent 1846-1848.* Madison: University of Wisconsin Press, 1973.

Schroeder, Seaton. *The Fall of Maximilian's Empire as Seen from a United States Gunboat.* New York, 1887.

Singletary, Otis. *The Mexican War.* Chicago: University of Chicago, 1960.

Smith, Arthur D. Howden. *Old Fuss and Feathers.* New York: Greystone Press, 1937.

Smith, Justin H., *The Annexation of Texas.* New York: Baker & Taylor, Co., 1911.

———. *The War With Mexico.* 2 vols. New York: Macmillan Co., 1919.

Sobieski, John. *The Life Story and Personal Reminiscences of Col John Sobieski (Lineal Descendant of King John II of Poland).* Miami: Hard Press, 2014.

———. *Life of President Benito Juárez: The Savior and Regenerator of Mexico.* Charleston, SC: Nabu Press, 2011. Reproduction of original.

Stahr, Walter. *Seward: Lincoln's Indispensable Man.* New York: Simon and Schuster, 2012.

Stephens, David R. *Sin Perdón: Acquiescence with Murder, The Wholesale Betrayal of Maximilian,* Vol. II, Bloomington, IL: AuthorHouse, 2008.

Stephens, John Richard. *Commanding the Storm: Civil War Battles in the Words of the Generals Who Fought Them.* Guilford: Lyons Press, 2012

Stinson, Byron. "They Went Over to the Enemy," *American History Illustrated* 3 (1968): 30-36.

Thomas, Benjamin P. *Abraham Lincoln. A Biography.* Carbondale: Southern Illinois University, 2008. Kindle Edition.

Thorpe, Francis N. *The Civil War: The National View.* Charleston: Nabu Press, 2010.

Tuttleton, James. "Lincoln's generals: Sherman and Grant in their memoirs," *The New Criterion,* October 1990.

Turner, Frederick C. *The Dynamic of Mexican Nationalism.* Chapel Hill: University of North Carolina, 1968.

Turner, Frederick Jackson. *The United States, 1830-1850: The Nation and Its Sections.* New York: Henry Holt and Company, 1935.

Vallier, Ivan. *Catholicism, Social Control, and Modernization in Latin America.* Englewood Cliffs: Prentice Hall, 1970.

Vásquez, Josefina Zoraida. *Mexicanos y Norteamericanos ante la Guerra del 47.* México: Ediciones Ateneo, 1977.

———. "The Texas Question In Mexican Politics, 1836-1845," *Southwestern Historical Quarterly* 89 (1986): 309-44.

Vigness, David M. *The Revolutionary Decades.* Austin: Steck-Vaughn, 1965.

Waldrop, M. Mitchell. *Complexity: The Emerging Science At The Edge of Order and Chaos.* New York: Simon and Schuster, 1992.

Wallace, Edward S. "The Battalion of St. Patrick in the Mexican War," *Military Affairs,* vol. xiv (1950): 84-91.

———. "Deserters in the Mexican War," *Hispanic American Historical Review* 15 (1935): 374-83.

Weems, John Edward. *To Conquer A Peace: The War Between the United States and Mexico.* Garden City/New York: Doubleday, 1974.

Wilson, Douglas L. and David, Rodney O. eds. *Herndon's Informants.* Chicago: University of Illinois Press, 1998.

Wittke, Carl. *The Irish in America.* Baton Rouge: Louisiana State University, 1956.

Woodham-Smith, Cecil. *The Great Hunger: Ireland 1845-49.* New York: New American Library, 1962.

Wortham, Louis J. *A History of Texas.* Glendale: Arthur H. Clarke Co., 1924.

Wynn, Dennis J. "The San Patricio Soldiers: Mexico's Foreign Legion," *Southwestern Studies,* Monograph 74. El Paso: University of Texas at El Paso.

——. "The San Patricios and the United States-Mexican War of 1846-1848," Ph.D. diss, Loyola University of Chicago, 1982.

Yoakum, H. *History of Texas.* Austin: Steck Co., 1935.

Zinn, Howard. *A People's History of the United States.* New York: HaperPerennial, 2001.

Zorrilla, Luis. *Historia de las relaciones entre México y los Estados Unidos de América, 1800-1858.* 2 vols. México: Editorial Porrúa, 1965.

VII. Miscellaneous Articles and Internet Sources

Auer, Jeffrey J. "Lincoln's Minister to Mexico" in *Ohio State Archeological and Historical Quarterly 57* (1950).

Carney, Stephen A. *The Occupation of Mexico May 1846-July 1848.* (West Point. US Army Center of Military History (2015).

Civil War, African American Medal of Honor Recipients. http://www.buffalosoldier.net/CIVILWARAFRICAN-AMERICANMED-ALOFHONORRECIPIENTS.htm

Corwin, Thomas. *Speech to the United States Senate,* February 11, 1847. http://www.bartleby.com/268/910.html

"Death of Maximilian." http://www.heritage-history.com/

Doblado, Manuel quoted by Kristen Arias in "Ley Juárez." http://historicaltextarchive.com/print.php?action=section&artid=572.

Emancipation Proclamation, http://www.civilwar.org/education/history/emancipation-150/10-facts.html

Galeano, Eduardo. Una entrevista en el 2013 con periodista Gary Young. "a historia nunca dice adiós. La historia dice hasta luego. http://www.masde131.com/2015/04/el-arte-de-la-memoria-indomita-para-recordar-a-eduardo-galeano/

General Lew Wallace Study and Museum, http://www.ben-hur.com/meet-lew-wallace/soldier/

Harper's Weekly, The Presidential Elections 1860-1912. http://elections.harpweek.com/1860/Overview-1860-2.htm

Hanke, Louis. *A Note on the Life and Publications of Colonel George Earl Church,* (Providence: Transportation Engineers, 1965). 1-33.

History Net: Sheridan. http://www.historynet.com/philip-sheridan

John Brown's Body/Battle Hymn of the Republic. *Library of Congress.* www.loc.gov/teachers/lyrical/songs/john_brown.html

JSTOR, Obituary, Colonel George Earl Church, JSTOR, 35: 303-205. http://www.jstor.org/stable/1777010

Latin American History. The Biography of William Walker, The Ultimate Yankee Imperialist, updated December 2014. http://latinamericanhistory.about.com/od/historyofcentralamerica/a/wwalker.htm

Lincoln, Abraham. The Emancipation Proclamation, January 1, 1863. http://www.archives.gov/exhibits/featured_documents/emancipation_proclamation/transcript.html

Lincoln, Abraham to William Herndon. February 15, 1848. *Classic Literature in the Public Domain Library.* Great Britain. http://www.classic-literature.co.uk/american-authors/19th-century/abraham-lincoln/

Lincoln, Abraham. Cooper Union Speech. http://www.abrahamlincolnonline.org/lincoln/speeches/cooper.htm

Lundy, Benjamin. "Anti-Texass Legion: Protest of some free men, states and presses against the Texass rebellion, against the laws of nature and of nations. "(Albany: n/p, 1845.) http://texashistory.unt.edu/ark:/67531/metapth2356/

Mendez, Luciana. "American School has largest U.S. history class in Latin America." *The Guadalajara Reporter.* Dec. 27, 2014.

Miller, Robert Ryal. "American Legion of Honor in Mexico." *Pacific Historical Review,* Vol. 30, No. 3 (Aug. 1961).

Obama, Barack. Address to the Nation. Office of the Press Secretary. The White House. December 01, 2009. https://www.whitehouse.gov/the-press-office/remarks-president-address-nation-way-forward-afghanistan-and-pakistan

Polk, James K. Address to Congress, May 11, 1846. http://www.dmwv.org/mexwar/documents/polk.htm

Quinlan, Casey. "College Board Caves to Conservatives, Changes U.S. History Curriculum." July 30, 2015. http://thinkprogress.org/economy/2015/07/30/3686060/conservatives-get-major-win-fight-ap-history-classes/

Richmond *Daily Inquirer,* 24 December 1860. 1860 Presidential Returns. http://www.virginiamemory.com/docs/1860_election_returns.pdf

Robert Gould Shaw Memorial. http://ctmonuments.net/2010/05/robert-gould-shaw-memorial-boston/

Schultz, Kathryn. "American Chronicles: Henry David Thoreau's Moral Myopia." *The New Yorker,* October 19, 2015.

Signal Corps Association. "Weaponry of 1860-1965." http://www.
civilwarsignals.org/pages/signal/signalpages/weapons.html.

Stanton, E. Cady, et al. "Form letter from E. Cady Stanton, Susan B. Anthony, and Lucy Stone asking friends to send petitions for women's
suffrage to their representatives in Congress, 12/26/1865," Records
of the US House of Representatives, National Archives and Records
Administration, Washington. ARC Identifier 306686.

Statutes of the United States. Gadsden Purchase. Yale Law School. http://
avalon.law.yale.edu/19th_century/mx1853.asp

Stevenson, Sara York. *Maximilian in Mexico: A Woman's Reminiscences of the
French Intervention* (New York: Century, 1899). http://www.executed-
today.com/tag/carlos-fuentes/

"Treaties of Velasco. 14 May 1836." *Lone Star Junction.* www.lsjunction.
com/docs/velasco.htm

Truman, Harry. "Address in Mexico," The Presidency Project. http://
www.presidency.ucsb.edu/ws/?pid=12841

Tuck, Jim. "Mexico's Lincoln: The Ecstasy and Agony of Benito Juárez
," MexConnect. http://www.mexconnect.com/articles/274-mexi-
co-s-lincoln-the-ecstasy-and-agony-of-benito-juarez

Upton, George P. "Siege of Querétaro," *Maximilian in Mexico* (Chicago:
A.C. McClurg & Co., 1911). Siege of Querétaro," http://www.her-
itage-history.com/

US Department of State. Office of the Historian. "Gadsden Purchase".
https://history.state.gov/milestones/1830-1860/gadsden-purchase
———. https://history.state.gov/milestones/1861-1865/french-interven-
tion.

Vásquez, Josefina. *The Texas Question in Mexican Politics, 1836-1845*, in
Southwestern Historical Quarterly 89 (1986).

Volkmann, Carl and Roberta. Benito Juárez Bust. "Springfield's Sculpture,
Monuments and Plaques." http://springfieldsculptures.net/Juarez.
html

West Virginia Archives and History. "John Brown's Raid." http://www.
wvculture.org/history/johnbrown.html

Whitman, Walt. "Year of Meteors," public domain. http://www.bartleby.
com/142/100.html

VIII. List of Maps

Map 1. "Coming of Age, 1821." Cartographic division of National Geographic Magazine. Copyright 1987.

Map 2. Untitled map in Chapter 3 showing the Nueces River as the boundary between Texas and Mexico. Courtesy of Wikicommons.

Map 3. Territory Ceded to the United States by the Treaty of Guadalupe Hidalgo, February 2, 1848. Courtesy of the Robinson Library.

IX. Photo Credits

Fig. 1. "Zachary Taylor, circa 1846." Cropped 8 x 10 version. Daguerreotype Division. Library of Congress.

Fig. 2. "General Antonio López de Santa Anna, circa 1830." Official portrait. Museo de Intervenciones.

Fig. 3. "Abraham Lincoln, 1846." Daguerreotype Division. Library of Congress.

Fig. 4. "Twenty-two days Siege of Veracruz," 1847 by William Henry Powell, 1867. Image Duplication Division. Library of Congress.

Fig. 5. "Close up of Abraham Lincoln at the time of his election to Congress," 1846. Courtesy of the Daguerreotype Collection, Library of Congress.

Fig. 6. John Brown, 1859. Photo by Black and Batchelder. Photo Duplicating Division. Library of Congress.

Fig. 7. Pierre G.T. Beauregard, Brigadier General, CSA, 1861.

Fig. 8. Jefferson Davis, President of the Confederate States of America. Photo by Matthew Brady, 1861. Public domain. National Archives.

Fig. 9. "Sheridan" by Alex Gardner - File from The Photographic History of The Civil War in Ten Volumes: Volume Four, The Cavalry. The Review of Reviews Co., New York. 1911. p. 268. Licensed under Public Domain via Commons.

Fig. 10. Congratulatory 1864 letter of Lincoln's pasted in Sheridan's *Memoirs*. Public domain. Philip H. Sheridan, *Personal Memoirs of P.H. Sheridan, General, United States Army*. New York: Charles Webster, 1888.

Fig. 11. Matías Romero, Special Mexican Envoy to the US *Carte de visite*, 1863. Age 26. Photographer unknown. Provided by the Republic Mexico. Public domain.

Fig. 12. Company E, 4th US Colored Infantry. Washington, D.C. Photo by William Morris Smith. Courtesy of Library of Congress.

AUTHOR BIOGRAPHY

Michael Hogan is the author of twenty-four books, including the best-selling *Irish Soldiers of Mexico* and the controversial *Savage Capitalism and the Myth of Democracy*. He is Emeritus Humanities Chair at the American School Foundation of Guadalajara, and a former professor of International Relations at the Autonomous University of Guadalajara. He is a member of the Organization of American Historians, the American Historical Association, and the Sociedad de Geografía y Estadísticas de Jalisco. Please visit the author's website at http://www.drmichaelhogan.com/

OTHER AVAILABLE WORKS BY THIS AUTHOR

History and historical fiction
The Irish Soldiers of Mexico, 1997
Los Soldados Irlandeses de México (Spanish Edition), 2014
Molly Malone & the San Patricios, 1999
Molly Malone y los San Patricios, Spanish Edition, 2012

Essays and other non-fiction
*We Never Know How High We Are Till We Are Called to Rise: Fifteen
    Five-Minute Speeches for Induction Ceremonies*, 2016
A Metaphorical Piano and Other Stories, 2013
A Writer's Beginnings, 2012
*Teaching from the Heart: Essays and Speeches on Teaching at American
    Schools in Latin America*, 2011
Twelve Habits of the Creative Mind, 2011
*Intelligent Mistakes: An English Grammar Supplement for Latin American
    Students*, 2011
A Writer's Manual: For Inmates in Correctional Institutions, 2011
*Savage Capitalism and the Myth of Democracy: Latin America in the Third
    Millennium*, 2009
Mexican Mornings: Essays South of the Border, 2006

Poetry
In the Time of the Jacarandas, 2015
A Lion at a Cocktail Party, 35th Anniversary Edition, 2013
Winter Solstice, 2012
Imperfect Geographies, 2011

The broken face of summer: Poems, 1981
Letters For My Son, 1975

Fiction
A Death in Newport, 2011

Anthologies
Mexico: Sunlight & Shadows, 2015 (contributor and co-editor)

ACKNOWLEDGEMENTS

The author and publisher wish to acknowledge the interest, time, and efforts by numerous people who received Advance Reader Copies of the manuscript and who offered feedback about this book project. We are especially indebted to author/professor Robert J. DiYanni of New York University, author/professor emeritus Robert E. May of Purdue University, author Elizabeth Maul Schwartz (a ninth-generation Texan, summer intern Jasmine Ortiz from the University of San Diego, and author Margaret Van Every.

Others we wish to thank include: Ronald Barnett, John Steven Beauchamp, William Beezley, Victoria M. Breting-Garcia, Lauren Brisbon, Wes Borucki, Marlene Brown, Tony Burton, Ana Sofia Carbonell, Marsh Cassady, Peter Catapano, Alfredo Corchado, Susan Dawson, Joel Dennstedt, Renee Drake, Dennis Fitter, Victor Gonzalez Pérez, Paul Grasmehr, Carlos Hernández, Eva M. Hunter, Richard Jensen, William Kaliher, C.M. Mayo, Matthew McCarty, Carol M. Merchasin, Christopher Minster, Sascha Möbius, Liam O'Hara, Fernando Ortiz, Jr., Margaret Porter, Jennifer Redmond, John Scherber, Joshua Shiver, Richard Stafford, Philip Stover, Joan F. Suttle, Loida Tapia, Carroll Trosclair, Luis Alberto Urrea, Heribert Von Feilitzsch, Carol Wheeler, Dawn Wink, and Christy Wiseman.

EDITOR'S EPILOGUE

Around the world, more than 400,000 students take the Advanced Placement US History (APUSH) exam every year, making it one of the most studied and tested advanced subjects in the high school curriculum. As mentioned in the author's preface, this book grew out of his APUSH class at the American School of Guadalajara—one of the largest such classes outside the United States.

His Mexican students were eager to learn more than the standard history textbooks contained about Abraham Lincoln's support for Mexico, not only in the 1840s but also well into the 1860s during the US Civil War. The author began working on this book project at the end of the 2012-2013 academic year, using his research and writing about the Mexican War for over two decades as a starting point.

Based on his new research and ensuing classroom discussions, the remarkable APUSH students at the American School of Guadalajara are perhaps better informed about relationships between the United States and Mexico during that period than any other group of students in the world. And, because of their hunger for education and the professor's desire to satisfy their appetite, this resulting book will also increase your own knowledge and understanding of why—more than 150 years after Lincoln's death—this great American president is still the most respected US political figure in Mexico.

For history teachers and students, high school or college, I'm certain the professor and his students would be honored if you use this book to supplement your other course materials. The appendix contains actual texts of government and private documents from archives in the United States and Mexico, the extensive bibliography contains almost three hundred citations to external authoritative references, and the illustrations include twelve photographs of important figures and three historic maps. I'm also confident the author would welcome the opportunity to answer any questions about the material, and you can contact him through his website http://www.drmichaelhogan.com/contact.php.

For history aficionados beyond the classroom, I believe this subject will resonate with readers far beyond that school in Guadalajara, and can facilitate a better understanding of relationships between the United States and Mexico that began in 1821 when Mexico declared its independence from Spain. What sets this book apart from almost 15,000 other books about Abraham Lincoln is the author's ability to shine new light on Lincoln's courage, intrigue, and unlikely friendships in furthering these relationships.

Publication of the eBook version in the spring of 2016 coincided with the 170th anniversary of the May 13 date the US Congress declared war on Mexico. Even before publication of the eBook, the overall project produced plans for a paperback edition for educators and students in Latin America, a separate USA paperback edition for educators and students, an audio book, and future Spanish-language editions.

In addition, the project spawned a script for a play to be performed by high school students in Mexico marking the 150th anniversary of the year Mexico finally defeated the French forces of Emperor Napoleon. As the book reveals, Lincoln was a staunch supporter of Mexico in its struggles against the French occupation from 1861-1867, even as he was preoccupied with the political and military challenges of the US Civil War during the same time period.

Thanks for reading the book. If you enjoyed it, help spread the word about it by writing reviews on Amazon and Goodreads and let your friends know by posting something on Facebook and on

Twitter. Also, I invite you to visit the official Facebook page for the book at https://www.facebook.com/MexicoLincoln/?fref=ts and give it a like so you can follow posts and comments from around the world. Best regards.

Mikel Miller, EgretBooks.com
San Diego, California, United States of America

INDEX

C

CPSIA information can be obtained at www.ICGtesting.com
Printed in the USA
LVOW07s0349230816

501431LV00005B/209/P